WHAT IS
HYPNOSIS?

WHAT IS HYPNOSIS?

Current Theories and Research

edited by
Peter L. N. Naish

Open University Press
Milton Keynes · Philadelphia

Open University Press
Open University Educational Enterprises Limited
12 Cofferidge Close
Stony Stratford
Milton Keynes MK11 1BY, England
and
242 Cherry Street
Philadelphia, PA 19106, USA

First Published 1986

British Library Cataloguing in Publication Data
What is hypnosis?: current theories and research.
  1. Hypnotism
  I. Naish, Peter L. N.
  154.7   BF1141
  ISBN 0-335-15338-0
  ISBN 0-335-15337-2 Pbk

Library of Congress Cataloging in Publication Data
What is hypnosis?
  Bibliography: p.
  Includes index.
  1. Hypnotism. I. Naish, Peter L. N.
BF1141.W49   1986   154.7   86-12632
ISBN 0-335-15338-0
ISBN 0-335-15337-2 (pbk.)

Text design by Carlton Hill
Typeset by Mathematical Composition Setters Ltd, Salisbury
Printed in Great Britain at the Alden Press, Oxford

A heavy summons lies like lead upon me,
And yet I would not sleep.

Macbeth, II.i.6

Contents

INTRODUCTION

Peter L. N. Naish

Throughout the history of what we now call hypnosis, beliefs about the effects
it can produce and explanations of the processes involved have ranged from
the naively gullible to the unshakably sceptical. These two extremes are still
apparent today, at least among lay people. When the average person is asked
what hypnosis is, or what it can do, either the reply is likely to describe the
imparting of superhuman abilities, or the topic will be dismissed as a
fraudulent stage trick. Opinions as extreme as these are seldom based on any
good evidence, and a satisfactory view can be reached only after careful
scientific investigation of the hypnosis phenomenon. This book will present a
number of such views of hypnosis, from contributors with an active interest
in the field. This compilation does not pretend to be an exhaustive catalogue
of all the current theories of hypnosis. However, it is hoped that the reader
will obtain a reasonably balanced picture of the kinds of thinking on the topic
generally to be found today. It will be discovered that the views still cover a
range along what might be called the gullible-sceptical continuum, although
the range is not as extreme as that described above. No author will suggest that
truly miraculous effects can be ascribed to hypnosis. Nor on the other hand,
will suggestions be made that hypnotic behaviour is always, and without
exception, a simple and deliberate attempt to deceive.

The beginnings of the scientific study of hypnosis

The scientific study of hypnosis is not new; it started in Paris, before the French
Revolution. At that time, before the term 'hypnosis' had been coined, the great
Mesmer was practising his skills. From his name the term 'mesmerism' was
later derived, but in those days the phenomenon was referred to as
'magnetism'. The motives behind Mesmer's work were of the best; he attempted to use his magnetism therapeutically. His beliefs and expectations about
it were a curious amalgam of ideas prevalent at the time. For example, there
was a distinct flavour of exorcism, expressed in the belief that patients would
not be cured without an internal struggle, reflected in a period of convulsive
writhings. Further, it was commonly supposed that the human body had

poles, rather like a magnet, and that illnesses were the result of a faulty distribution of the associated 'magnetic fluid'. Mesmer would make passes along the length of a patient's body, in much the same way as a magnet is passed over another piece of steel when it is required that the latter should become magnetised. In this way Mesmer believed that he could realign the field associated with a sick person, and hence effect a cure. Mesmer saw the practising 'magnetist' as an important and active agent in this cure. His treatment became increasingly popular, to the extent that he had to employ assistants and devise methods for passing the magnetic fluid into a number of people simultaneously. For the poor, who could not afford to attend his fashionable magnetic meetings, the worthy Mesmer placed his influence upon strategically located trees! The afflicted then had merely to come and touch a tree to experience the benefits of the magnetic miracle.

Mesmer's growing popularity brought him to the attention of the authorities. More for political than medical reasons, Royal Commissions were set up to investigate his practices. This was the first formal attempt to investigate the mechanisms of what we now call hypnosis. The commissions had a number of august members. One was led by the distinguished American scientist and statesman Benjamin Franklin. (It was Franklin who tempted fate by flying a kite in a thunderstorm, to collect electricity from the clouds.) Another notable individual in the team was Dr Guillotin, who subsequently lent his name to a machine for separating the French aristocracy from their heads.

Mesmer was investigated by what today would still be considered sound scientific practice, although the reasoning was blinkered. It was decided, in advance, that people may or may not be cured by magnetism. However, if magnetism could be shown not to exist in the context, then it would follow that it could not have cured anything. Such a finding would represent an end to the matter. Thus Mesmer's claims for magnetic effects were carefully tested, using sensitive instruments, such as magnetometers. Naturally enough, these failed to detect any magnetism. The commissions also carried out exactly the kind of experiment that modern research psychologists would use. For example, people known to be sensitive to Mesmer's ministrations were taken blindfold to several trees. Only one of these had been 'magnetized', but the unsuspecting experimental patients obligingly provided the expected manifestations of magnetism at any tree. The inevitable conclusion reached by the Royal Commissions was that there was no substance in the idea of magnetism. The unfortunate Mesmer had to leave Paris, to spend the remainder of his life in relative obscurity.

Thus ended the first scientific investigation of hypnosis. The honesty and accuracy of the commissions' methods and results were laudable, but it was unfortunate that they chose to address such a restricted question. For example, they gave little consideration to the fact that some of Mesmer's patients might genuinely have been cured – if not by magnetism, then by some other mechanism worthy of investigation. A rather disparaging mention was made that some effects might be ascribed to suggestion.

Implications for modern theories

In spite of the disappearance of Mesmer from the scene, interest in the use of hypnosis and investigation into its nature continued. However, although the theory of magnetism had been thoroughly discredited by the French Royal Commissions, it was to be many years before the magnetic explanation of mesmerism was laid to rest. The reason for this is not hard to find; for, as long as the hypnotist was seen as the essential active participant in the hypnotic situation, then it was necessary also to believe in the existence of some mysterious force flowing from him into the patient. In the absence of any other obvious mechanism, some kind of invisible magnetic fluid was an excellent candidate for this unseen power. With the rejection of beliefs in undetectable yet potent forces following from hypnotist to patient, it would have been logical for practitioners to constrain their theories of hypnosis within certain boundaries. In practice, however, it has been only relatively recently that theories have embodied the full implications of the rejection of magnetism as a viable explanation. The implications can be deduced by reasoning as follows.

In the absence of anything like a magnetic fluid, almost the only thing transmitted by a hypnotist is his or her speech. The recipient of the hypnotist's words can deal with them only in the same way as with any other spoken material. That is, the sounds are analysed, and recognized by the brain as words. These are assembled to form an intelligible communication. Words can have powerful effects upon their hearer. Consider, for example, the effects upon a listener of hearing the sentences, 'You have passed your exam', or 'You are terminally ill.' The natural responses to such words are in no way mysterious, the effects being due entirely to the personal implications of the information for the listener. Thus the character in the book *Doctor in the House*, who received an annuity only for as long as he was a student, would have been disappointed to learn that he had passed his final examination. The point is that the hypnotist's only 'weapon' is his words; and, outside stories of wizards and magic, words have no intrinsic power – they are merely what the listener makes of them.

Words are not in fact the only source of information available to modify the behaviour of a person being hypnotized. The patient can pick up various cues from the situation in which he or she is placed. This must have been important for the patients of the Mesmerists, since these practitioners would have used more 'magnetic passes' than words. Also, as with the hypnotist's words, it is what the recipient makes of this information that determines the resultant behaviour. This fact is clearly demonstrated by the way in which 'classical' hypnotic responses have changed over the years. It must be presumed that Mesmer's patients expected to have a 'crisis'; a room was actually provided in which they could have their convulsions in peace and safety. Readers considering exploring hypnosis, perhaps to break the smoking habit, will be relieved to know that today's patients do not have the same expectations;

consequently, neither do they have the same convulsions. Situations certainly can affect behaviour, but the precise effects depend upon the person placed in the situation, not upon the one who engineers it.

It is essential to appreciate that the important behaviour-determining agent in the hypnotic situation is the one who is hypnotized. The recipient of the treatment determines the responses produced. The effects must be generated by the same mechanisms that lead to any other behaviour, in any other non-hypnotic situation. Consequently, hypnotic responses must be drawn from the patient's normal behavioural repertoire; and since no mysterious force is available to modify the responses, it follows that the behaviour can never be truly unique or exceptional. This conclusion can be reached without even considering hypnosis research. The Darwinian concept of 'survival of the fittest' requires that, in general, all organisms make full use of every ability at their disposal. In this way they increase their chances of surviving and passing on their genes in a competitive world. Suppose for a moment that humans truly had a special mode of operation available. Let us presume that in this condition we possessed all the powers popularly attributed to hypnosis: astonishing strength, infallible memory and so on. The benefits for survival that would be imparted by such abilities are self-evident. Were the superhuman mode available to us, evolutionary pressures would have forced humanity to adopt it permanently many millennia ago. It must be concluded that we are in practice as 'super' as we can ever be.

There are many accounts of astonishing feats performed under the influence of hypnosis. How can these be reconciled with the above assertion that no supernormal feats can be expected? In practice, it is very difficult to demonstrate any kind of hypnotic behaviour that cannot be encountered in some non-hypnotic situation (see, for example, Wagstaff 1981). The contributors to this book cite various examples that support this statement, but one will be given here by way of illustration. One of the more apparently spectacular demonstrations performed by stage hypnotists is the human plank trick. There are variations, but the show normally starts with the hypnotist putting his volunteer into what is claimed to be a hypnotic trance. The guinea-pig is then instructed to become straight and rigid, like a plank. In this condition it is possible for the 'plank' to be rested between two chairs, head on one and heels on the other. This looks very impressive to an audience, and the observers make the rather natural assumption that the feat could not have been performed without the aid of hypnosis. However, surprising as it may seem, this is not the case, and the reader is invited to test this personally. The would-be plank (who must not, of course, have any back problem) should stretch out on the floor or a table, with hands by the sides, endeavouring to be as stiff and unbending as possible. Two assistants are then required, one to lift the human plank by the ankles, the other with the hands underneath the back of the head. The volunteer will not find it too hard to remain effectively straight for a short while.

The state of hypnosis

The reader may feel that the foregoing has been a rather merciless debunking of what begins to look like a hypnosis myth. However, although people can be shown to exhibit the same type of behaviour outside the hypnosis situation as they do in it, this does not automatically imply that hypnosis never plays any part in engendering the behaviour. For example, in the case of the human plank feat, the hypnotic component of the situation is at least instrumental in giving a doubting volunteer sufficient faith to carry out the task. Some theorists have gone as far as to suggest that enough differences exist between the kind of behaviour exhibited in the hypnotic situation from that to be found in everyday life for hypnosis to be seen as a distinct 'state'. It is sometimes said that a hypnotized person is in an 'altered state of consciousness'. (Waxman presents this viewpoint, in Chapter 2.)

People with this kind of view have been referred to as 'state theorists'. Their position implies that there is something fundamentally different about the condition of a person who has been hypnotized, in the sense that a sleeping person can be said to differ physiologically from one who is awake. In the case of hypnosis, however, such easily demonstrated physiological differences are not displayed. Indeed, as has already been pointed out, it is not easy to find any very clear difference between the hypnotic and non-hypnotic conditions. This being the case, there are today very few thoroughgoing state theorists to be found (Fellows 1982). Most researchers see themselves as non-state theorists, or perhaps somewhere between the two extremes. The reader will be beginning to see that, although there is reasonable conformity between theorists about what hypnosis is *not*, there is still a lack of unanimity when it comes to deciding what it *is*. The precise nature of hypnosis remains a matter for healthy debate, as do so many other topics of psychology. The reader should not be disenchanted by this, but rather enter into the spirit of the arguments, and try to assess for himself or herself the merits of the various views put forward in this book. The Chapter 8 will offer some assistance, by attempting to draw together the different threads.

Techniques and terminology, fallacies and fears

Before we launch into the technicalities of hypnosis theory and research, a little more guidance will be offered for those unfamiliar with this field in particular, or with psychology in general. It is necessary to have some idea of the methods used by researchers, both to induce hypnosis in their experimental volunteers, and to test its effects. There will be a brief discussion of what should be understood by some of the specialist terms used in this book. An attempt will also be made to answer a number of more general questions about hypnosis that are frequently asked by members of the public.

When hypnosis is put to practical use, it is often in the therapeutic context.

The practitioners are likely to refer to the people being hypnotized as 'patients' or 'clients'. However, when for example an experimental psychologist is investigating hypnosis, the people he uses are, as far as he is aware, quite healthy. The term 'patient' would be inappropriate, so researchers refer to their guinea-pigs as 'subjects'. This is one of a number of possibly unfamiliar terms used in the following chapters. Some terminology is of a general nature, but perhaps the most important terms to clarify from the outset are those related spcifically to hypnosis. So far in this Introduction expressions such as 'hypnotized' and 'hypnotic trance' have been used freely. Such terms are familiar to the average reader, and used in this way are adequate to convey the impressions required. However, in recent times there has been a certain resistance among theorists to the employment of such words in this ill-defined manner (e.g. Fellows 1984, Naish 1985). The problem with such terminology is that it implies the existence of definable processes and conditions, uniformly applicable to all cases, meaning the same to all theorists. Suppose an experimenter simply states that he 'hypnotized' a subject, and that while the subject was 'under hypnosis' he performed certain tasks. Other researchers will want to ask: 'What do you mean by "hypnotized"; what did you actually do? How did you know that the subject was "under hypnosis"? In what way was the subject's behaviour different from the point in time preceding this condition?' It is preferable to avoid these difficulties by stating simply that a particular induction procedure was used with the subject, and that following this induction certain tests were performed. Thus no statement is made about the condition of the subject following the induction process. The procedure is not even claimed to produce hypnosis, although the implication is there, since it is generally described as a 'hypnotic' induction. For simplicity, terms like 'hypnosis' and 'hypnotized' will continue to be used in this book, without elaboration, but it should be borne in mind that they are being employed as convenient labels. They are not intended to imply the presence of some well-defined condition.

To facilitate comparison between the work of different researchers, standardized hypnotic induction procedures have been developed. These are frequently combined with a scale of susceptibility for hypnosis. The subject is given a set of standard suggestions, and the extent to which he or she responds to them is noted, so yielding a measure of responsiveness. References to these scales will be found in the following chapters. An example is the Harvard Group Scale of Hypnotic Susceptibility (Shor and Orne 1962). This measure saves the time of a busy researcher by enabling a group of subjects to be tested simultaneously.

For the therapeutic use of hypnosis there is no particular need for uniformity of induction procedure. Most clinical techniques revolve upon the concept of relaxation, perhaps in part because the idea that hypnosis is somewhat like sleep still lingers on. Thus the induction may have a good deal in common with an antinatal relaxation class. The therapist will ask the patient to begin by sitting or lying comfortably; instructions may be given to take a few deep breaths; and then, progressively, the client is encouraged to relax various parts of the body. The progressive relaxation frequently starts with the feet, then the patient is instructed to let the calf muscles go limp, then the thighs. The same is done for fingers, hands, arms and shoulders. Eventually the whole body is supposed to feel relaxed and heavy. The client is asked to close the eyes and is frequently then given a relaxing scene to visualize as vividly as possible. This might entail picturing lying on a sunny beach, with the therapist drawing attention to various sensory aspects of the scene, such as the blue of the sky, the whiteness of the sand and the sound of the surf. Most people report the experience as a pleasant one, and, perhaps not surprisingly in view of the induction technique, patients describe themselves as feeling extremely relaxed. In many cases this is the total of experiences reported, but some subjects and patients will go further and describe curious sensations, in response to the instructions of the hypnotist. Certain researchers would discount the value of such subjective reports, because, for a variety of reasons, it may be unwise to accept at face value all personal accounts of unverifiable experiences. A subject may be attempting to report accurately but fail to be objective. It is also possible that subjects will tend to tell the experimenter what they believe he or she wants to hear. For these reasons some researchers try to use only objective observable data when assessing the effects of hypnosis.

Susceptibility scales often use ratings based upon the objective observations of the experimenter. But since a hypnotist cannot watch several people simultaneously, the group scale mentioned earlier has to sacrifice this level of objectivity in the interests of speed. The subjects are asked at the end of the test to rate their own responsiveness. The assessment of susceptibilities is usually done by noting the extent of the responses to different types of test suggestion. One class of suggestion, for example, examines motor effects – that is, effects relating to the subject's muscles and powers of movement. Suggestions of immobility might be made; for example, a subject can be told to put the hands together, to link the fingers and then to discover that he or she is unable to separate the hands. A high-scoring subject would be observed to struggle, yet fail to move the hands apart. A low scorer would separate the hands without apparent difficulty. Another example of a motor suggestion is the arm levitation test. The subject is instructed that one arm, with hand and fingers, will begin to grow lighter and lighter, and gradually float up towards the ceiling. Frequently the suggestions are augmented with instructions to visualize some appropriate scenario, such as having balloons attached to the fingers by long strings, which are gently tugging upwards, taking the fingers with them.

As well as motor responsiveness, sensory effects are generally tested during hypnotic susceptibility assessment. In this type of test an attempt is made to induce a sensation in a subject by means of suggestions. For example, a subject may be told that a taste of lemon will be experienced, and then responses like sucking and swallowing are monitored. Another frequently used suggestion is of a fly walking on the subject's face. In response to this, the hypnotically susceptible may be observed to make facial movements suggestive of irritation. Some subjects may raise a hand to brush away the imaginary fly. In the days before chemical anaesthesia, attempts were made to use hypnosis for pain management in surgery (see Waxman, Chapter 2). The possibility of producing this kind of analgesia has also been investigated in the experimental setting, but care naturally has to be taken in the choice of painful stimulus for the testing. In a commonly used technique, the subject is required to immerse an arm in a tank of ice-cold water. This very quickly leads to severe discomfort. Under hypnosis a subject may be given suggestions that the situation is entirely bearable, and a measure of susceptibility may be obtained by noting for how much longer the subject will tolerate the experience. The appropriate interpretation for results derived from this kind of experiment will be considered in later chapters.

Another property of hypnosis often used in the measurement of susceptibility is that of memory manipulation. Attempts have been made to induce memory enhancement by hypnosis, for example to improve the memory of eyewitnesses in police investigations. However, for a test procedure it is easier to examine memory impairment rather than any alleged improvement. The subject is generally told that upon awakening from hypnosis it will not be possible to remember certain events. The effectiveness of the instruction can then be tested at the conclusion of the session. Again, whatever the result, its interpretation is a matter for some debate, and the issues will be raised later in the book.

Can anybody do it?

Three related questions are often asked by the lay person regarding hypnosis. They are: Can anybody be hypnotized? Can anybody hypnotize? Is it possible to hypnotize oneself? A brief answer to the first question is that most people seem to be somewhat responsive. The use of susceptibility scales is a reminder that people are not uniformly 'hypnotizable'. The second question has in effect already been answered, when it was pointed out that the hypnotist is not imbued with any magical powers. If no special ingredient is required, anyone should be able to hypnotize. On the other hand, some people display a 'hypnotizing knack' to a greater degree than others. The subject's perceptions of the would-be hypnotist are clearly important to the result. For example, if the milkman suddenly announced to a customer that he could hypnotize her, she might find herself unresponsive to his induction procedure. On the other hand, if she were taken to a hospital and confronted by a white-coated bearded gentleman with a mid-European accent, then the lady might be found to respond readily to an identical induction technique.

The same person can find subjects to be more or less responsive, depending upon the mode of presentation. The author has on a number of occasions given lectures about hypnosis, concluding the sessions with the administration of a group induction procedure. Naturally, not all members of the audiences are responsive, but the number showing the traditional signs of 'being hypnotized' depends very much upon the style of the preceding lecture. If this has tended to focus on the 'mystery and magic' of hypnosis, then many people seem to be responsive. On the other hand, a rather 'debunking' approach appears to render many of the audience unsusceptible to the suggestions.

Those with an aptitude for hypnotizing others must be presumed to possess some skill in conveying an impression of ability and appropriateness. This indication that subjects' responses depend upon their perceptions of the situation underlines the fact that hypnosis comes from within. Moreover, it effectively answers the third question, regarding the possibility of hypnotizing oneself. There would be a good deal of truth in the statement 'all hypnosis is self-hypnosis', since the hypnotist is merely acting as a guide. In view of this, it is not surprising that many people are able to experience the same kind of sensation alone. This is often facilitated by an initial period of instruction by someone in the role of hypnotist, and some people find it helpful to use a tape-recording of this person's directions when they attempt hypnosis at home. This technique is sometimes used therapeutically, so that a patient need not attend a clinic frequently in order to experience the benefits of a hypnotic induction.

The details given above touch upon a paradoxical issue. Reference was made to the therapeutic use of hypnosis, and it was also pointed out that all hypnosis is effectively self-induced, and this only when the patient perceives the situation and practitioner as appropriate for hypnotic induction. However, some patients fear hypnosis, thinking that the condition implies loss of control. Therapists not wishing to provoke this anxiety will sometimes avoid alarming their patients by omitting to use the term 'hypnosis' and instead describing their procedures as a form of relaxation training. It must be presumed that the therapy employed under the new name is still effective, otherwise therapists would not continue to use the ploy. Does the maintaining of efficacy imply that the patients are nevertheless hypnotized? If so, how do they reach this condition, when it was earlier suggested that it is achieved only because the patient perceives it as being appropriate? This apparent paradox can be answered in a number of ways. A non-state view would claim that the only thing achieved by a so-called hypnotic induction is a good level of relaxation for the subject. Since many conditions for which medical help is sought can be attributed to anxiety and stress, it follows that this relaxation will be beneficial. Consequently, even if a situation is not labelled as hypnosis, as long as it remains effective in inducing relaxation it will continue to be beneficial. A state view of hypnosis would deny that it is essential to define the situation as hypnosis before an effective induction can occur. Merely to remove the label 'hypnosis' does not prevent it taking place, as long as the practitioner continues to use most of the ingredients of the traditional induction. So a patient undergoing the so-called relaxation training is nevertheless hypnotized, and it follows that he or she will derive the usual benefits from the procedure. An alternative position for the non-state theorist is to accept the state view, that merely changing the name leaves the procedure effectively intact. As a result, the non-state view would be that almost all the ingredients remain, and they would continue to be effective in encouraging a person to adopt the kind of behaviour traditionally referred to as 'hypnotic'. The type of ingredient that might achieve this is discussed by Wagstaff, Chapter 4, in the context of compliance.

There are many difficult-to-resolve issues such as the above, in the subject of hypnosis. Ultimately they can often be seen as questions of semantics and definitions.

The abuse of hypnosis

Newcomers to hypnosis are understandably often nervous. They tend to enquire: can they be hypnotized without knowing it? Can they be hypnotized against their will? If hypnotized, can they be made to do things against their will? The first of these questions is effectively two in one. It might be asking whether it is possible to be 'under hypnosis' without being aware of the fact. More probably the questioner has in mind the possibility that one could suddenly discover oneself to have been 'hypnotized'. The glib reply to the question in the first form might be to ask how a person ever knows when he or she is 'under hypnosis'. As has been made clear, the hypnotic condition does not incorporate the rather wonderful aspects that the uninitiated tend to expect. As a result, it is not at all uncommon for subjects who have undergone an explicit induction procedure to express doubts as to whether they really were hypnotized (e.g. Kidder 1973). Subjects such as these have to learn to apply the label 'hypnotized' to a set of experiences different from the ones expected. Hence it could be said that there was a period during which those experiences pertained and the experimenter considered the subject to be hypnotized; but, since the subject had a different definition of hypnosis, he or she was unaware of being hypnotized. This is analogous to the situation of a patient learning from the doctor that he has a disease of which he had not previously heard. However, although such a patient would have been ignorant of the fact that he had that particular disease, he would have been aware of any symptoms arising from it. In the same way, there may be a situation in which, due to differing definitions of the condition, a subject may not believe himself or herself to be hypnotized, when the experimeter does. The subject has full self-awareness, nevertheless and cannot be said to be in a condition without knowing it.

Referring back to the issue of calling hypnosis 'relaxation', the answer to the second part of this question must depend upon the theoretical stance of the hypnotist. From a 'state' point of view, it might be argued that it is indeed possible for subjects or patients to discover themselves in the hypnotic condition, having had the fact that they were being hypnotized concealed from them. On the other hand, a 'non-state' view would claim that all aspects of a situation work together to cause a subject to display certain types of behaviour. Whether or not the situation was explicitly defined as 'hypnotic' might have some effect upon the subsequent behaviour, but it would certainly not affect the subject's degree of awareness of what was going on. However, this kind of ignorance of being hypnotized has already been shown to be an ignorance of definition. Thus a subject does not know that he is hypnotized, because it has not been called hypnosis; he is still aware of his condition. Similarly, when he is *being* hypnotized, although the subject may not know the name of his destination, he can still monitor his progress towards it.

It is generally accepted by hypnotists of all theoretical persuasions that people cannot be hypnotized against their will. It is also agreed that some people who at first will not 'let go' sufficiently to go along with a standard hypnotic induction can be rendered more susceptible by appropriate procedures. Some of these techniques, such as were advocated by Erickson (e.g. Rossi 1980), get round the difficulty not by renaming the situation 'relaxation' but by changing the suggestions themselves. The usual, rather direct induction suggestions are replaced with less obvious, indirect remarks. It is claimed by proponents of these procedures that previously 'resistant' patients can be helped by the technique. Acceptance of this claim does not imply that the patient should be seen as being forcibly hypnotized. Instead, the patient is effectively 'talked round' to the hypnotist's point of view. The patient's will is no more subverted in this situation than when the hypnotist has a reassuring talk to encourage a previously reluctant patient to 'have a go'.

The question of whether, once hypnotized, one can be made to perform some act against one's will is more controversial. Hypnotists tend to be ambivalent on the matter. On the one hand, they are prone to reassure patients that they cannot be made to perform any undesired action, but on the other, they often recommend patients to avoid the dangers of being hypnotized by untrained or unscrupulous people. If there is any justification for this warning, it implies that, even if subjects or patients will not *do* anything they do not like, they might at least be made to engage in mental experiences that they do not like and which are thus injurious. It might be argued that the distinction between mental events and overt behaviour is not great, and therefore hypnotists should not 'sit on the fence'. Either subjects cannot in any way be given bad experiences, or they can indeed be made to have experiences against their will.

It has been suggested that, if hypnosis ever has been implicated in the production of antisocial behaviour, then it has served only as an extra predisposing agent over and above other motivating factors (e.g. Conn 1981). This is effectively a restatement of the frequently made assertion that people cannot be made to day anything under hypnosis that they do not really want to do. However, is it possible in the context of hypnosis that what a person 'really wants' might be changed? Heap (1984) cites a young woman who consulted a lay hypnotist. Although it was not the presenting problem, the hypnotist announced that the client's underlying difficulty was sexual inhibition. He proceeded to 'remedy' this, by fondling her breasts. The unfortunate woman was severely embarrassed by the incident, and did not return for further 'treatment'. Since the victim would not normally have submitted to such behaviour, the question must be asked: was it the hypnosis that made her submit against her will? Most practitioners would agree that this was almost certainly not the case. Had the woman's assailant simply hypnotized her and said, 'Now you will submit to everything I do to you', it is most unlikely that she would have acquiesced in the same way. The man had to legitimize his actions, by couching them in therapeutic terms, directed at curing an alleged condition. In all probability, any other quack, not using the hypnosis context at all, could have achieved the same ends by adopting the same ploy. Nevertheless, whatever the role of hypnosis in this case, the clear lesson to be drawn is that those seeking to be hypnotized should consult only accredited hypnotists.

To conclude the matter of coercion, although it seems unlikely that hypnosis can ever reasonably be blamed for 'making' people do things, hypnotized subjects often do report a sense of non-volition and of being under the control of the hypnotist. Possible reasons for such a sensation will be discussed in later chapters. For the present it serves as one more warning. If the hypnotist seems to the client to be in control, then, even if that control is illusory, it is clearly wise for the patient to choose a trustworthy therapist.

Armed with the background presented in this Introduction, the reader should now be in a position to appreciate the points made in the following Chapters. Each examines a different aspect of hypnosis or offers a different kind of explanation for so-called hypnotic behaviour.

References

Conn , J. H. (1981) The myth of coercion through hypnosis. *International Journal of Clinical and Experimental Hypnosis*, 29: 95–100.

Fellows, B. J. (1982) Neglected issues in the debate over the use of hypnosis in criminal investigations. *Bulletin of British Society of Experimental and Clinical Hypnosis*, 5: 85–9.

⸻ (1984) Editorial comment. *British Journal of Experimental and Clinical Hypnosis*, (3): 2.

Heap, M. (1984) Four victims (newsletter). *British Journal of Experimental and Clinical Hypnosis*, 2: 60–2.

Kidder, L. H. (1973) On becoming hypnotized: how sceptics become convinced: a case study of attitude change? *American Journal of Clinical Hypnosis*, 16: 1–8.

Naish, P. L. N. (1985) The 'trance' described in signal detection terms. *British Journal of Experimental and Clinical Hypnosis*, 2: 133–7.

Rossi, E. L. (ed.) (1980) *The Collected Works of Milton H. Erickson on Hypnosis*. New York: Irvington.

Shor, R. E. and Orne, E. C. (1962) *Harvard Group Scale of Hypnotic Susceptibility*. Palo Alto, Calif.: Consulting Psychologists Press.

Wagstaff, G. F. (1981) *Hypnosis, Compliance and Belief*. Brighton: Harvester.

THE DEVELOPMENT OF HYPNOSIS AS A PSYCHOTHERAPEUTIC FORCE

David Waxman

Historically, hypnosis has always been associated with therapy. It is therefore appropriate that this aspect should be explored before the more experimental side is examined. This chapter is contributed by Dr David Waxman, who has for many years used hypnosis in his psychiatric practice. He holds office in a number of societies devoted to the study and applications of hypnosis, including the presidency of the European Society of Hypnosis in Psychotherapy and Psychosomatic Medicine, the presidency of the British Society of Medical and Dental Hypnosis and the vice-presidency of the British Society of Experimental and Clinical Hypnosis.

Introduction

The use of hypnosis in various guises has emerged through the pages of history to become an effective and accepted instrument of psychotherapy. Its origins are obscure, and its earlier techniques and miracle cures are shrouded in mystery. As a result of the total lack of understanding of the mode of achievement of the hypnotic state and of its nature, methods of induction varied from the seemingly magical to the bizarre or the overtly authoritarian, only to compound the ideas of wizardry that were attributed to the hypnotist. In addition, from its earliest discovery, hypnosis has been subjected to abuse and misuse by charlatans and entertainers, and the dramatic effects that may often be produced have enhanced the folklore with which it has been surrounded. Consequently any serious study of the subject has been neglected until recently. Its clinical applications and the claims of research workers have been either viewed with suspicion and incredulity or summarily rejected.

When Freud discarded the use of hypnosis as a technique for the exploration of the unconscious mind, further investigation into the nature and uses of hypnotherapy remained in limbo. Only slowly has it emerged, with considerable pangs of labour, into a world challenged by high-technology medicine. With the reawakening of interest, experimental psychologists have taken hypnosis into the laboratory, to 'place under the microscope' and examine more closely its effects and phenomena. The development of the electroencephalograph has enabled neurophysiologists to formulate ideas of a specific neurophysiological state. Its uses have spread to many disciplines of medicine. National and international societies have sprung up, and exciting new avenues of treatment have developed. Dynamic exploration, having replaced suggestive therapy, has additionally added a page from the book of learning theory; and hypnosis has been shown to be an acceptable, valid and effective instrument for the treatment of a wide range of nervous disorders.

Origins and theories

Animal magnetism

As explained in Chapter 1, it all really began with Franz Anton Mesmer. Born in 1734 in the small town of Iznang on Lake Constance, he was the son of a gamekeeper with good contacts amongst the aristocracy. After a temporary flirtation with studies in philosophy and theology he decided upon a career in medicine, and qualified at the University of Vienna at the mature age of thirty-three.

Many of the physicians of Mesmer's Europe, following the teachings of Galen, believed that there was some invisible fluid that filled the universe and, traversing the planets, reached the earth and every mortal being therein. It was necessary, so the idea went, to maintain a balance of this fluid between the mind, the body and all external forces, in order to maintain good health, both mental and physical. Another idea, which had existed since the days of Paracelsus, was that specific healing properties were possessed by magnets. With their powers of polar attraction and repulsion, here was a force that could harness this ethereal fluid. Healing by touch and healing by stroking were yet other methods practised at the time. Why not combine them all? Could it not be that by the application of magnets and by the appropriate stroking movements this fluid could be coaxed through the human body in order to restore good health? All was now revealed. With the help of Father Maximillian Hell, the professor of astronomy at his old university, Mesmer designed an assortment of magnetized plates, which were made to fit over various parts of the body. These could be placed over the affected area and would attract the fluid to generate that artificial force required for healing. Later, invoking Newton, Mesmer maintained that gravitation was also involved, but he afterwards concluded that he himself was the magnet; by his touch alone, he could guide the healing fluid through the human body to enter the 'substance of the nerves' of his patients and affect them immediately. He had 'discovered' animal magnetism!

It was perhaps because he believed so much in his own theories that Mesmer was able to achieve so considerable a success in his treatment. Perhaps it was because of his convictions that his powers of suggestion were so effective. Possibly also the suggestibility of his subjects contributed in no small manner to the cures that resulted. In spite of the scepticism of prevailing medical opinion, Mesmer's fame spread far and wide. But because he had no real scientific basis for his theories his eventual downfall was inevitable. Paradoxically enough this was brought about as a result of one of his greatest successes and yet greatest errors, a case that must be on record as a classical example of psychotherapeutic myopia.

Maria Theresa Paradis, then aged eighteen, was the patient who could claim this doubtful fame. Her father had been appointed private secretary to the Empress of the Holy Roman Empire, whose namesake she was. This young girl had been stricken with total blindness at the age of seven, but she was nevertheless a brilliant professional pianist. As a result of this unique combination, as well as her undoubted talent, she was in great demand throughout the concert halls of Europe. All attempts to restore her vision, by such methods as existed at that time, had failed until Dr Mesmer was brought in for consultation. Since ophthalmological and neurological examination had revealed no abnormality, Mesmer could safely assume that he would be dealing with a condition that was certainly not organic in nature. In view of the important position of the family and the fact that so many other physicians had failed to cure this girl, the case was of considerable importance to his credibility. He accepted the challenge, and animal magnetism was the therapy dispensed. The patient regained her sight, and Mesmer's methods were vindicated. His triumph was short-lived. His classical omission was his failure to explore and to understand the reason for Maria's blindness. The restoration of her sight was to be accompanied by the withdrawal of the state pension she had received because of her condition. Additionally she was no longer unique as a pianist, and her popularity waned. Mesmer had neglected the family dynamics and the manner in which the girl had been manipulated. The wrath of the parents descended upon the hapless magnetizer, and the real victim, poor Maria Theresa, again lapsed into blindness. Mesmer's popularity fell into a rapid decline; the medical heirarchy of Vienna were triumphant.

Mesmer fled the country. Arriving in Paris, he soon set up a salon for the treatment of the sick. Quickly re-establishing his charisma, he maintained that soft lighting, heavy curtaining and the strains of music in the background all enhanced the effect, and mirrors on the walls reflected the magnetism. The centrepiece was a large wooden vat, the *baquet*, filled with water in which were suspended iron filings. Iron rods projected from the depths, and seated around and in contact with a rod and with each other were his patients. The doctor himself circumnavigated this weird group and as he touched each with a 'wand' that patient swooned, went into a convulsion and was taken away to a side room. The convulsion was the 'crisis', an essential part of the treatment, without which there could be no cure. Once again Mesmer's popularity soared but once again it was short-lived. King Louis XVI, in response to popular demand, set up a Royal Commission, under the presidency of the newly appointed United States Commissioner to France, Benjamin Franklin, to investigate animal magnetism. The enquiry was thorough and systematic. The verdict returned was that 'the imagination does everything, the magnetism nothing'. Once more defeated, Mesmer retired to the town of Meersburg near to his birthplace on Lake Constance, where he died on 5 March 1815.

One eminent French physician, Alexandre Bertrand, was later responsible for supporting and explaining Mesmer's theories (Bertrand 1823). He admitted to the effectiveness of the magnetism treatment, although he disputed that magnetism existed. Rather it was Mesmer's suggestions that were responsible for his success. It was, Bertrand maintained, the influence of the imagination of patients *acting upon themselves*. In this way he pre-empted Emile Coué that great pioneer of therapy through suggestions (Coué 1922). Although Mesmer had firmly believed in the idea of animal magnetism, little did he realize his own ability as a psychotherapist. Much of his work was involved with the treatment of the neuroses and for the relief of psychosomatic and conversion symptoms where the 'imagination' plays a very considerable part. It was only later to be appreciated how important was the role of concentration, suggestibility and trust.

Somnambulism

Mesmer was dead, but magnetism lived on. New theories and techniques abounded. Mesmer's magnetism spread from Europe across the world. The more scientific-minded stressed the importance of imagination, belief and the will to achieve the expected results. The Marquis Chastanet de Puységur discovered the somnambulistic state in which the patient was able, whilst under the influence of magnetism, to open the eyes, move about and generally obey commands. Mesmerism was considered to be a form of sleep-walking. Psychic as well as physical factors were involved. The *baquet*, the iron rods and the need for the crisis, in fact the entire facade of the mesmeric stage-setting, were rejected. The Royal Commission of Louis XVI was right. However, the somnambulistic state can be achieved only in certain deeply hypnotizable subjects, and such patients respond extremely well to suggestion under hypnosis. Fortunately we know today that a light trance is usually sufficient to enable successful therapy to be carried out.

Mesmerism for diagnosis

Great Britain was not to be forgotten in this new 'science', which was spreading so rapidly. In 1788 J. B. de Mainauduc, a pupil of one of Mesmer's principal disciples, Charles d'Eslon, lectured on magnetism in London and the West of England, influencing many doctors to adopt the technique. In 1829 Richard Chenevix, a follower of de Puységur, demonstrated its use at St Thomas' Hospital. Amongst the many eminent physicians present was Dr John Elliotson. He was a great innovator, always ready to try out new ideas, and he soon became one of the foremost protagonists of what was still known as 'mesmerism' or 'magnetism'. He was a leading physician of the time, had established the new University College in London and was elected Professor of Medicine in 1831. He subsequently witnessed demonstrations by the Baron Dupotet and then freely used the ideas he had gained. In addition to the many cures that could be achieved, he also believed that special diagnostic powers could be attained through the forces of magnetism. Using two highly suggestible young ladies known as the Okey sisters, diagnosis by somnambulism became one of the instruments of his medical practice. He gave public demonstrations of his methods, although his work was strongly discouraged by the authorities. He was eventually dismissed from his post, only to be later rehabilitated.

A type of sleep

In 1813 a Portuguese abbot, José Custodio di Faria, gave public demonstrations of magnetism in Paris. He had anticipated Bertrand and many who followed by emphasizing the subject's ability to go to sleep on command. Although the magnetists had recognized the need for the fixation of attention and for an understanding between the mesmerizer and the mesmerized, for di Faria, mesmerism was due to concentration and nothing else. Attention was focussed only on the words that were used; when the command was given, the patient closed his or her eyes. The mesmeric state was just a form of 'lucid sleep' (Faria 1819).

In 1841 the Marquis de Lafayette, who had pleaded Mesmer's cause before George Washington, toured England instructing groups of doctors throughout the provinces. Magnetism was hailed as a panacea for a wide variety of ills, and a great battle of correspondence was waged in the medical press.

One man who was rather less gullible and more scientific was a Scottish surgeon named James Braid. Born in Fifeshire in 1795, he practised in Manchester. He learned magnetism from a Frenchman named Charles de la Fontaine and interested himself in the work of di Faria and Elliotson. He too rejected the idea of magnetism and cosmic forces, and later his own theories on the subject were published (Braid, 1899). Braid agreed that the total concentration of attention of the subject was the first requirement and that this would produce a particular psychological condition of 'nervous sleep'. This was 'hypnos', a word derived from the name of the Greek god of sleep and 'neurypnology' or 'hypnology' was henceforth to replace 'magnetism'.

Magnetism as an anaesthetic

The production of anaesthesia or analgesia was one of the many inexplicable features of magnetism known at the time of Elliotson. Many major operations were performed by this method throughout the world, and Mesmeric institutions were established in Britain, where surgery using this virtually safe and painless procedure was undertaken. In his Harveian oration, given in 1846, Elliotson had referred to one of the indisputable phenomena of mesmerism, that in which 'wounds give no pain' (see Waxman 1978). One of the most prominent surgeons of that time was James Esdaile. He practised in Calcutta and carried out hundreds of painless operations, using magnetism alone as the anaesthetic. These are reported extensively in issues of Elliotson's journal, *The Zoist*. The advent of the use of ether and chloroform, however, proved time-saving for the surgeon, and mesmerism was abandoned. Nevertheless many dentists today perform extractions and doctors perform minor operations using hypnosis. There are also many reports of the more recent use of hypnosis for abdominal operations.

'Hypnos' or suggestibility

A new phase was now reached in the development of hypnosis as a psychotherapeutic force. Magnetism in its new guise of respectability was to retrace its journey across the Channel to reach the town of Nancy in north-eastern France. It was here re-established in 1860 in the clinic of a general practitioner named Dr Ambroise August Liébault. Outraged by the apparent success he achieved, Professor Hippolyte Bernheim of the local university decided to investigate Dr Liébault, only to be totally won over to the study of hypnosis. Working together, the two men evolved the theory that the state of hypnosis was produced by suggestion alone and that hypnosis itself was a state of increased suggestibility. Expectation, they maintained, was the primary factor in the causation of the hypnotic state; the influence of the hypnotist was via the mental processes of the subject, rather than by bodily channels. Furthermore, one of the main factors in hypnotic suggestion was auto-suggestion. Their theories are outlined in their book on suggestive therapeutics (Bernheim 1900). Bernheim additionally thought that all hypnotic phenomena may be produced without hypnosis and by suggestion alone. This claim has been made by more recent adversaries of hypnosis, as if, were it proven, it would automatically deny the existence of a specific hypnotic state.

Hypnosis and hysteria

In opposition to the Nancy school, Jean Martin Charcot at the Salpêtrière Hospital of Paris claimed that hypnosis was a condition of abnormal pathology akin to hysteria. Charcot had a large number of patients available to him, many suffering from epilepsy as well as hysterical symptoms. He compared these symptoms with those of hypnosis, and concluded that they were similar. The only subjects who could be successfuly hypnotised, he insisted, were those who exhibited some hysterical symptoms. His conclusions are to be found in his treatise on the subject (Charcot 1890). It was due to Charcot's experiments with hypnosis that hysteria was distinguished from any form of pathological disease, as is implicit in the name by which the condition is described since it used to be considered the result of movement or 'wandering' of the womb. (Greek, 'hystera' the womb). It was left to Freud to discover, through the use of hypnosis, why a particular neurosis may be expressed in this particular way.

The Bernheim–Charcot conflict had its effect. Great psychologists of the latter half of the nineteenth century embraced the teachings of one school or the other. Moll, Babinski, Krafft-Ebing and Forel reported enthusiastically of their successes. Surgical and dental operations continued to be performed under hypnosis even with the increasing use of the newly discovered inhalation anaesthetics. Whether by magnetism or concentration, the patient would be put into the hypnotic 'trance', powerful suggestion removed the symptoms, and cure was claimed. Little had changed. The total reliance upon the suggestibility of the patient remained the method of the day.

A dissociation

One of those interested in the theories and practice of hypnosis was Pierre Janet, a pupil of Charcot at the Salpêtrière, author, philosopher and subsequently professor at the College de France (Janet 1925). He developed the idea of hypnosis as a dissociation – that is, a splitting of the conscious part from the unconscious part of the mind. Although this may occur in normal circumstances it may also be deliberately achieved. Here then was a possible means of reaching the subconscious in hysterical personalities, which were themselves 'split'. This, he felt, explained Charcot's view of hypnosis and hysteria.

Dynamic hypnosis

Another of the many celebrated students attached to the school of Charcot was Sigmund Freud. After numerous sessions at the Salpêtrière he travelled to Nancy to explore the ideas of Liébault and Bernheim, and then on to Professor Forel in Switzerland for further study. By now the interests of Dr Freud had extended to the field of research in psychology, and he recognized in the use of hypnosis the key to that hitherto sparsely explored science. He began to investigate the phenomena of hypnosis, to assess the theories of his predecessors in this area and to develop fresh ideas for the use of hypnosis in psychotherapy. Was it animal magnetism, a form of sleep, a condition of increased suggestibility, an hysteria, a dissociation? Was it any or all of these things? Freud set out to establish the true nature of the hypnotic state. He returned to Vienna, to his old friend the Viennese general practitioner Dr Joseph Breuer, and began to explore with him the hidden msyteries of the mind.

At about the time that Janet was working on his idea of a dissociation, Dr Breuer was treating a young girl aged twenty-one named Bertha Pappenheim. She had become ill whilst nursing her sick father, who had died in 1881. She had devoted herself to him unselfishly through the previous two years, frequently remaining by his bedside throughout the night. She presented numerous bizarre and unaccountable symptoms, and Breuer diagnosed that she suffered from what he called 'a psychosis of a peculiar kind'. He attempted to work on the 'psychical traumas' of this young patient as Charcot had worked to relieve the somatic traumas. Janet had found that his hypnotized patients could recall events that they had been unable to remember in the normal state. He had said that a forgotton emotional shock might thereby be revealed, which could give a clue as to the cause of the neurosis. The fears, obsessions or compulsions of his patients could then be made to disappear by further strong suggestion. Working together, Breuer and Freud, almost simultaneously with Janet, launched themselves into full-scale research of this new technique of 'regression'. Their efforts were inspired by a dramatic turn of events in the treatment of Bertha Pappenheim. Using hypnosis, Breuer had originally treated her in the established fashion with suggestions of deep trance and loss of symptoms. But his efforts were to no avail until at one point the patient herself spontaenously spoke of her problem whilst in the hypnotic state. As she regressed she was able to pin-point the origin of each symptom, simultaneously ventilating the feelings that had been associated with that situation. When this occurred the symptoms seemed to disappear. Bertha, appropriately enough, called the treatment 'chimney-sweeping' or 'the talking cure'.

Breuer and Freud began to compile a case-book history (Breuer and Freud 1955). Bertha Pappenheim was to become the famous 'Anna O'. The interpretation of her symptoms, as revealed by her whilst in hypnosis, became the foundation stone upon which Freud was to build his new school of psychoanalysis. Symptoms had appeared, explained Freud, because her emotions had been repressed below the level of consciousness. Hypnosis had allowed the uncovering of such repressed material, and the ventilation of her feelings had been the purging or catharsis that had resulted in the cure. Their patient, he maintained, had passionately wanted to seduce her doctor as, she had implied, her father had seduced her. Some time later Freud discovered that seduction by her father is one of the commonest fantasies of young girls. Nevertheless, this was the focus from which Freud evolved his ideas of the transference, positive or negative, or the counter-transference, which he additionally maintained Breuer had developed for Miss Pappenheim. She had revealed, in the reversal of roles, her own infantile sexual desires. Hypnosis, stated Freud, was nothing more than a particular 'loving relationship'.

Inspired by this case, Freud was to venture further. But he was soon to counter a major obstacle, that of resistance. Patients often blocked and would not or could not recall repressed memories even with the use of hypnosis. Although he had discovered the value of regression and all that followed, he was to learn to his cost that on many occasions the 'memories' that would surface during an hypnotic session could be entirely fanciful or fantasy. Nevertheless he also realized that, whether fact or fantasy, what was important from the point of view of therapy was that the patient wanted to believe these revelations to be true. As such, the symptoms were still attributable to them and it was necessary that the reasons for any such belief were exposed and explained. Thus interpretation, explanation and insight-directed therapy all developed as an essential addition to hypnotherapy.

Frau Emmy von N., a lady of forty, was Freud's first attempt to use hypnosis without the help of Breuer. She was a highly anxious person with a facial tic, and her words were punctuated by a curious clacking sound from her mouth. She stammered when frightened and suffered from numerous other complaints, with vivid hallucinations of mice and other animals. Freud maintained that some earlier mental experience, which was too traumatic for the patient to tolerate, had been unconsciously reinterpreted by her and converted into physical symptoms. He adopted the term 'conversion'. By this means the unacceptable memory could be hidden from conscious recall, and the gain resulting from the conversion symptoms could be used by the patient for her own protection. Such was the case with Frau Emmy, Freud concluded. The cathartic process under hypnosis failed in this case to produce permanent relief. The patient repeatedly relapsed, indicating the guarding and resistance that protected her repressed memories. This conversion was the hysteria, so fashionable in Charcot's Salpêtrière and so prevalent amongst the young female patients of the psychologists of the nineteenth century. But the obstacle that halted Freud with his researches in hypnosis was that of resistance. In many patients he was unable to penetrate the defences protecting the repressed material.

He moved on to fresh investigations, to open up the hidden territory of the unconscious through his newly developed technique of psychoanalysis. He abandoned hypnosis and treated patients by the methods of free association and dream interpretation that are used to this day. Further serious research into hypnosis, which Freud had so enthusiastically developed was laid to rest for almost half a century. Hypnosis became the victim of the non-qualified and lay therapists, of charlatans and entertainers. Some limited research did in fact continue. Ferenczi, Wilhelm Stekel, Morton Prince and a few others remained faithful to their interest in hypnosis. The great Pavlov certainly looked at its possibilities. The condition of hypnosis, he thought, was a conditioning into a special form of sleep.

It was because of this interest, however minimal, that the use of hypnosis was to save from ruin the life of many a solider during and after the First World War. The Freudian techniques of regression, ventilation and catharsis were once more resuscitated for the treatment of men suffering from shell-shock, later known as combat reaction or battle fatigue. Whilst under hypnosis, these men were encouraged to relive the emotional component of their battle experiences, often with a dramatic and considerable therapeutic effect. This work, championed in Britain by psychiatrists J. A. Hadfield, H. E. Wingfield and W. McDougall, stimulated some interest once more, and sporadic papers on the subject appeared, although they were hardly sufficient to revitalize hypnosis as a regular form of therapy.

More recent theories

In the early 1930s the work of Clark Hull, one of the foremost US authorities on learning, revived the study of hypnosis and established it on a sound experimental basis. A considerable amount of investigation has since then been conducted into its nature and uses. One controversial viewpoint was that of Robert White, (1941) who stressed the importance of good positive motivation and called hypnotic behaviour 'meaningful, goal-directed striving' (White 1941). T. X. Barber maintained that there was no reason to assume the existence of such a state as hypnosis, although he admitted that hypnotic effects had been elicited through the simple power of suggestion (Barber 1969). Spanos and Barber talked of 'role-playing' and 'goal directed fantasy'. Certainly a good deal of scepticism still existed as to whether there was in fact a specific state of hypnosis (Spanos and Barber 1974).

An interesting hypothesis was formulated by Ainslie Meares (1960). This is known as the atavistic theory. It maintains that there occurs in hypnosis a regression of the mental functions of the subject, to a primitive level where the power of suggestion operates and ideas are accepted without criticism. He also suggested that some patients who consciously desired hypnotherapy developed an unconscious psychological defence mechanism to prevent the return to this primitive level. Perhaps this explains some of Freud's difficulties. However, Meares also explained regression and cartharsis by his statement that in hypnosis 'the mechanism which keeps the uncomfortable thing repressed, ceases to function properly and the patient is able to bring out the repressed matter'.

A neurophysiological state

Although psychology and psychiatry progressed along the main fronts of research and treatment, the study of hypnosis remained in limbo until 1957. This was a year of great advancement, both experimentally and clinically.

The breakthrough was achieved when electroencephalography was used to explore and record the electrical impulses emanating from the brain in various altered states of consciousness and in pathological conditions of the brain. This was at last to establish a neurophysiological basis for the hypnotic state, to reinforce the numerous psychological ideas that had been argued for almost two hundred years. It was known that characteristic patterns of brainwaves could be recorded during the various levels of sleep, in coma and in similar states. (Berger 1930, Bremer 1935, Loomis, Harvey and Hobart 1938, Dynes 1947, Barker and Burgwin, 1949, Morazzi and Magoun 1949, Aserinsky and Kleitman 1953, Chertok and Kramarz 1959; but it was Barry Wyke of the Department of Applied Physiology of the Royal College of Surgeons of England who described clearly the neurological changes that take place in hypnosis (Wyke 1957). He was able to trace alterations in general cerebral activity with variations in frequency and marked diminution in voltage, which he believed were specific to the hypnotic state. The brainwaves can be changed by suggestions of various sensory or emotional experiences or by the suggestion to go to sleep. Thus he showed that hypnosis and sleep are physiologically distinct states. Additionally, Rozhnov (1978) was able to demonstrate electro-encephalographic changes occurring during hallucinatory suggestions given to the subjects in hypnosis. More recently, Meszaros *et al.* (1980), using greatly improved techniques, were able to demonstrate a subjectively altered state of consciousness and also concluded that no signs of sleep can be shown in the hypnotic state.

The manner in which messages are conveyed to the brain was explored by Magoun (1951). He identified the working of a collection of nerve cells or neurones and their processes in the brain stem of all primitive vertebrates, and in the mammalian brain. This is called the reticular formation. It extends from the lower end of the part of the brain known as the fourth ventricle and upwards into the thalamus and hypothalamus. This system receives afferent connections from tracts of the spinal cord as they ascend to the brain, as well as from the cranial nerves. In the brain, connections reach an area known as the limbic system, which is responsible for monitoring our emotions. In a further paper, Wyke (1960) explained how, together with other impulses, the voice of the hypnotist will travel along this channel, and how, by strict concentration of attention, all other impulses are ignored. The single, steadily flowing sound of the voice reaches the limbic system and the subject will respond to suggestions of calmness. As this slow and monotonous input continues, the activation of the reticular system is gradually reduced, there is diminished awareness of the environment, and the state of hypnosis results. There is a direct, closed circuit of communication between the hypnotist and the subject, who, if suitably motivated and in a sufficiently deep state, will respond to any suggestions given. We now know that such suggestions must be reasonable, within the capability of the subject and such as he or she would be willing to carry out when in the awake and totally conscious state.

Research continues world-wide. It now seems that hypnosis is not in any way a form of sleep but a specific state in itself, in fact a neurophysiological reality, particularly incorporating that psychological condition of the mind of increased suggestibility. Hypnosis may be defined as an altered state of awareness effected by total concentration on the voice of the therapist. It will result in measurable physical, neurophysiological and psychological changes in which may be produced distortion of emotion, sensation, image and time (Waxman 1981).

Hypnosis and treatment

Psychodynamic techniques

Alongside experimental work and research into the true nature of the hypnotic state, treatment advanced from the authoritarian and originally purely suggestive methods to keep pace with modern psychotherapeutic procedures. Until the days of Breuer, once the mesmeric or hypnotic state had been induced, the therapist relied upon powerful suggestion for the relief of symptoms. Now another technique was revealed. Inspired by Janet and as spontaneously produced by Bertha Pappenheim, Breuer and Freud evolved the use of regression and catharsis. This was followed by explanation of the causes of the problem, and so insight and understanding were a necessary adjunct. Effective use of the transference was to become an integral part of the procedure. Eventually, although dream interpretation and free association were intended as non-hypnotic techniques, patients very often drifted into hypnosis if these were used. Freud himself noted this. All these methods may be combined today in what is known as psychodynamic or dynamic treatment.

The development of behavioural hypnosis

At the turn of the century, Pavlov, who had already researched into hypnosis, was experimenting with the behaviour of dogs at his laboratories in old St Petersburg. He discovered the conditioned reflex, later to be known as the conditioned response. These experiments were extended so that it was soon known that humans too could be conditioned to respond to certain stimuli. The ideas of conditioning reached to the United States and to J. B. Watson at the Johns Hopkins University. Further research led to the development of 'learning theory', which emphasized that all our behaviour is learned from our earliest days. Watson and his colleague Rosalie Rayner experimented with conditioning and showed that new responses could be established where they had not previously existed. It was subsequently found that conditioned responses could also be altered and replaced by other responses. Watson founded the new school known as behaviourism in 1914, and from this the form of treatment known as behaviour therapy evolved. In effect this means that, if a learned response is inappropriate or unacceptable for any reason, it can be 'unlearned', and a new and more acceptable response can be relearned in its place. The essence of 'unlearning' is to produce and to maintain in the patient a profound sense of relaxation so that anxieties, fears or other undesirable feelings can be neutralized. In this state, if confronted in imagination by the stimulus that had previously produced that unwanted response, the patient would remain calm and relaxed. Thus having 'unlearned' and relearned, he or she would subsequently react in this new relaxed manner in the real-life situation.

Many ideas of producing and maintaining relaxation so that treatment may proceed have been attempted, from that of learning to relax progressive groups of muscles, as taught by Jacobson (1938), to treatment with barbiturate drugs. Without doubt the simplest and most effective method is with the use of hypnosis. The patient can be relaxed and will usually readily visualize situations or specific anxiety-producing stimuli that may be suggested by the therapist. In this way, by remaining calm in what was originally a frightening or unpleasant experience, he or she has relearned a more acceptable response. Joseph Wolpe (1958) established the use of behaviour therapy, first in experimenting with cats and then with patients. He treated them along a graduated scale of experiences – from those producing the least fear to those that produced the greatest – reconditioning each at every stage on the scale or hierarchy. After each step the patient was sent away to practise in real life what he or she had newly learned under hypnosis. This method, known as 'desensitization', can be adapted to treat a wide range of neuroses.

Do-it-yourself hypnosis

Another technique that has evolved is known as self- or auto-hypnosis. Although many specialists will argue that all hypnosis is auto-hypnosis – in other words that the patient produces the hypnotic state by himself or herself – for the purposes of treatment this must be more specific. Patients are taught by the therapist whilst actually under hypnosis to produce the state for themselves in their own time, and to practise what has been learned at each session of therapy twice daily at home, and in this way to reinforce the new learning. When they are well versed in this technique they may use it additionally without further instruction, by pre-empting situations in which they think they may develop adverse emotions. By continuous use, patients will over time lose their dependence upon the therapist as well as any transference that may have been produced. Instruction in self-hypnosis should be a *sine qua non* in most conditions treated by hypnosis.

Positive thinking and hypnosis

Yet other techniques recently evolved are those of ego strengthening (Hartland 1971) and ego-assertive retraining (Waxman 1981). The former is perhaps an extension of the ideas of Coué (1922) of 'getting better and better every day', but learned whilst in hypnosis. It was devised by Dr John Hartland. In the Hartland method, the patient is repeatedly given, at every session, strong suggestions of feeling better, stronger, more alert, more positive, etc. The suggestions are individually tailored to suit each subject. Hartland himself was convinced that eventually these suggestions would become effective.

The technique of ego-assertive retraining, in addition to those suggestions of improvement of self-image, incorporates a behavioural technique in which patients are shown that they can assert themselves when confronted by some authority or figure who would normally produce in them feelings of anxiety or inferiority. This could possibly be any person of importance or even some apparently unremarkable individual – boss, girlfriend or shop assistant.

It is not suggested that all of these techniques be utilized in the treatment of every patient. Each method, or any combination of them, may be incorporated with hypnotherapy today. Every patient is an individual and must be properly assessed and diagnosed before any particular remedy is attempted.

Uses of hypnosis

The neuroses

Taken together, the neurotic group of illnesses constitute some of the commonest problems met with in everyday life. Neurotic reactions are an indication of mental conflict and are the most frequent mode of faulty response to stress. There appears to be a constitutional factor present, but a neurosis may also arise as a result of early environmental difficulties or in response to unsatisfactory relationships with other people.

If we turn back the pages of history we may realize that most of the patients treated by Mesmer suffered from some form of psychoneurosis. Psychotherapy remains today the main form of treatment of neurotic reactions. Additionally tranquillizer drugs are frequently prescribed but these are not curative, and the unsatisfactory long-term effects of such medication are well known. Hypnotherapy remains a form of psychological treatment for the common neuroses, and some of these are noted below.

ANXIETY

We all require a level of anxiety that will warn us when to take heed, when to stop, look and listen. We can all tolerate stress up to a certain level. But when the level, which varies with each person, is exceeded, then symptoms begin to appear. The common and normal responses to anxiety include blushing, stammering, rapid breathing, palpitations, 'butterflies' in the stomach, excessive bowel activity, frequency of micturition and the overall feeling of being paralysed with fear. Although these are primitive protective responses, when they become chronic the continuous mental and physical symptoms can make life intolerable. We know that the persistent use of tranquillizer drugs, once hailed as the answer to these problems, may result in dependency, which will only compound the original problem. Relaxation in hypnosis can offer relief from anxiety symptoms, and the regular use of self-hypnosis will bring down the level of anxiety so that stressful situations can be confronted without any adverse effect. Such treatment may not be sufficient, since other neurotic behaviour is common in highly anxious people and this must be dealt with additionally.

PHOBIC RESPONSES

A phobic fear is an irrational fear, and classically all the symptoms of anxiety may manifest themselves at once. *Blakiston's Medical Dictionary* (1972) lists some 275 different types of phobia but this is far from complete. Phobias are invariably associated with symptoms of anxiety and/or depression. Either or both of these conditions may precede the onset of phobic symptoms. It is therefore of the greatest importance to taken an accurate and extensive psychiatric history. If the patient is depressed it is then essential to prescribe the correct antidepressant medication, and much research has been carried out on the treatment of phobias where the latter condition additionally exists (Waxman 1975). Once the depression is under control, the anxiety and phobic symptoms can be dealt with by means of hypnosis. The original treatment as described by Wolpe continues to be the method *par excellence* in spite of numerous other behavioural techniques that have been devised (see the section above, on 'the development of behavioural hypnosis'). In addition to desensitization along a hierarchy of anxiety-provoking situations visualized whilst in hypnosis, the patient must be taught to use self-hypnosis and to practise each stage twice daily in the interval between weekly meetings with the therapist. The most common phobias are agoraphobia, illness- and death-phobias, and social phobias, although a fear of flying is rapidly overtaking them. Many patients have irrational fears in many areas. Isolated phobias rarely exist and easily generalize into other associated fears. For example, a fear of heights, lifts and flying will frequently occur in the same person.

Phobic fear may not necessarily involve a response in all systems simultaneously. One or more symptoms may occur separately, and where this happens the condition may be referred to as psychosomatic.

PSYCHOSOMATIC ILLNESSES

These isolated responses may occur in any system of the body in people confronted with some stressful situation. It is when such a symptom becomes recurring and incapacitating that treatment is required. In some people the symptoms seem to have a predilection for a particular part of the body, and there is evidence of a constitutional and emotional factor involved in determining this. This is known as 'organ inferiority' (e.g. Adler 1917, Wolberg 1948).

The central nervous system. Recurrent headaches are frequently self-diagnosed as migraine. Often these are of nervous origin and should be correctly labelled tension headaches. Nevertheless true migraine may also be triggered by tension, and many sufferers recognize this. One lady of forty-two gave a twenty-year history of such attacks, which had become more frequent and severe. Talking through her problem in the relaxed state of hypnosis resulted in a greater understanding of her difficulties. She had commenced a new job, which involved close and concentrated work in a poor light. When she complained of headache her boss said, 'You give *me* a headache'. She left the job but took the headaches with her. These subsequently appeared not only in stress situations associated with work but generalised into all other areas in her life in which she experienced anxiety. Thorough medical and ophthalmic examination revealed no abnormality. Moreover, understanding what was thought to be the origin of the problem made no difference to her symptoms. She was hypnotized and proved a good and co-operative subject. She regressed to her earlier days and suddenly spoke of a school-friend who had died of a cerebral tumour. It was because of the underlying fear and the association of her own headaches with a possible tumour that her symptoms had persisted. Desensitization to a wide range of anxiety situations in her life brought symptom relief in six sessions. Instruction in self-hypnosis was given, and in follow-up after four years she had been free of headaches.

A highly anxious young man aged thirty-four suffered from *grand mal* epilepsy. Attacks were occurring every two or three weeks and were invariably triggered by situations of stress. The regular use of self-hypnosis reduced his level of anxiety, and during regression he revealed many problems of his early childhood, which had shaped his persisting anxious personality. Full discussion during and after the session was an essential part of therapy. He has been free from attacks for three years. It is essential to follow up all patients, as an occasional 'booster' may be required.

The respiratory system. The problem of nervous asthma is well known and may affect people of all ages. Treatment is based mainly on the use of self-hypnosis. This must be used regularly and, in addition, immediately an attack is anticipated. A full account of the treatment is given by Maher-Loughnan (1970).

The cardiovascular system. Chest pains simulating angina or coronary attacks are common, as is also a rise in blood pressure associated with situations of anxiety. The young man whose friend drops dead on a golf course is a frequent visitor to his GP, complaining of chest pains or palpitations. Flatulence and indigestion may often be mistaken for cardiac pains, and the fear of death that results is sufficient to make the cardiovascular system a common target for psychosomatic symptoms. Thorough physical examination is always essential, and if negative, the prescription of self-hypnosis is the most positive form of therapy likely to help this patient.

The gastro-intestinal system. Many highly anxious people 'internalize' their problems, and the gut is an all too common focus. Symptoms of peptic ulcer may result, or at the other end of the intestinal tract the irritable bowel syndrome is extremely common. Extensive research has been undertaken, and a good deal of nonsense has been spoken and written about this simple and primitive response to anxiety, which every schoolboy has long recognized. Diarrhoea may also be explained as the somatization of feelings of anger and aggression, and this aspect should be thoroughly explored, particularly in so far as patients' relationships with their parents are concerned. Relaxation in hypnosis, dynamic exploration, desensitization, self-hypnosis and ego-assertive retraining, if efficiently carried out, will bring symptom relief. Another technique recently used omitted any attempt at hypnoanalysis and introduced suggestion of warmth by asking the patient to place a hand on the abdomen whilst relating this to asserting control over bowel function. (Whorwell *et al.* 1984).

The genito-urinary system. Psychosexual difficulties should be brought under this heading, since they are so frequently physical responses of emotional origin. In the male these include erectile difficulties and premature ejaculation. Both conditions are due to fear of failure. Vaginismus and frigidity in the female are due to fear of attack. Orgasmic problems may be related to anxiety. After excluding organic illness all of these problems must be extensively investigated and will respond to the hypnotherapy techniques outlined above as used for other fear responses. Sexual deviations are in a special group; more than for any other condition, real positive motivation must be present if treatment is to be effective.

One young woman of twenty-four was distressed by her own lesbian practices. She had always enjoyed friendships with young men but could not allow nor evisage any physical relationship with any of them. She was unable to account for this. She had often thought of marriage but was terrified lest her sexual problem would manifest itself. Under hypnosis she spoke, with considerable release of affect, of the vigorous corporal punishment meted out by her stepfather in her childhood, of his later attempt to seduce her and her own desire to retreat into the shelter of her mother's arms, which was always repulsed. A sexual approach by an older girl at school was at first rejected; but she obtained solace from the relationship and eventually succumbed, and other relationships followed. She was confused as to the reason for this and for her inability to allow a close relationship with a young man she had learned to trust. After a frank discussion of her problem the patient was sensitized whilst under hypnosis, to a series of lesbian sexual situations and simultaneously desensitized to a hierarchy of heterosexual situations until she was able to permit, in imagination, full and satisfactory intercourse. Her relationship with her male friend improved; she married and now enjoys a happy and fruitful life. Follow-up was by post. When last heard from, she had admitted to her husband her earlier sexual problems. He had understood, and she claimed not the slightest desire to relapse into her former habits. However, it must be emphasized again that, while many patients think they want to change these habits, where there is any doubt at all, treatment, particularly of psychosexual problems, is bound to fail.

Nocturnal enuresis (bed-wetting) is also a condition that will respond to hypnotherapy. It is essential to explore fully the family relationships and the understanding by the parents of the problem. During hypnosis, emphasis is given to ego-strengthening with ideas of adult development and mastery over the body and its functions, increase in bladder capacity and bladder control and to becoming alerted and awakening when the bladder is distended. The child is instructed not to empty the bladder for at least three hours before each treatment session and is told that he or she will awaken during the hypnotic session when the bladder feels full, just as he or she will awaken at night under similar circumstances. He or she is allowed to go to the toilet and on return is rehypnotized, and further powerful post-hypnotic suggestion is given.

The musculoskeletal system. Muscular and joint pains limit movement, and as a consequence fear of movement will aggravate the pain. Reduction of anxiety under hypnosis will do much to reduce fear as well as any accompanying muscular spasm. Chronic backache, for example, is one of the major causes of absence from work; hypnotherapy can be a useful adjunct to other forms of treatment for this condition.

The skin. As one of the most exposed features of the body, the skin will often reveal underlying emotional problems. Many skin conditions are aggravated, if not caused, by anxiety; and most dermatologists treating eczema or psoriasis, for example, will often simulteneously prescribe some anxiety-reducing medication. Hypnotherapy has been used successfully for such conditions (Waxman 1973), with exploration and behaviour therapy as the main themes.

THE OBESSIONAL/COMPULSIVE NEUROSES

Problems of repetitive thoughts, words, ideas and images and compulsive deeds are amongst those grouped under this heading. The patient usually retains insight but is unable to resist the repetition. There are often other personality difficulties, and depression may be a further feature. The unusual failure of so many different forms of treatment that have been used for this condition is witness to the extreme difficulties that arise for the therapist. Certain antidepressant drugs are helpful in obsessional problems (Waxman 1975) and should invariably be prescribed. Hypnosis may be used additionally, especially for the process of dynamic exploration, discussion and conditioning. In the latter, the patient is shown in imagery that the day can continue in a perfectly normal way without recourse to the particular obsessional activity.

HYSTERICAL/CONVERSION SYMPTOMS

Although a relic of the era of Charcot, these problems frequently appear amongst the many other symptoms of anxiety. They tend to mimic other conditions in their physical manifestations, and thorough investigation to eliminate organic disease is essential. Since the symptom has a definite meaning, this should be explored in depth, understood and explained to the patient if treatment is to be successful. Hypnotherapy lends itself particularly to this technique. Symptom removal by suggestion under hypnosis, as in the days before Breuer and Freud, is definitely contraindicated and may well result in reinforced substitution symptoms. A true Freudian abreaction is a rare but rewarding experience, but this effect is not always necessary and even if it does occur will not always result in relief of the problem. It is worthwhile to recall poor Mesmer at this stage and how failure to explore fully the family dynamics involving Miss Paradis resulted in her relapse and and his downfall.

Sleep problems

The treatment of insomnia with the use of hypnosis is overall based on the relief of the anxiety that is preventing sleep. The problem may manifest itself in initial or intermediate sleep difficulties or early-morning waking. The latter is frequently, although not always, a symptom of depression; and once again this possibility must be investigated by taking a complete and detailed history. Other sleep difficulties may also occur with depression, and if this diagnosis is reached it is essential to prescribe antidepressant medication. Hypnosis may then be used additionally when the drug has taken effect. However, the therapist must remember that the depressed patient is often suicidal. It could be possible to reduce the patient's accompanying anxiety so he or she can appraise the situation in the light of the non-anxious day. With everything appearing hopeless, suicide may appear to be the only solution. Other factors must also be considered where there are sleep difficulties. These include pain, physical discomfort and the effect of drugs or stimulants. Death-fears preventing sleep are not uncommon. If these problems are excluded, hypnotherapy can be an effective means of removing the overlay of anxiety that is responsible for the sleeplessness. The essential factor is instruction in self-hypnosis and in showing the patient that, if he or she is in bed and ready to go to sleep, it is possible to 'switch off' whatever thoughts or preoccupations were previously keeping him or her awake. Also during self-hypnosis the patient may visualize anticipated events that could be the cause of anxiety, and yet remain relaxed and calm. Self-hypnosis each morning in addition will help to lower the general level of anxiety.

Personality problems

These involve particularly problems of self-image. There may be difficulty in seeing oneself feeling comfortable in relationship to other people and the world around. For some reason, there is a feeling of inadequacy, and some physical response may occur because of the emotional stress that results. Many of these symptoms are due to this fear; blushing, stammering and nervous tics are readily recognized and can be dealt with by desensitization. Other responses may help the sufferer to escape from threatening life situations, and these include alcoholism, drug addiction and other acting-out behaviour. Just as complicated are eating and weight problems – that is, problems of body image that may manifest themselves in the conditions known as anorexia and bulimia. The techniques using hypnosis are unchanged. Considerable difficulties arise however when the unacceptable response or habit becomes additionally an addiction. The physical and psychological problems of withdrawal will compound any existing symptoms and will often result in the patient abandoning treatment. Hospitalization and drug therapy must always be considered as well as all the supportive measures that should be undertaken (Waxman 1985). Here particularly, if the patient really does not wish to recover, certainly hypnosis will not *make* him or her do so; real positive motivation and long-term follow-up are essential.

Obstetrics

Hypnosis and self-hypnosis are ideal methods that may be used to teach expectant mothers to relax. Additionally, suggestions of perineal analgesia may be effective if the patient is fortunate enough to be a somnambule. It is necessary however for the therapist, if he or she is not also the obstetrician, to work in close co-operation with the latter as well as with the theatre staff; in addition, the therapist should be present during the delivery. Where successful, such treatment can be as useful as any anaesthetic. Deliveries are safer, and babies are healthier (Davidson 1962).

Dentistry

The most effective use of hypnosis in dentistry is for the reduction of fear. In addition, hypnosis can be used to reduce needle and instrument phobias (see the section above, on 'the neuroses'). It is also used for that most intractable problem known to dental surgeons, that of bruxism or tooth grinding. Treatment of the latter however is not for the amateur. There may be very deep-rooted problems associated with suppressed anger, and long-term analysis may be indicated. In certain susceptible patients, hypnosis may be used to produce local analgesia so that dental work may proceed without the patient being aware of pain. When hypnosis is used in dentistry, additional bonuses are the reduction of gagging, salivation and bleeding (Smith 1977).

The relief of pain

It is not known when hypnosis was first used for the relief of pain, but certainly this method flourished well into the second half of the nineteenth century. A considerable amount of research is being carried out today into the nature and physiology of pain, the relationship with anxiety and depression as well as environmental, racial and other factors. It must also be understood that pain and the manner in which it is experienced can have a considerable meaning. The manner in which pain is expressed or suppressed should be taken into account before treatment is commenced. Recently pain clinics have been established in many centres in the world where numerous techniques of treatment are practised and assessed. Hypnosis may not only be used in minor operations, in obstetrics and dentistry, as has been shown, but can also be of value in the relief of pain in terminal illness.

About twenty years ago morphine-like substances known as the endorphins were found to be present in the brain. Shortly afterwards it was thought that hypnosis may act by stimulating the release of these substances and in this way produce analgesia. A substance known as naloxone will reverse the effects of morphine, and a good deal of investigation has been undertaken to examine the effects of hypnotically induced analgesia and the use of naloxone in reversing those effects. Results were equivocal. In one small study naloxone was found to completely reverse analgesia of the hand artificially induced by hypnosis (Stephenson 1978). Other extensive studies (Finer 1982) demonstrated that naloxone did not act in this way in hypnotized subjects, suggesting that hypnosis does not result in a release of endorphins.

That hypnosis may be an effective analgesic must be accepted. Whether this is because of the result of suggestion or due to some as yet hidden factor or chemical change remains unknown. In general terms the more anxious the individual the more intense will he or she report the pain. In addition to the reduction of anxiety, other techniques may be employed, for example the suggestion of warmth and comfort and the relief of pain by placing, say, the palm of the hand over the affected site; or, conversely, by the suggestion of placing ice over the area, resulting in numbing of sensation including the sensation of pain. According to Bond (1984) only 20 per cent of patients are susceptible to pain relief by hypnotherapy.

Memory recall

The treatment of this problem derives from the earlier Breuer–Freud technique of regression. William James had claimed that the most trivial thought or memory must affect the brain structure in as much as it had left some imprint on the brain. Modern research has shown this to be far from the truth. Memories fade with the passage of time and some are totally lost; recall itself may be poor, or the result of lack of concentration, or it may be clouded by anxiety. Memories associated with events that are too frightening or humiliating, or which in some way have been too traumatic to tolerate, may be repressed below the level of consciousness and can sometimes be retrieved with the use of hypnosis. Under the effect of hypnosis, relaxation is achieved, and any anxiety surrounding the original event, or that has developed since, may be neutralized. Additionally, using techniques of regression some patients are able to go back in time and relive the actual episode, even with the emotional content that was experienced or repressed at that time. However, not all patients have the ability to regress to this extent, and memory recall may simply be a process of remembering.

Patients do not necessarily tell the truth during recall under hypnosis, as Freud discovered. They may lie deliberately or unwittingly; they may confabulate or try to help by modifying any true recall. Thus what any person 'remembers' whilst under hypnosis may not be a true record of events as they happened. This is all very well in therapy, for what the patient believes or wants to believe or wants the therapist to believe is as important as the truth and must be taken into account. Where hypnosis is used in criminology, however, what the subject says must be regarded only as information, and can be taken only as a possible clue. Hypnosis has not the infallibility of a finger-print. It can never be acceptable as real evidence in a court of law and must always be supported by hard facts.

Moreover, leading questions must never be put to the person under hypnosis in a way that may invite a certain reply. The technique is to take the person back to the day of the event in question and to allow him or her to talk freely, and with as little interruption as possible, about that day. Any bias must be totally avoided. Thus no suspect should ever by hypnotized in an attempt to arrive at the 'truth'. The person carrying out the hypnosis should be a psychiatrist or psychologist with special training in its use and must be totally impartial. A full medical and psychiatric assessment of the person undergoing the hypnosis should be made beforehand. It is of value if the session is recorded so that the proceedings are not in dispute at any time. A very considerable amount of literature has been published on the subject of memory recall and its uses (e.g. Waxman 1983).

Summary

The revival of the use of hypnosis in treatment has been a major advance in psychotherapy. There is no doubt that it is successful in its correct clinical application. There is equally no doubt that its use is often abused. Before hypnotherapy is even contemplated, correct diagnosis is essential and this can be made only by a qualified medical practitioner, a dentist or a qualified psychologist. There is no qualification in hypnosis as such. It is part and parcel of a postgraduate curriculum that is usually undertaken by individual societies. The development of hypnosis to its present place in medicine and psychiatry has been traced in this chapter, but in spite of the wide range of problems for which it may be applied it is certainly no panacea. There are considerable limitations to its uses, and dangers exist for example when inadequate assessment and incorrect diagnoses are arrived at. Nevertheless if correctly applied there is no doubt that hypnotherapy has become not only a most useful adjunct to other recognized therapies but in many instances a specific treatment in its own right.

References

Adler, A. (1917) Study of organ inferiority and its psychical compensations. *Nervous and Mental Disease Monograph Series*, 24. New York.
Aserinsky, E. and Kleitman, N. (1953) Regularly occurring periods of eye mobility and concomitant phenomena during sleep. *Science*, 118: 273–4.

Barber, T. X. (1969) *Hypnosis: A Scientific Approach.* New York Van Nostrand Reinhold.

Barker, W. and Burgwin, S (1949) Brain wave patterns during hypnosis, hypnotic sleep and normal sleep. *Archives of Neurology and Psychiatry,* 63: 412–20.

Berger, H. (1930) Uber das Elektrenkephalogram des Menschen, 11. *Journal of Physiology and Neurology,* 40: 169–79.

Bernheim, H. (1900) *Suggestive Therapeutics: A Treatise on the Nature and Uses of Hypnotism.* New York: Putnam.

Bertrand, A (1823) *Traite du Somnambulism.* Paris.

Blakiston's Medical Dictionary (1972), ed. A. Osol. 3rd Edition. New York McGraw-Hill.

Bond, M. R. (1984) *Pain: Its Nature, Analysis and Treatment.* Edinburgh Churchill Livingstone.

Braid, J. (1899) *Neurypnology or the Rationale of Nervous Sleep Considered in Relation with Animal Magnetism.* London: Redway.

Bremer, F. (1935) *Cerveau Isolé et Physiologie du Sommeil C. R.* Paris: Societe Biologique: 118, 1235–42.

Breuer, J. and Freud, S. (1955) Studies on hysteria. *Standard Edition of Complete Work of Sigmund Freud,* Vol. II, 1893–5, ed. J. Strachey. London: Hogarth Press.

Charcot, J. M. (1890) *Oevres Completes IX.* Paris: Bourneville et Brissaud.

Chertok, L. and Kramarz, P. (1959) Hypnosis, sleep and electro-encephalography. *Journal of Nervous and Mental Diseases,* 128: 227–38.

Coué, E. (1922) *Better and Better Every Day.* London: Unwin.

Davidson, J. A. (1962) An assessment of the value of hypnosis in pregnancy and labour. *British Medical Journal,* 11: 951–3.

Dynes, J. B. (1947) An objective method of distinguishing sleep from the hypnotic trance. *Archives of Neurology and Psychiatry,* 57: 84–97.

Faria, J. C. di (1819) *De la Cause du Sommeil Lucide.* Paris.

Finer, B. (1982) Endorphins under hypnosis in chronic pain patients: some experimental findings. Paper read at Ninth Congress of Hypnosis and Psychosomatic Medicine, Glasgow.

Hartland, J. (1971) *Medical and Dental Hypnosis and its Clinical Applications,* 2nd edition. London: Baillière Tindall.

Jacobson, E. (1938) *Progressive Relaxation.* Chicago: University of Chicago Press.

Janet, P. (1925) *Psychological Healing, I and II.* London: Allen & Unwin.

Loomis, A. L., Harvey, E. N. and Hobart, G. (1938) Brain potentials during the onset of sleep. *Journal of Neurophysiology,* 1: 24.

Magoun, H. W. (1951) An ascending reticular activating system in the brain stem. Archives of Neurology and Psychiatry, 67: 145–54.

Maher-Loughnan, G. P. (1970) Hypnosis and auto-hypnosis for the treatment of asthma. *International Journal of Clinical and Experimental Hypnosis,* 18 (1): 1–14.

Meares, A (1960) *A System of Medical Hypnosis,* Philadelphia and London: Saunders.

Mészáros, I., Bányai, E. I. and Greguss, A. C. (1980) Hypnosis, EEG and evoked potential. In M. Pajntar, E. Roškar and M. Lavrič (eds.), *Hypnosis in Psychotherapy and Psychosomatic Medicine.* Ljubljana: University Press.

Moruzzi G. and Magoun, H. W. (1949) Brain stem reticular formation and activation of the EEG. *Electroencephalography and Clinical Neurophysiology,* 1: 455–73.

Rozhnov, V. E. (1978) Towards understanding the nature of hypnosis. In F. H. Frankel and H. S. Zamansky (eds.), *Hypnosis at its Bicentennial.* New York and London: Plenum.

Smith, S. R. (1977) *A Primer of Hypnosis*. Bristol: John Wright & Son.

Spanos, N. P. and Barber T. X. (1974) Toward a convergence in hypnosis research. *American Psychologist*, 29 (7): 500–11.

Stephenson, J. B. P. (1978) Reversal of hypnosis induced analgesia by naloxone. *Lancet*, 11: 991–2.

Waxman, D. (1973) Behaviour therapy of psoriasis: a hypnoanalytic and counter-conditioning technique. *Postgraduate Medical Journal*, 49: 591–5.

(1975) An investigation into the use of anafranil in phobic and obsessional disorders. *Scottish Medical Journal*, 20: 61–6.

(1978) Wounds give no pain. Presidential address given at Inaugural Meeting of Section of Medical and Dental Hypnosis of the Royal Society of Medicine, London.

(1981) *Hypnosis: A guide for Patients and Practitioners*. London: Allen & Unwin.

(1983) Use of hypnosis in criminology: *Journal of the Royal Society of Medicine*, 76: 480–4.

(1985) The treatment of alcohol and drug additions: an overview. In D Waxman, P. C. Misra, M. Gibson, and A. Basker (eds.), *Modern Trends in Hypnosis*. New York and London: Plenum.

White, R. W. (1941) A preface to the theory of hypnotism. *Journal of Abnormal Psychology*, 36: 477–505.

Wolberg, L. R. (1948) *Medical Hypnosis*. New York: Grune & Stratton.

Whorwell, P. J., Prior, A. and Faragher, E. B. (1984) Controlled trial of hypnotherapy in the treatment of severe refractory irritable bowel syndrome. *Lancet*, 11: 1232–4.

Wolpe, J. (1958) *Psychotherapy by Reciprocal Inhibition*. Stanford, Calif: Stanford University Press.

Wyke, B. D. (1957) Neurological aspects of hypnosis. *Proceedings of the Dental and Medical Society for the Study of Hypnosis*. London: Royal Society of Medicine.

(1960) Neurological mechanisms in hypnosis. *Proceedings of the Dental and Medical Society for the Study of Hypnosis*. London: Royal Society of Medicine.

THE CONCEPT OF TRANCE

Brian J. Fellows

Chapter 2 was contributed by an author whose primary interest is the practical use of hypnosis. David Waxman is more concerned with assessing the appropriateness of using hypnosis as an adjunct to therapy than with trying to establish the exact nature of the processes involved. He has described the phenomenon as he witnesses it in his everyday work. In many situations it is not essential that the mechanisms of a therapeutic procedure are understood; it is sufficient that they work. Aspirin was used for many years before the nature of its physiological action was established. The remaining chapters of this book are contributed by theoretical psychologists, whose interests are directed towards establishing viable theories of hypnosis. There will undoubtedly be critics who would wish to claim that it must be a sterile theory that is not founded on the rich data available to medical practitioners. However, the pure researcher is frequently able to use a broader perspective, and has the advantage of being able to experiment on his or her subjects in a way that is often not reasonable with patients. Of course, the researcher's theories must take account of medical findings too.

Waxman's description of hypnosis was physiological in style, as might be expected from a medical practitioner. He sees hypnosis as a 'state', and mentions the condition of 'trance'. Brian Fellows is a 'non-state' theorist, and in this next chapter he questions the need for the concept of trance. He presents evidence suggesting that many of the characteristics commonly associated with trance are absent from hypnosis, whereas qualities often associated with hypnosis can in fact be found in other non-hypnotic conditions.

Dr Fellows is lecturer in psychology at Portsmouth Polytechnic. His psychology department was one of the first in Britain to offer the subject of hypnosis as part of the degree course. He is editor of the British Journal of Experimental and Clinical Hypnosis.

If you were to ask someone what they thought was involved in hypnosis or what it meant to be hypnotized the answer would most likely include some reference to a trance state. A dictionary definition of hypnosis, although avoiding the term 'trance', will stress that it is 'an artificially induced state resembling sleep and characterised by extreme suggestibility' (Garmonsway 1965). Standard textbooks on the subject also tend to talk of hypnosis as a unique and special state of mind, and the terms 'hypnotic state' and 'hypnotic trance' are often used interchangeably (e.g. Hilgard 1965, 1). This conception of hypnosis as a trance state is thus popular and widespread, both in our everyday understanding and in the professional literature. However, as I hope to demonstrate in this chapter, this conception is not without its problems. The link between hypnotic behaviour and the trance state has been the subject of a number of critical attacks from researchers, particularly during the past twenty years or so. Two of the leading critics of what has come to be called 'the state theory' of hypnosis are contributors to this book (Nicholas Spanos and Graham Wagstaff); but probably the most important figure in this movement (and he could probably be called its 'father') is Theodore X Barber, who, in a large number of experimental and theoretical papers and books, presented the main case against seeing hypnosis in terms of a trance state. Later in this chapter I will attempt to summarize Barber's views and findings and discuss their implications for how we think and talk about hypnotic behaviour and experience. Let us first examine the trance concept.

Definition of trance

The *Penguin English Dictionary* defines trance as 'a condition of unawareness of external things in which visions, hallucinations, etc., are experienced and any acts peformed are unconscious' (Garmonsway 1965). A more technical definition would be as follows:

> A sleep-like state marked by reduced sensitivity to stimuli, loss or alteration of knowledge of what is happening, substitution of automatic for voluntary activity. Trances are frequent in hysteria and they may be hypnotically induced. In extreme form trance resembles (or is) coma. Religious or emotionally marked trances are called ecstasy. (English and English 1958).

Both of these definitions emphasize certain important characteristics of the meaning of the term 'trance', which we should note. (1) The individual is relatively unaware or insensitive to the external environment. However, this feature by itself is not enough to define a trance state since there are many situations in which a person may be said correctly to be unaware of the surrounding environment without being in a trance; for example, during deep concentration, when deeply absorbed in a book or when engaged in lively conversation. (2) Unusual experiences may occur during a trance, including hallucinations and false beliefs. Again, this feature is not sufficient for the definition, since such experiences may occur without a trance. (3) Actions are performed unconsciously or automatically rather than being voluntary. As before we need to question the sufficiency of this characteristic, since the fact that action occurs unconsciously or automatically does not necessarily mean the person making the action is in a trance state. For example, many well-practised skills (such as walking, riding a bicycle or driving a car) are performed largely at an automatic level, but one would hesitate to describe the performer of such skills as being in a trance state. The definition clearly oversimplifies the distinction between voluntary and involuntary actions that occur in varying degress and combinations in our everyday lives.

The main question to be considered in this chapter is whether it is appropriate to use the concept of trance, as defined above, in the description and explanation of hypnotic behaviour. Are hypnotized subjects aware of their environment? Do they have unusual experiences? Are their actions involuntary and unconscious? These are some of the central questions that we will need to answer. In order to do this we will need to examine in some detail the nature of hypnotic behaviour and experience and the conditions under which they occur. But first let us explore the range of experiences that typically come under the heading of 'trance'.

The trance in a religious context

As one of the above definitions indicated, trances occur in certain pathological states, such as hysteria. They may also occur in a religious or emotional context, in which case they are usually referred to as ecstasy. One of the most important studies of the latter kind was that undertaken by William Sargant (1957, 1973). Sargant collected a large number of religious conversion and possession experiences from a variety of mainly primitive cultures throughout the world, emphasizing the role of rhythmic stimuli (such as drumming, hand clapping, chanting and dancing) and hyperventilation (overbreathing) in their production. For example, in his first book Sargant (1957) quotes the first-hand experiences of Maya Deren (1953) of her involvement and response to voodoo ceremonies and rituals on Haiti. She told how the drumming induced uncontrollable bodily movements, until she felt the experience of possession:

> My skull is a drum; each great beat drives that leg, like the point of a stake, into the ground. The singing is at my very ear, inside my head. This sound will drown me! . . . I cannot wrench the leg free. I am caught in this cylinder, the well of sound. There is nothing anywhere except this.
> (Quoted by Sargant 1957: 94)

In his second book Sargant (1973) reports on a series of fascinating personal studies of possession, trance, religion and primitive healing methods in various parts of the world including Kenya, the Sudan, Zambia, Nigeria, Brazil, the West Indies, Haiti and the USA. The term 'trance' is freely used by Sargant to describe a range of behaviours mainly brought about by rhythmic dancing, overbreathing or fear (e.g. snake handling). Unfortunately, Sargant tends to neglect the important role of the social context and variables such as expectations in these experiences. He also tends towards a naive and simplistic view of hypnosis; for example, he states that on waking the hypnotized subject 'seldom remembers what has happened during the hypnotic sleep' but 'may remember all sorts of facts about his past life which he cannot remember when he is awake' (Sargant 1973: 27). Such beliefs are understandable, and very widespread in the popular mind. However, as I hope to show, they betray a serious misunderstanding or lack of knowledge about the nature of and variables affecting hypnotic behaviour. Unfortunately for the theory, it simply is not true that 'hypnotized' subjects remember nothing of their experiences or that they are able to remember more about their past when 'hypnotized' than when not (Barber 1969).

The concept of trance also figures prominently in the description of contemporary Western religious experiences and of trance mediumship (Gauld 1982) and speaking in tongues (Goodman 1972). However, a recent study of Spanos and Hewitt (1979) has shown that glossolalia (speaking in tongues) can be performed without the usual indications of a trance state, i.e. with eyes open, with no trembling or shaking and with no obvious memory deficits. As we shall see, essentially the same conclusions apply to hypnosis.

The trance in creative work

Another major activity with which the trance concept is frequently linked is that involving creative work of various types. For example, Jaime Sabartes (1948) provided numerous descriptions of the trance-like state used by Picasso during painting. Here is one such account, of when Picasso was working on the painting *Night Fishing in Antibes* in 1939 (now in the Museum of Modern Art, New York):

> This piece of canvas was so huge it took him hours to cover it . . . It is possible that his speed could be matched; but that anyone could beat him at covering a surface with a brush is rather improbable, for his gestures are guided by the intensity of his emotions and his entire thought is concentrated upon what he is doing. That is why he is not to be distracted; for that is tantamount to destroying his delerium, to interrupting the flood of his ideas, to wakening him in the middle of his sleep . . . When he creates, he is like a somnambulist and obeys only the imperious intuition that governs him.
> (Sabartés 1948: 179)

What we do not know is whether such trance states helped the painting and produced better work, or whether they were more in the nature of an incidental accompaniment. Picasso would perhaps have been an equally great artist without them.

The observations by creative artists of their own experiences are an interesting and under-utilized source of information for psychologists. T. S. Eliot (1933), one of the most reflective of writers, has this to say about automaticity in creative writing: 'Some forms of ill health, debility or anaemia may (if other circumstances are favourable) produce an efflux of poetry in a way approaching the condition of automatic writing.' Eliot goes on to suggest that what happens is 'something negative', not inspirational; rather more like the 'breaking down of strong habitual barriers'. In Pavlovian terms this might be called 'disinhibition'. However, it would seem that Eliot here was referring specifically to his own problems in overcoming intellectual constraints of the sort that would not inhibit writers of a more liberal style, such as Dylan Thomas. It is interesting that Thomas was frequently accused of composing his poetry in a 'quasi-automatic' manner, and that he was not concerned whether his poetry meant anything precise or not but rather that it made a 'nice noise' (Wain 1966). Although this criticism does not do full justice to the power of Thomas's poetry, it usefully illustrates the contrast in creative approach between Thomas and someone like T. S. Eliot, and points to the probability that trance experiences are more a matter of style than essential to the activity.

The trance in literary appreciation

It is a common belief that trance-like states, if not necessary for the appreciation of art, music, literature, poetry and the like, are at least frequent and welcome accompaniments to such appreciation. T. S. Eliot (1930) pointed to the need for a relatively non-intellectual, passive attitude of mind in the reading of poetry: 'The reader has to allow the images to fall into his memory successively, without questioning the reasonableness of each at the moment so at the end a total effect is produced.' Eliot referred to this as the 'logic of imagination', a concept closely resembling that of 'trance logic', introduced by Martin Orne (1959) to describe the apparent tolerance for logical incongruity displayed by 'hypnotized' subjects – i.e. seeing two images of the same person, one real and the other a suggested hallucination. Orne went on to propose that the 'essence of hypnosis' was the subject's tendency to 'mix freely his perceptions derived from reality with those that stem from his imagination . . . These perceptions are fused in a manner that ignores everyday logic' (Orne 1959: 118–19). Orne's proposals have generated a good deal of controversy in hypnosis research (see Sheehan and Perry 1976). Many subsequent better-controlled studies have failed to show any differences between 'hypnotized' subjects and those who are simulating hypnosis (Spanos *et al.* in press). Although this finding throws considerable doubt over the idea that 'trance logic' is the 'essence of hypnosis' it nevertheless does not destroy the validity of the concept for our general approach to imaginative experiences of the sort Eliot was writing about.

The link between hypnosis and poetry was originally proposed by Edward Snyder, who published a little-known book called *Hypnotic Poetry* in 1930. In this book he argued that a number of poets during the nineteenth century Romantic era wrote poems that, when read aloud, had a decidedly trance-inductive effect. Snyder distinguished between trance-inductive poems (e.g. Gray's 'Elegy Written in a Country Churchyard', Coleridge's 'Kubla Khan' and 'Rime of the Ancient Mariner') and intellectualistic poems (e.g. Browning's 'Christina') that had little or no trance-inductive effect. Snyder's work is discussed in the context of modern hypnosis research in a paper by Snyder and

Shor (1983), who also attempt to analyse the techniques used in trance-inductive poetry. These include (a) freedom from abruptness, (b) regularity of soothing rhythm, (c) refrain and frequent repetition, (d) ornamented harmonious rhythm, (e) vagueness of imagery and (f) fatiguing obscurities. It is instructive to consider these trance-inductive characteristics in the effect of a poem such as Coleridge's 'The Rime of the Ancient Mariner', in which the reader or listener assumes the role of the hapless wedding-guest who is held 'like a three years' child' by the glittering eye of the mariner. One can readily appreciate the power of the poem particularly when delivered in a dramatic form as in the recording by Richard Burton:

> The ship was cheer'd, the harbour clear'd
> Merrily did we drop,
> Below the kirk, below the hill
> Below the lighthouse top . . .

What is needed now is a detailed empirical study of the effects of such poems upon a range of people. The work of Josephine Hilgard (1970) on the relationship between hypnotic susceptibility and imaginative involvement could provide a basis for such an enterprise. Hilgard found, as a result of interviews with several hundred university students, that those students who responded well to traditional hypnotic procedures (i.e. 'highly susceptibles') were also disposed towards deep emotional and imaginative involvements in reading novels, drama, listening to music, watching films and the like. This work not only emphasized that there were large differences between people in their involvements (maybe the low involvers would prefer intellectual or factual literature?) but that similar abilities or predispositions were brought into play, both in hypnosis and in everyday imaginative situations, thus establishing an important continuity between hypnotic and imaginative experiences. As we shall see, looking at hypnosis as an aspect of imagination provides an important alternative paradigm to the traditional state theory.

An alternative empirical approach to the problem is exemplified in a study by Fellows and Armstrong (1977). Two groups of subjects, one group scoring high on tests of hypnotic susceptibility and one scoring low, were asked to read a short story in the laboratory and then to rate their experiences on a number of seven-point scales (e.g. degree of absorption, pleasure, identification with characters, vividness of imagery, emotional involvement, awareness of external events). Subjects were also asked to rate their usual experiences when reading imaginative literature. The advantages of this approach were that it avoided the problem of subjects not being able to remember the required experiences, and that it enabled control to be exerted over the material subjects were exposed to. The findings in general confirmed Hilgard's work. The highly hypnotizable subjects become more involved in the story and rated their usual involvements higher than the lowly hypnotizable subjects. However, there was some indication in the data that the lowly hypnotizable subjects regarded the story-reading task in the laboratory as being untypical of the level of involvement obtainable in more naturalistic settings. This indicates (1) that good hypnotic subjects may have a special ability to have trance-like experiences 'to order' in laboratory settings, and (2) the need for more research into naturally occurring and self-regulated trance-like experiences.

The trance in mesmerism

Although there is some evidence that hypnotic-like methods were in use in the early Egyptian, Greek and Roman civilizations, as explained in Chapter 2, the history of hypnosis as we would now recognize it began in France in the late eighteenth century with the work of Franz Anton Mesmer. The report of the 1784 Royal Commission of Inquiry into animal magnetism (Franklin *et al.* 1785) describes the most prominent effect of Mesmer's animal magnetism as a type of convulsive seizure, referred to as a 'crisis', which was a sign of the success of the treatment. The Franklin Report provides a graphic account of these crises:

> The convulsions are rendered extraordinary by their frequency, their violence and their duration. As soon as one person is convulsed, others presently are affected by that symptom . . . These convulsions are characterised by precipitate and involuntary motions of all the limbs or of the whole body, by a distraction and wildness in the eyes, by shrieks, tears, hiccuppings and immoderate laughter. They are either preceded or followed by a state of languor and reverie, by a species of dejection, and even drowsiness.
> (Franklin *et al.* 1785: 87)

The Franklin Report goes on to demonstrate, by a series of clever blind control experiments, that the effects attributed to the power of animal magnetism often occurred when patients thought that they were being magnetized but were not (see Chapter 1). Moreover, 'magnetic' effects did not occur when patients did not realize they were being magnetized when in fact they were. The report concludes that the important factor in producing the crises was not whatever the magnetist was allegedly doing to them, but what the subject *believed* he was doing. The emphasis, therefore, passed from a physical effect to a psychological explanation: 'The inevitable conclusion is that the imagination simply produces all the effects attributed to the magnetism and that where the imagination ceases to be called forth, it has no longer the smallest efficacy' (Franklin *et al.* 1785: 115). As is indicated by Sheehan and Perry in their excellent review of the Franklin Report and its aftermath: 'It is perhaps one of the great ironies of the history of hypnosis that these conclusions are only now, almost 200 years later, beginning to be taken seriously' (Sheehan and Perry 1976: 13–14).

There are a number of contemporary theorists who are converging upon the central role of imaginative skills and abilities in the explanation of hypnotic behaviour (see, for example, the discussion by Spanos and Barber 1974). What must be learned from the Franklin Report, however, is not to throw the baby out with the bath water. By dismissing animal magnetism as imagination the

1784 commissioners implied that the mesmeric procedures had no therapeutic value. What they failed to do was to distinguish between the *procedures*, which clearly did have some therapeutic value, and the mesmerists' *explanation* of how the procedures worked. In the same way, to reinterpret hypnotic behaviour in terms of imagination does not imply that the procedures should be dismissed or that the behaviour is in some way invalid. Rather, the thrust of the alternative interpretation is to draw our attention to the links between hypnosis and other imaginative experiences, as well as to the therapeutic value of imaginative techniques (for further discussion see Sheikh 1983).

Braid and the sleep metaphor

The person primarily responsible for what we now recognize as hypnosis was the English doctor James Braid (1843), who was the first to use the term 'neurypnology' (or nervous sleep), which later became simply 'hypnosis' or 'hypnotism'. Braid's procedures usually involved having the subject fix his or her eyes on an object above eye level so as to produce strain on the eyes, which, if successful, had the following effects:

> In three minutes his eyelids closed, a gush of tears ran down his cheeks, his head dropped, his face was slightly convulsed, he gave a groan and instantly fell into profound sleep, the respiration became slow, deep and sibilant, the right hand being agitated by slight convulsive movements.
> (Braid 1843: 17)

Although Braid was inclined to look for physiological explanations for these effects he was willing to concede that 'the oftener patients are hypnotized, from association of ideas or habits, the more susceptible they became; and in this way they are liable to be affected entirely through the imagination' (Braid 1843: 36).

Although contemporary hypnosis research generally would not support Braid's statement about the effects of practice on hypnotic susceptibility (Perry 1977), his view about the role of imagination was warmly received. However, the evidence is firmly against any simple link between hypnosis and sleep. Although many modern hypnotic induction procedures employ traditional 'go-to-sleep'-type terminology their aim is certainly not to produce sleep. A subject who is asleep is unlikely to respond to any hypnotic suggestions (If a subject fails to 'wake-up' to instructions at the end of a hypnotic session, he could be asleep!) Sleep and the effects of a hypnotic induction (which does not lead to sleep) are physiologically distinct. The fact that there is no reliable physiological index for the effects of an induction procedure also raises doubts about the adequacy of the trance-state interpretation (Barber 1961). Behaviourally and subjectively sleep differs from hypnosis. Although the 'hypnotized' subject is often inert and inactive as if asleep, he or she certainly does not have to be like this. There are induction procedures in which the subject is encouraged to be alert and active (e.g. Banyai and Hilgard 1976,

Gibbons 1979) and these work just as well. In fact there is evidence to suggest that performance on some hypnotic tasks might be better *without* the traditional induction telling subjects to relax and go to sleep. For example, recent work reported by Barber and Wilson (1977) has shown that it is often more effective simply to tell a subject directly how to respond to (or how to think along with and imagine) the things suggested (e.g. that your arm is a rod of iron or that you are now having your fifth birthday party) rather than using an indirect procedure, such as a traditional trance induction. Spanos, in Chapter 5, describes how subjects may be instructed how to be more responsive, but is this simply cheating and not really hypnosis? This question brings us to the central question: what exactly is hypnosis?

The popular view of hypnosis

The popular view of hypnosis, which has its origins in the work and ideas of Mesmer, Braid and other nineteenth century hypnotists, is that it is a specially induced trance state in which the subject, at least partially, loses awareness of reality, is controlled by the suggestions of the hypnotist and becomes able to perform and experience a variety of activities that in the normal waking state would not be possible. This is an interesting and exciting view of the subject, which has been considerably reinforced and embellished by popular writers, the media, stage performers and also professional therapists, anxious that the magic and curative appeal should not be removed from their methods. The existence of stereotyped and common misconceptions of hypnosis in the work of many prominent literary writers has been well documented by Ludwig (1963). One of the most powerful influences upon the public image of hypnosis was that of Svengali the malevolent hypnotist in George du Maurier's (1894) novel *Trilby*. Unfortunately it seems that the negative attitudes associated with this view have also tended to inhibit the development of research and teaching in this subject. A recent survey (Fellows 1985a) revealed that in only 4 out of 50 university and polytechnic departments of psychology in Great Britain was there any serious attempt to introduce students to the methods and theories of what H. J. Eysenck (1976) once referred to as 'one of the most striking phenomena in the whole of their science'. The survey also revealed that there were a number of departments that were opposed to practical instruction in hypnosis on principle. Such an attitude, though understandable, flies in the face of modern research, which indicates the innocence of hypnotic procedures, particularly when employed in academic or research settings (Orne 1965, Coe and Ryken 1979).

The coercive power of hypnosis

This discussion raises the issue of the coercive power of hypnosis. Popular mythology would have us believe that once a person is 'hypnotized' (i.e. is in a hypnotic trance) then there is nothing much that person can do to resist the hypnotist's suggestions. The evidence, again, is firmly against such a simplistic view (Barber 1961, Orne 1972). A recent review of the research was presented by Perry (1979), who also analysed the court transcript of a case in Australia in which a lay hypnotist was found guilty of three sexual offences against two female clients. This case was interesting in that it pitted the two main viewpoints on hypnotic coercion against each other. The hypnotist admitted the acts, but argued that hypnotic coercion was impossible since a hypnotized person would immediately resist suggestions of an unwanted nature. The women involved stated that they were aware of what was happening but that, because they were hypnotized, they were unable to resist the hypnotist's advances. Perry concluded that neither explanation was entirely adequate and that other factors needed to be considered. For example, the patients' *belief* in their inability to resist may be sufficient to create a self-fulfilling prophecy. Alternatively, the behaviour of the two women might be seen as constituting a motivated helplessness in which their subsequent testimony was a 'rationalization in retrospect'.

Thus, like alcohol, it is possible that hypnosis might be used by some people as a way of disowning responsibility for their own behaviour, which is otherwise perceived by them as being taboo. This type of explanation may help to explain the often uncharacteristic behaviour of volunteers on stage for a hypnosis show – although here, as in the clinical situation, there are also powerful social factors demanding compliance with suggestions (see Wagstaff, Chapter 4). It is much easier to go along with the wishes of the hypnotist (particularly when an audience is present and wanting to be entertained) than to resist and let the hypnotist down. The importance of loyalty to the hypnotist and a subject's willingness to resist suggestions is also highlighted in a recent study by Levitt and Baker (1983) in which subjects were given financial incentives to resist hypnotic suggestions. Their findings point towards the need to consider social-interactional factors in the explanation of hypnotic behaviour.

Hypnosis as a trance state

The main conclusion to emerge from the above discussion is that the behaviour of a subject during hypnosis cannot simply be interpreted in terms of a hypnotic trance state. Maybe some subjects do have unusual experiences of the sort that might be labelled 'trance-like', but these experiences in themselves cannot adequately explain the observed behaviour. Let us now look in more detail at the role of the trance concept in the traditional picture of hypnosis and at some suggested alternative interpretations.

Figure 3.1 shows a schematic picture of the traditional view of hypnosis, which is widely held by professionals and lay people alike. It assumes that the subject or patient starts out in 'a waking state' and is transformed by means of an induction procedure into a hypnotic trance state. The presence of this trance state is then thought to make possible the production of various

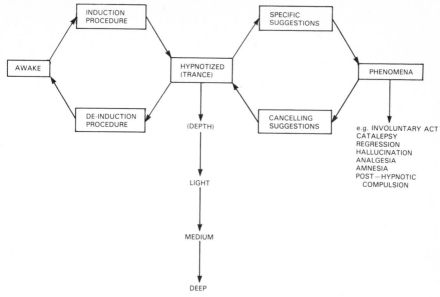

Figure 3.1   The traditional view of hypnosis as trance.

experimentally and therapeutically suggested effects including involuntary action, catalepsies, regression, hallucination and analgesia. It is further assumed that this trance state varies in depth from light to deep (or somnambulistic) and that different hypnotic phenomena are characteristic of different depths. Thus simple arm levitation and eyelid catalepsy may be possible with only a light trance (or even by 'waking suggestibility'), whereas a deeper trance is required for hallucinations and amnesias.

Although this basic picture has not been accepted by everyone, it is only in the past thirty years or so that it has come under severe critical attack from researchers such as T. X. Barber (1969, 1979), Sarbin and Coe (1972) and most recently Wagstaff (1981). Modern theorists now divide into two basic schools according to whether or not they are sympathetic to this picture of hypnosis. There are 'state theorists' who, with some reservations, would tend to go along with the traditional picture; these include notably Leon Chertok (1981), Milton Erickson (Rossi 1980), Ernest Hilgard (1965, 1977) and Spiegel and Spiegel (1978). Another theorist who would appear to fit into the state school is Edmonston (1981), who has presented a strongly argued case for interpreting hypnosis purely in terms of relaxation. The main problem with Edmonston's proposal, as is pointed out by Sarbin (1983), is that it deals solely with the first half of the formula presented in Figure 3.1. His focus is upon what he terms 'neutral hypnosis', which is what happens to the subject as a result of the induction procedure before other suggestions, challenges, etc. are presented. Thus Edmonston equates the hypnotic trance with relaxation. He even goes so far as to coin the term 'anesis' for the state of neutral hypnosis. As he says: 'Perhaps what is needed now, as in the days of Braid, is not so

much a confrontation of theorists as a relabelling of neutral hypnosis'
(Edmonston 1981: 219). Edmonston's emphasis upon nomenclature and relabelling is important and I shall return to it shortly. But the fact remains that
his relaxation theory deals with only a small part of the domain of hypnosis,
and perhaps not a particularly important part at that.

Non-state approaches

The alternative non-state view of hypnosis rejects the picture presented in
Figure 3.1, or at least the central portion of it, relating to trance state. For
example, in his review of Edmonston's book mentioned earlier, Theodore
Sarbin (1983), who together with T. X. Barber has been the main proponent
of the non-state viewpoint, asks us to consider another perspective than that
proposed by Edmonston. Rather than seeing the induction as a force that in
some way transforms the body (and/or the mind), preparing it to emit very
special behaviours,

> Suppose one were to begin from another perspective; that the subject and the
> hypnotist are each enacting roles appropriate to their conceptions of a developing
> script. To enter into the role of a hypnosis subject calls for an entrance ritual.
> The induction serves as such a ritual . . . Having completed the ritual, the actor
> is then ready to perform the work of the hypnotic subject – that is, to utter
> counter-factual statements, to demonstrate multiple personalities, to expose a
> hidden observer, to become analgesic, etc.
> (Sarbin 1983: 58)

Although such a formulation is not completely incompatible with the view
of hypnosis as a form of relaxation, it points towards other questions, like
what meanings the subject assigns to the self-observed changes in his or her
body. Such questions have no part to play in the essentially mechanistic
formula proposed by Edmonston and other state theorists. The main thrust of
Sarbin's position (most fully presented in Sarbin and Coe 1972) is that
hypnosis may be most parsimoniously considered as a form of role-playing in
which the subject endeavours to play the role of a hypnotized person to the
best of his or her ability. This is not to say that all hypnotic behaviour is sham
or faked, which is a common misinterpretation; for some subjects may become
so involved in their role as to accept the suggested events as really happening.
A parallel may be drawn with actors 'losing themselves' in their part on stage.
Rather, the aim of Sarbin's approach is to draw parallels with other features
of human imaginative activity and to raise the possibility of alternative ways
of interpreting hypnosis, which do more justice to the complexity of the
experience than the simple trance model does.

Barber's attack on the trance concept

As I have mentioned, the most strident critic of the trance-state viewpoint has
been T. X. Barber, whose empirical and theoretical contributions are usefully

summarized in the following references: Barber (1969, 1979), Barber, Spanos and Chaves (1974) and Sheehan and Perry (1976: ch. 3). The latter provides an excellent evaluation of Barber's work and also emphasizes the various phases in the development of his ideas. In his early work (prior to about 1960) Barber saw hypnosis primarily as a transactional process between subject and hypnotist in which the subject was selectively attentive to the words of the hypnotist, accepted them as being literally true and was cognitively set to carry out the instructions and to perform them successfully. At this stage Barber showed no reluctance about using the concept of trance. However, in what Sheehan and Perry (1976) refer to as his 'operational phase' (culminating in the book *Hypnosis: A Scientific Approach* in 1969) Barber attempted to make a thoroughgoing break with traditional conceptualizations that used concepts such as 'hypnotized', 'hypnotic state' and 'trance state' to refer to subjects responding to hypnotic-type suggestions. In contrast, his approach was to identify the relevant antecedent and dependent variables in the hypnotic situation and to determine experimentally the functional relationships holding between them.

In a later paper Barber (1979) likened his approach to a shift in scientific paradigm of the sort discussed by Thomas Kuhn (1962) in his history of scientific revolutions. Thus, just as the geocentric view of the solar system was replaced by the heliocentric view, the phlogiston conception of combustion by the oxygen conception and in current psychology the behavioural approach by the cognitive, so the special-state (or trance) paradigm of hypnosis would be replaced by .. what? The answer to this last question is yet to be decided. However, as already indicated in this chapter, a prime candidate is the imagination paradigm, although the concept of imagination is not without its problems and ambiguities (for a recent review see Sheehan 1979).

Barber's experimental work

The 1960s witnessed the publication of a remarkable number (well over one hundred) of experimental and theoretical papers by Barber and his colleagues from the Medfield Foundation in Massachusetts, USA. Their basic methodology was that of independent group design (see Coe 1973 for a good review of this work in comparison with other designs). In this, unselected subjects are randomly assigned to different treatment conditions. For example, in a series of studies Barber and Calverley (reported in Barber 1969: ch. 3) allocated subjects to one of three conditions: *hypnotic*, in which a traditional hypnotic induction procedure was present (so as to produce a 'trance state'); *task motivational*, in which subjects were instructed to do their best to imagine the things suggested (and so were not in a 'trance state'); *control*, in which no special preliminary instructions were given. Following this a series of eight test suggestions were administered to each subject: arm lowering, arm levitation, hand lock, 'thirst hallucination', verbal inhibition, body immobility, 'post-hypnotic-like' response and selective amnesia. These test suggestions comprise the Barber Suggestibility Scale (BSS), which is one of the many ways of measuring hypnotic responsiveness (see Fellows 1979 for British norms for this scale). However, Barber and Calverley used the scale as a dependent measure in their experiments. Their main findings were as follows.

(1) *Under base-level conditions most subjects responded to some of the test suggestions.* This is an important finding, which has been widely replicated by many researchers with a variety of test suggestions. It indicates that most, if not all, of the phenomena commonly associated with hypnosis can be produced without a hypnotic induction procedure. This clearly places the first part of the traditional formula shown in Figure 3.1 in some doubt, although we still need to explain how the suggestions work. This finding inclines one towards looking at hypnosis simply in terms of suggestibility (or response to suggestion), which was the position promoted by Hippolyte Bernheim (1890) and others at the end of the nineteenth century.

(2) *A small proportion of subjects (about one-sixth to one-fourth) showed a high level of base-rate response to test suggestions.* In other words there seem to be some people who are particularly adept at producing a whole range of hypnotic behaviours and experiences almost 'at the drop of a hat', in the absence of any trance-inducing preliminaries at all. Again, this is a surprising though well-established finding. Such people are often referred to as 'hypnotic virtuosos' (Kihlstrom 1985), and a good deal of research is currently underway to identify their characteristics. One interesting line of work reported by Wilson and Barber (1983) suggests that such individuals may be particularly prone to having fantasy (or one might say 'trance-like') experiences in their everyday lives, and so their hypnotic performance might be seen as a natural extension of skills and dispositions on display elsewhere. Such thinking fits in well with the work of Josephine Hilgard (1970) on imaginative involvements, although follow-up research suggests that the link is premature and simplistic (Lynn *et al.* 1985). Although some hypnotic virtuosos might be described as fantasy prone, there are others who cannot be so described. This research may also link up with that on the appreciation of poetry.

(3) *Hypnotic induction procedures facilitated responsiveness to test suggestions,* in that the average number of suggestions responded to in the hypnotic condition was 2.5 greater than that in the control condition. This finding also receives strong support from other research to the extent that some researchers have been tempted to point to this feature (hypersuggestibility) as the main defining characteristic of hypnosis (e.g. Hull 1933, Weitzenhoffer 1953). But are people hypersuggestible because they are 'hypnotized' or in a 'hypnotic trance state'? Unfortunately, no one has been able to demonstrate conclusively that when a subject responds well to test suggestions he or she is (or has to be) in a trance state. As Barber has frequently pointed out, there is an element of circularity in this argument. The subject is said to respond well because he or she is in a trance, but how do we know he or she is in a trance? Because he or she responds well. To break this circle it is necessary to have an independent index of the existence of a trance state, but none has been found despite a great deal of searching. Physiologically, a responsive ('hypnotized') subject

does not differ from an unresponsive ('not hypnotized') subject, provided adequate controls are made (Sarbin and Slagle 1979). All the other signs of trance, such as glazed look, slumped posture, slowed actions and testimony of 'having been hypnotized', are so subject to experimental distortion and manipulation as to be unreliable as indicators of a trance state (see Barber 1969: ch. 1, for a full discussion of trance-state characteristics).

(4) *Task-motivational instructions facilitate responsiveness to test suggestions to the same extent as the hypnotic induction procedure.* This finding emphasizes the value of having a motivational condition in addition to the other two, since it would be tempting (as was the case in many early studies) to conclude, on the basis of the superiority of the hypnotic over the control condition, that 'hypnosis' (or trance) was the factor responsible for the good hypnotic performance. But, of course, there are many differences between the hypnotic and control conditions that could be responsible for the observed differences in performance. Although we might be surprised by what people may perform when they are 'hypnotized', our surprise may be no more than a reflection of our ignorance of what they may be capable of without hypnosis. Thus audiences at stage hypnosis shows may gasp in wonder when they witness the 'hypnotized' volunteer being suspended like a plank between two chairs and the hypnotist sitting on his stomach. However, as described in the Introduction to this book, this is not proof of hypnosis. In a carefully controlled experiment Collins (1961; reported by Barber 1979: 224–5) demonstrated that control subjects were able to perform the feat just as easily as 'hypnotized' subjects. Interestingly, the control subjects expressed surprise at their own ability to perform the feat, which initially they did not think they would be able to perform. The message here is that our own surprise or incredulity at what apparently 'hypnotized' subjects are able to perform and experience should not lead us to ascribe these performances to the presence of a special hypnotic trance state, in the absence of appropriate control testing.

The same basic argument applies to the whole range of phenomena commonly associated with hypnosis. For example, it is often said that surely a person's ability to endure severe pain while 'under hypnosis' is good proof that a special hypnotic trance state exists. The issue is however not that simple. Barber and Hahn (1962) demonstrated that task-motivational instructions (to imagine vividly a pleasant situation) were as effective in reducing both subjective and physiological responses to painful stimuli as a hypnotic induction procedure with analgesic suggestions. Concerning the many anecdotal reports of hypnosis being used to control pain during major surgery there are also many other issues to consider; e.g. whether the amount of pain involved in surgical procedures is popularly overestimated (Lewis 1942) and whether 'hypnotized' subjects who undergo surgery experience pain that they do not report.

What seems to be emerging from contemporary research is a picture of pain not as a simple sensation but rather as a complex psychological response to a situation that includes expectation, anxiety, interpretation and suffering (Rachlin 1985). Hence the thrust of the pain therapist should be to reassure and give comfort and confidence to the patient rather than to put him or her into a trance. As Barber (1981a) describes in connection with the treatment of cancer patients by hypno-suggestive methods, what happens conflicts sharply with the popular notion of the hypnotist simply 'hypnotizing' the pain away. The true picture is more of a caring therapist who is prepared to spend time and effort to help the patient to come to terms with the illness. 'By showing the pain patient that someone truly cares for him or her and that something can be done for the pain, the therapist reduces the patient's lonliness, fear and hopelessness and, consequently, reduces the patient's discomfort' (Barber 1981a).

Convergence upon imagination as a central concept

As already indicated, the 1960s witnessed a flood of critical experimental and theoretical papers from T. X. Barber and his colleagues specifically aimed at undermining the traditional view of hypnosis as involving some sort of trance state. This essentially destructive period was followed by a mainly constructive phase in Barber's work, covering the 1970s, in which he asserted the central role that imaginative skills and abilities played in the production of hypnotic phenomena. In 1974 Barber wrote an important paper in conjunction with Nicholas Spanos (Spanos and Barber 1974) in which they drew attention to what they saw as 'a convergence in hypnosis research' among theoreticians of many different persuasions upon the central role of two factors in a subject's successful response to hypnotic suggestions. Firstly, there is need for a willingness on the part of the subject to co-operate with the experimenter in fulfilling the aims of the experiment. This is the motivation factor, which Barber emphasized so strongly in his operational phase and which brought so much criticism on his head (e.g. Ernest R. Hilgard 1970). Adequate motivation, although necessary, is clearly not sufficient for successful hypnotic performance (unless it leads to deliberate faking), and Barber now acknowledges this.

The second factor in hypnotic suggestibility is the importance of the subject's involvement in suggestion-related imaginings, which involves both (a) sustaining and elaborating imaginings that are consistent with the aims of the suggestions and (b) disregarding information that is inconsistent with these aims. Although this conceptualization would not be out of harmony with the developing positions of theorists such as Ernest Hilgard (1977), there still remains an enormous gap between Barber's new viewpoint and that of clinically oriented state theorists mentioned earlier.

Figure 3.2 presents in schematic form what Barber's alternative model of hypnosis looks like. There is now provision for an antecedent input from the skills and abilities that a person brings into the hypnotic situation. In this operational phase Barber was forced to explain away consistent individual differences in hypnotic responsiveness in terms of situational factors, which left him very open to criticism (e.g. Ernest R. Hilgard 1970). The same problem

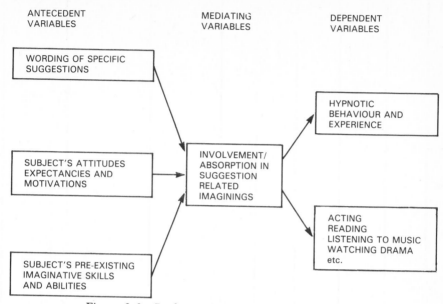

ANTECEDENT
VARIABLES

MEDIATING
VARIABLES

DEPENDENT
VARIABLES

WORDING OF SPECIFIC
SUGGESTIONS

SUBJECT'S ATTITUDES
EXPECTANCIES AND
MOTIVATIONS

SUBJECT'S PRE-EXISTING
IMAGINATIVE SKILLS
AND ABILITIES

INVOLVEMENT/
ABSORPTION IN
SUGGESTION
RELATED
IMAGININGS

HYPNOTIC
BEHAVIOUR AND
EXPERIENCE

ACTING
READING
LISTENING TO MUSIC
WATCHING DRAMA
etc.

Figure 3.2   Barber's alternative view of hypnosis.

faces theorists of a social-psychological orientation, such as Wagstaff (1981); and there is some indication that they, like Barber, are moving towards some acknowledgement of an imaginative-skills input in their formulations (e.g. Wagstaff 1985 and Chapter 4 below). As shown in Figure 3.2, the central concept is now involvement or absorption in the suggestion-related imaginings, which replaces the trance concept in Figure 3.1, but which like trance is an aspect of the person's subjective experience. We are to some degree back with the perennial problem of how to validate subjective experiences.

An interesting example of Barber's recent tolerance towards experiential and trance-like concepts in interpretation of hypnosis occcurs in his surprisingly sympathetic review of the collected papers of Milton Erickson (Barber 1981b). In this review he points out that Erickson in common with all other trance theorists failed to distinguish between the two distinct trance-like experiences. Under what Barber labels 'Trance A' are various degrees of relaxation, calmness, passivity and unconcern or detachment from reality. Thus Trance A would be equivalent to Edmonston's (1981) notion of 'neutral hypnosis' and similar to Hilgard's (1977) 'dissociation'. In contrast, 'Trance B' refers to the absorption, involvement, etc. in the ideas and words communicated by the hypnotist. Thus Trance B incorporates concepts such as being entranced, fascinated, captivated, enthralled and enraptured. Barber argues that Trance B is an essential part of hypnotic responding (as opposed to faking) but that Trance A is not. Such a formulation would help to avoid the criticisms of theories equating hypnosis with relaxed states and would be consistent with experimental work showing that traditional induction procedures are unnecessary for successful hypnotic responding. The problem that now remains is how to specify the nature and range of Trance B experiences.

An important step towards this goal has recently been made by Sheehan and McConkey (1982) through the detailed analysis of subjects' experiences whilst responding to hypnotic suggestions. They have used a special 'Experiential Analysis Technique' (EAT), which involves going over a video play-back of the hypnotic session with the subject and encouraging him or her to describe and comment upon the experiences. Their work points to the fact that subjects employ a variety of strategies in order to get the suggestions to work. There is no evidence for any universal Trance A or Trance B experiences, although hypnotic subjects frequently report feeling relaxed or engrossed in the suggestions. The traditional picture of the hypnotized person as being in a zombie-like state of complete subjection and unawareness is certainly wide of the mark. Hypnotic subjects cannot be simply conceptualized as passive recipients of hypnotic suggestions. Rather, as Barber and Wilson (1977) stress, subjects do, and need to, work at the suggestions in order to realize them, at least in the early stages. The same applies to reading a novel; some mental work is usually required to get into the story, but subsequently the story should 'take over', leaving the subject to enjoy the experience.

Concluding remarks about terminology

The picture I hope to have conveyed in this chapter is not so much one of confusion but rather of uncertainty about how best to interpret hypnotic performance. The lessons of T. X. Barber's empirical and theoretical attack on the usefulness of the trance concept in hypnosis cannot be ignored. The simple traditional picture that most of us seem to have about hypnosis is clearly questionable. However, as Thomas Kuhn (1962) pointed out, scientific paradigms die hard, and this is particularly the case in a subject like hypnosis, where the basic beliefs and assumptions underlying the paradigm are widely held in the general population. In order that false beliefs and misconceptions are not unnecessarily reinforced and sustained, researchers and other professionals in the field must exercise particular care and vigilance in the terminology they use to talk about the subject; for the traditional picture of hypnosis is embedded both in our thinking and in our language. Hence, I conclude this chapter with a plea for more care and precision in the use of traditional hypnotic terminology, particularly (although not only) when professionals are talking to other professionals. Therapists may well see a need, for clinical purposes, to go along with a patient's belief system and maintain the aura of magic; but to talk to other professionals in the same manner is not justified.

The main problem with talking about 'hypnotizing' someone, or putting them 'into or under hypnosis', is that the language begs the question; it makes implicit assumptions about what is happening. Students frequently ask me (with awe) if I can hypnotize people. The answer is not easy to give since their question is embedded in a model or paradigm of hypnosis that I cannot accept. I have to give them a lecture (although I can perhaps now tell them to read this chapter). The simplest strategy, is to translate the question into operational terms, in which case the answer is 'yes'. I can certainly administer a traditional (or a non-traditional?) induction procedure. But this is only half of the formula: Edmonston's (1981) 'neutral hypnosis'. To hypnotize properly we need to go on to administer other test suggestions like arm levitation, eye catalepsy and regression; and then the subject's responses will be assessed. Such an operational strategy is probably the easiest way to cope with the terminological problem. Thus when we talk about 'hypnotizing' someone what we really mean is that we administer certain procedures, which have certain measurable effects. Traditional hypnotic terminology is not simply descriptive, it also has interpretative components, which we need to acknowledge.

Views relating to the imprecise use of hypnotic terminology in professional journal writing have been recently expressed by editors of the *American Journal of Clinical Hypnosis* (Mott 1985) and the *British Journal of Experimental and Clinical Hypnosis* (Fellows 1985b). Journal authors are often not clear what they mean when they talk about 'using hypnosis', or about a patient being 'deeply hypnotized'. There are literally hundreds of different procedures that might be labelled 'hypnotic'. To talk simply of 'using hypnosis' implies that all such procedures result in a common state or experience, an assumption that, in the light of Sheehan and McConkey's (1982) work, seems very unlikely. One way in which the concepts may be sharpened up is by distinguishing between hypnosis as a state or experience ('neutral hypnosis') and hypnosis as a set of phenomena. For example, Naish (1985) wrote a paper entitled 'The "Trance" Described in Signal Detection Terms'. One might assume that he was interested in describing the effects of an induction procedure (a 'trance state'), but a close reading of the paper indicates that what Naish was really concerned with was the ability, which some people had, to produce a variety of hypnotic phenomena in response to test suggestions. This is but one example of the terminological confusion in current hypnosis writing over which we need to be vigilant.

References

Banyai, E. I. and Hilgard, E. R. (1976) A comparison of active-alert hypnotic induction with traditional relaxation induction. *Journal of Abnormal Psychology*, 85: 218–24.

Barber, T. X. (1961) Physiological aspects of hypnosis. *Psychological Bulletin*, 5: 390–491.

(1969) *Hypnosis: A Scientific Approach*. New York and London: Van Nostrand Reinhold.

(1979) Suggested ('hypnotic') behaviour: the trance paradigm versus an alternative paradigm. In E. Fromm and R. E. Shor (eds.), *Hypnosis: Developments in Research and New Perspectives*. New York: Aldine.

(1981a). Hypnosuggestive procedures in the treatment of clinical pain. In T. Millon (ed.), *Handbook of Health Care*. New York: Plenum.

(1981b) Innovations and limitations in Erickson's hypnosis: a review of the collected papers of Milton H. Erickson. *Contemporary Psychology*, 26: 825–7.

Barber, T. X. and Hahn, K. W. Jr (1962) Physiological and subjective responses to pain producing stimulation under hypnotically suggested and waking-imagined 'analgesia'. *Journal of Abnormal and Social Psychology*, 65: 411–18.

Barber, T. X., Spanos, N. P. and Chaves, J. F. (1974) *Hypnotism, Imagination and Human Potentialities*. New York and Oxford: Pergamon.

Barber, T. X. and Wilson, S. C. (1977) Hypnosis, suggestions and altered states of consciousness. In W. E. Edmonston (ed.), *Conceptual and Investigative Approaches to Hypnosis and Hypnotic Phenomena. Annals of the New York Academy of Sciences*, 296: 34–477.

Bernheim, H. (1890) *New Studies in Hypnotism*. Translated by R. S. Sandor in new edition 1980. New York: International Universities Press.

Braid, J. (1843) *Neurypnology: or the Rationale of Nervous Sleep Considered in Relation with Animal Magnetism*. London: Churchill; reprint edition 1976, New York: Anne Press.

Chertok, L. (1981) *Sense and Nonsense in Psychotherapy: The Challenge of Hypnosis*. New York and Oxford: Pergamon.

Coe, W. C. (1973) Experimental designs and the state–nonstate issue in hypnosis. *American Journal of Cliniccal Hypnosis*, 16: 118–28.

Coe, W. C. and Ryken, K. (1979) Hypnosis and risks to human subjects. *American Psychologist*, 34: 673–81.

Collins, J. K. (1961) Muscular endurance in normal and hypnotic states: a study of suggested catalepsy. Honours thesis Department of Psychology, Unniversity of Sydney, Australia.

Deren, M. (1953) *Divine Horsemen. The Living Gods of Haiti*. London: Thames & Hudson.

Du Maurier, G. (1894) *Trilby*. London: Dent; reprint 1931, Dent Everyman's Library.

Edmonston, W. E. (1981) *Hypnosis and Relaxation. Modern Verification of an Old Equation*. New York: Wiley.

Eliot, T. S. (1930) Preface to 'Anabasis'. In St John Perse, *Collected Poems*. Princeton: Princeton University Press, 1971.

(1933) *The Use of Poetry and the Use of Criticism*. London: Faber.

English, H. B. and English, A. C. (1958) *A Comprehensive Dictionary of Psychological and Psychoanalytical Terms*. New York and London: Longmans.

Eysenck, H. J. (1976) Foreword to W. S. Kroger and W. D. Fezler, *Hypnosis and Behaviour Modification: Imagery Conditioning*. Philadelphia: Lippincott.

Fellows, B. J. (1979) The British use of The Barber Suggestibility Scale: norms, psychometric properties and the effects of the sex of the subject and of the experimenter. *British Journal of Psychology*, 70: 547–557.

Fellows, B. J. (1985a) Hypnosis teaching and research in British psychology departments: current practice, attitudes and concerns. *British Journal of Experimental and Clinical Hypnosis*, 2: 151–5.

(1985b) Editorial comments. *British Journal of Experimental and Clinical Hypnosis*, 2: 132.

Fellows, B. J. and Armstrong, V. (1977) An experimental investigation of the relationship between hypnotic susceptibility and reading involvement. *American Journal of Clinical Hypnosis*, 20: 101–5.

Franklin, B. *et al.* (1785) Report by Dr Benjamin Franklin and the other commissioners, charged by the King of France, with the examination of animal magnetism, as now practised in Paris. Translated from the French with an historical introduction by W. M. Godwin, London, 1785. In M. M. Tinterow (ed.), *Foundations of Hypnosis from Mesmer to Freud*, Springfield, Ill.: Thomas, 1970.

Garmonsway, G. N. (1965) *The Penguin English Dictionary.*

Gauld, A. (1982) *Mediumship and Survival.* London: Heinemann.

Gibbons, D. E. (1979) *Applied Hypnosis and Hyperemperia.* New York and London: Plenum.

Goodman, F. D. (1972) *Speaking in Tongues: A Cross-Cultural Study of Glossolalia.* Chicago: University of Chicago Press.

Hilgard, E. R. (1965) *Hypnotic Susceptibility.* New York: Harcourt, Brace & World.

———(1970) Review of *Hypnosis. A Scientific Approach* by T. X. Barber. *American Journal of Clinical Hypnosis.* 12: 272–4.

———(1977) *Divided Consciousness: Multiple Controls in Human Thought and Action.* London and New York: Wiley.

Hilgard, J. R. (1970) *Personality and Hypnosis.* Chicago: University of Chicago Press.

Hull, C. L. (1933) *Hypnosis and Suggestibility: an Experimental Approach.* New York: Appleton-Century-Crofts.

Kihlstrom, J. (1985) Hypnosis. *Annual Review of Psychology,* 36: 385–418.

Kuhn, T. (1962) *The Structure of Scientific Revolutions.* Chicago: University of Chicago Press.

Levitt, E. E. and Baker, E. L. (1983) The hypnotic relationship – another look at coercion, compliance and resistance. *International Journal of Clinical and Experimental Hypnosis,* 31: 125–31.

Lewis, T. (1942) *Pain.* New York: Macmillan.

Ludwig, A. M. (1963) Hypnosis in fiction. *International Journal of Clinical and Experimental Hypnosis,* 6: 71–80.

Lynn, S. J., Rue, J., Montgomery, R. and Snodgrass, M. (1985) Fantasy proneness: developmental aspects, personality correlates and psychopathology. Paper presented at tenth Internal Congress of Hypnosis and Psychosomatic Medicine, Toronto, August.

Mott, T. (1985) Editorial, Are hypnotherapy patients hypnotized? *American Journal of Clinical Hypnosis,* 27: 151–2.

Naish, P. (1985) The 'trance' described in signal detection terms. *British Journal of Experimental and Clinical Hypnosis,* 2: 133–7.

Orne, M. T. (1959) The nature of hypnosis: artifact and essence. *Journal of Abnormal and Social Psychology,* 58: 277–99.

———(1965) Undesirable effects of hypnosis: the determinants and managements. *International Journal of Clinical and experimental Hypnosis,* 13: 226–37.

———(1972) Can a hypnotized subject be compelled to carry out otherwise unacceptable behaviour? *International Journal of Clinical and Experimental Hypnosis,* 20: 101–17.

Perry, C. (1977) Is hypnotizability modifiable? *International Journal of Clinical and Experimental Hypnosis,* 25: 125–46.

———(1979). Hypnotic coercion and compliance to it: A review of evidence presented in a legal case. *International Journal of Clinical and Experimental Hypnosis,* 27: 187–218.

Rachlin, H. (1985) Pain and behaviour. *Behavioural and Brain Sciences,* 8: 43–85.

Rossi, E. H. (1980) *The Collected Papers of Milton H. Erickson on Hypnosis.* New York: Irvington.

Sabartés, Jaime (1948) *Picasso. An Intimate Person.* Trans. from the Spanish by Angel Flores. New York: Prentice-Hall.

Sarbin, T. R. (1983) Review of *Hypnosis and Relaxation* by W. E. Edmonston. *International Journal of Clinical and experimental Hypnosis*, 31: 57–8.

Sarbin, T. R. and Coe, W. C. (1972) *Hypnosis: A Social Psychological Analysis of Influence Communication*. New York and London: Holt, Rinehart & Winston.

Sarbin, T. R. and Slagle, R. W. (1979) Hypnosis and psychophysiological outcomes. In E. Fromm and R. E. Shor (eds.), *Hypnosis: Developments in Research and New Perspectives*. New York: Aldine.

Sargant, W. (1957) *Battle for the Mind*. London: Heinemann.

(1973) *The Mind Possessed*. London: Heinemann.

Sheehan, P. W. (1979) Hypnosis and the processes of imagination. In E. Fromm and R. E. Shor (eds.), *Hypnosis: Developments in Research and New Perspectives*. New York: Aldine.

Sheehan, P. W. and McConkey, K. M. (1982) *Hypnosis and Experience: The Exploration of Phenomena and Process*. Hillsdale, N. J.: Lawrence Erlbaum.

Sheikh, A. A. (ed.) (1983) *Imagery: Current Theory, Research and Application*. New York and Chichester: Wiley.

Snyder, E. D. (1930) *Hypnotic Poetry: A Study of Trance-Inducing Techniques in Certain Poems and its Literary Significance*. Philadelphia: University of Philadelphia Press.

Snyder, E. D. and Shor, R. E. (1983) Trance-inductive poetry: a brief communication. *International Journal of Clinical and Experimental Hypnosis*, 31: 1–7.

Spanos, N. P. and Barber, T. X. (1974) Toward a convergence in hypnosis research. *American Psychologist*, 29: 500–11.

Spanos, N. P., de Groot, H. P., Tiller, D. K., Weeks, J. R. and Bertrand, L. D. (in press) 'Trance logic' duality and hidden observer responding in hypnotic, imagination, control and simulating subjects: social psychological analysis. *Journal of Abnormal Psychology*.

Spanos, N. P. and Hewitt, E. C. (1979) Glossoalia: a test of the 'trance' and psychopathology hypotheses. *Journal of Abnormal Psychology*, 88: 427–34.

Spiegel, H. and Spiegel D. (1978) *Trance and Treatment. Clinical Uses of Hypnosis*. New York: Basic Books.

Wagstaff, G. F. (1981) *Hypnosis, Compliance and Belief*. Brighton: Harvester.

(1985) Hypnotic susceptibility: a socio-cognitive perspective. Paper read at the Annual Conference of the British Psychological Society, University College, Swansea, 29 March – 1 April.

Wain, J. (1966) Dylan Thomas: a review of his Collected Poems. In C. B. Cox (ed.), *Dylan Thomas: A Collection of Critical Essays*. Englewood Cliffs, N. J.: Prentice-Hall.

Weitzenhoffer, A. M. (1953) *Hypnotism. An Objective Study in Suggestibility*. New York: Wiley.

Wilson, S. C. and Barber, T. X. (1983) The fantasy prone personality: implications for understanding imagery, hypnosis and parapsychological phenomenar. In A. A. Sheikh (ed.), *Imagery: Current Theory, Research and Application*. New York and Chichester: Wiley.

HYPNOSIS AS COMPLIANCE AND BELIEF: A SOCIO-COGNITIVE VIEW

Graham F. Wagstaff

In the previous chapter Fellows disputed the need for the traditional trance concept, to explain hypnotic effects. In Chapter 4 Graham Wagstaff launches an even stronger attack upon conventional assumptions about hypnosis. He is a social psychologist, and couches his account in social psychological terms, suggesting that, at least in some cases, hypnosis is merely an example of compliance. Wagstaff also argues that there may sometimes be a cognitive component to hypnotic experiences. Cognitive psychologists are concerned with the mechanisms by which we make use of the information we extract from our environment, to arrive at an understanding of our world. Many of the contributors to this book touch on the theme, and its association with hypnosis implies that what a person makes of his or her hypnotic experience may depend upon the way the situation is analysed and understood.

Dr Wagstaff lectures in the University of Liverpool Department of Psychology. He has published widely on the subject of hypnosis, and has been particularly concerned with the controversial issue of forensic hypnosis.

A major problem in applying ordinary psychological concepts to hypnotic phenomena is that hypnotic effects appear so diverse that any attempt to apply a single explanation is doomed to failure. We have to consider not only simple responses to suggestions such as arm levitation and postural sway, but also hallucinations, amnesia, regression, extraordinary strength and endurance, post-hypnotic responses, and relief from clinical problems such as asthma, migraine and distressing skin conditions, as well as the striking demonstration of hypnotic analgesia, especially painless surgery. Consequently, throughout the whole history of hypnosis the 'state' or 'trance' view has remained with us; for if we cannot explain these phenomena by reference to mundane psychological processes, they must be explicable in terms of something 'else', something unique and possibly mysterious, about which we still know little (Wagstaff 1982a). However, in this chapter it will be argued that this view may be unnecessarily pessimistic, and that perhaps the reason why we have been unable to find *the* essence of hypnosis is that there is no single explanation of all hypnotic phenomena (Wagstaff 1981a). There may be no central 'essence' of hypnosis; instead different phenomena may require different explanations to different degrees, and a range of processes may interact to give rise to the phenomena. The interactions may differ from situation to situation, and from person to person. Nevertheless, if an interactive interpretation is to be offered, it is necessary to suggest some central core processes that may be useful. In this chapter the discussion will centre upon two processes from social psychology: compliance and belief.

In view of this orientation, throughout this chapter terms such as 'hypnosis', 'hypnotic' and 'hypnotizable' are used parenthetically to define operations or responses to operations. They do not imply the existence of, or susceptibility to, a special state of hypnosis or 'trance'.

Compliance and belief

Within social psychology the term 'compliance' is a special form of conformity (Kiesler and Kiesler 1970, Aronson 1977). It refers to overt behaviour that becomes like the behaviour that a group or person wishes an individual to show; it refers solely to outward actions and does not consider the private convictions of the actor. As Orne (1966) has emphasized, in the context of hypnosis, compliance is *volitional* in nature, whereas a traditional feature of much hypnotic behaviour is that it is allegedly non-volitional or involuntary (Bowers 1983). Accordingly Wagstaff (1981a) has distinguished two categories of response to hypnotic suggestions which would constitute 'compliance only':

(1) Where a volitional act is supposed to reflect an underlying subjective experience but this is not the case; for example, in response to a pain stimulus subjects say they are not feeling pain, when privately pain is felt, or they move their hands as if brushing away a fly, but do not experience an hallucinated fly at all.

(2) Where an act explicitly or implicitly is supposed to be performed non-volitionally, but the subject consciously and deliberately performs the act. For example, a subject may deliberately raise an arm in response to an arm-levitation suggestion without feeling that the arm 'rises by itself'.

The arguments in this chapter will emphasize compliance as an important element in hypnotic responding. However, we also need a concept that will deal with veridical reports and experiences of hypnotic suggestion. Wagstaff (1978, 1981a) has suggested that the term 'belief' may be useful in this respect.

The main dictionary definitions of 'belief', which when applied to the area of hypnosis seem particularly appropriate in this role, are 'full acceptance of a thing as true; trust in a statement or person; faith'. Belief essentially concerns the private convictions or experiences of the individual; and in the context of hypnosis, beliefs can be concordant or discordant depending on the expectations of the subject. This concept allows subjects to state that certain experiences are 'true' without the necessity of postulating that the premises on which such statements are made are objectively valid. For example, as Barber, Spanos and Chaves (1974) have suggested, a shaman may behave in unusual ways, maintaining odd postures, frothing at the mouth and talking in a strange voice. The shaman's explanation of his behaviour may be that he is possessed by a spirit, yet few anthropologists would agree with this as an explanation. Nevertheless few would argue either that he is lying or faking; instead the interpretation would be that he behaves in this manner because he *believes* he is possessed by a spirit. In the same way it is possible for subjects to report honestly that they 'felt hypnotized' not because they had fallen into some objectively verifiable unique 'state' or 'trance', but because they sincerely believe that their experiences were concordant with their expectations of 'being hypnotized', even though such experiences may be readily explicable in terms of ordinary psychological processes (Wagstaff 1978, 1981a).

The power of compliance

To some investigators the idea that subjects in the hypnosis situation are likely to exhibit compliant 'sham' responses is untenable. This was the view of one of the champions of hypnotic surgery, J. Esdaile. When Esdaile was asked how he could account for the number of patients coming for treatment he replied:

> I see two ways of accounting for it; my patients on returning home either say to their friends similarly afflicted, 'What a soft man the doctor is! He cut me to pieces for twenty minutes and I made him believe that I did not feel it. Isn't it a capital joke? Do go and play him the same trick.' Or they may say . . . 'Look at me, I have got rid of my burden.'
> (Quoted in Marcuse 1976: 48–9)

Marcuse (1976) says: 'The problem of shamming or conscious simulation is most clearly answered in this question of anaesthesia' (1976: 49).

The comments of Esdaile and Marcuse typify two fundamental misconceptions about the a priori probability of compliance or shamming in hypnosis. Firstly, Esdaile assumed that the only motive for shamming was a desire on the part of the patient to fool the hypnotist as some kind of joke. Secondly, Marcuse seems to give the impression that, since subjects cannot fake hypnotic anaesthesia during surgery, it is unlikely that other hypnotic phenomena are attributable to shamming. The second of these propositions contains a number of inherent difficulties. Although it is very unlikely that all people undergoing surgery with hypnosis fake anaesthesia, there is sometimes no concordance between the ability to undergo hypnotic surgery painlessly and hypnotic susceptibility as assessed by other criteria; a patient may be poor at performing other hypnotic behaviour characteristic of 'deep trance' subjects but be good at tolerating clinical pain with hypnotic procedures, and vice versa (Barber 1969, Rock, Shipley and Campbell 1969). Similar anomalies occur with the hypnotic treatment of other medical problems where clinical success can sometimes be unrelated to hypnotic susceptibility (Gill and Brenman 1959, Frankel 1976).

It is thus dangerous to assume that we can simply generalize from one area of hypnotic behaviour to another. Yet it may also be misleading to assume that *within subjects* compliance or faking is all-or-none. Just because a subject genuinely experiences arm lowering, it is possible he or she may still fake amnesia. However, none of these alternatives can be taken seriously if we assume that the sole motivation to sham is some attempt to put one over on the hypnotist for a laugh. Consequently, a more sophisticated view of faked or sham behaviour is necessary, and misconceptions about the viability of compliance as an influence on hypnotic behaviour may continue for as long as hypnosis as an area remains divorced from a very closely allied context: that of the psychology of social influence.

One of the best-known social influence studies was conducted by Milgram (1974). He demonstrated how ordinary people could be readily induced to administer supposedly dangerous doses of electric shock to a screaming 'victim' if ordered to do so by an experimenter in a laboratory situation. In actuality the shocks were not real and the victim was an actor, but according to Milgram the 26 out of 40 subjects who did this believed they were giving real shocks. When Milgram described the experiment to a mixed group of students, psychiatrists and middle-class adults, not one said that he or she would fully obey the experimenter, and a similar group predicted that only a pathological fringe of 1 or 2 per cent would respond (Milgram 1974). In other words, there was a vast decrepancy between how people thought they would behave and how they actually did.

According to Milgram his subjects were confronted with a conflict between their own private attitudes about administering the shocks and their wish not to commit a severe social impropriety by disobeying the experimenter and ruining the experiment. Milgram's analysis includes the following quote from Goffman:

> Society is organised on the principle that any individual who possesses social characteristics has a moral right to expect that others will value and treat him in a correspondingly appropriate way ... When an individual projects a definition of a situation and then makes an implicit or explicit claim to be a person of a particular kind, he automatically exerts a moral demand upon the others, obliging them to value and treat him in the manner that persons of his kind have a right to expect.
>
> (Goffman 1959: 185)

Thus to disobey the experimenter in Milgram's situation would amount to a severe social impropriety. On the other hand, to obey would result in the fulfilment of role obligations and expectations, the promotion and defence of the self-image and the successful conclusion of the encounter. In order to arouse these sentiments in an individual it is not even necessary to employ an authority figure; peer-group pressure can readily induce individuals knowingly to give erroneous responses when non-conformity would produce social embarrassment. Thus subjects in group situations were prepared to tell what really amounted to lies, simply because others were making similar statements (Kiesler and Kiesler 1970).

In the obedience studies of Milgram behaviour was explicitly demanded; however, social rules that govern the experimenter–subject relationship may also evoke behaviours which are only implicitly demanded by the experimental situation. The idea that experiments can be biased by the subjects' desire to look 'good' is not a recent one. As early as 1908 Pierce commented:

> It is to the highest degree probable that the subject's . . . general attitude of mind is that of ready complacency and a cheerful willingness to assist the investigator in every possible way by reporting to him those very things that he is most eager to find, and that the very questions of the experimenter . . . suggest the shade of reply expected.
> (Quoted in Orne 1962)

Orne (1962) uses the term 'demand characteristics' to refer to those cues that influence the subject's behaviour in this way and he emphasizes that the role of a 'good' subject is to validate the experimental hypothesis in accordance with the experimenter's expectations. Orne provides a variety of evidence to illustrate how easy it is to get subjects to comply with ridiculous requests when the context is appropriate. In one example, by Menaker, subjects were required to perform serial additions on sheets filled with random digits. This required 224 additions per sheet, and subjects were given 2,000 sheets to complete. Each subject's watch was taken away and he was told: 'Continue to work; I will return eventually.' The result of this impossible task was that 'Five and a half hours later, the experimenter gave up' (Orne 1962). Orne regards his observations as consistent with those of Frank (1944), who also failed to find resistance to disagreeable and nonsensical tasks. Frank accounts for this 'primarily by the subject's unwillingness to break the tacit agreement he had made when he volunteered to take part in the experiment, namely, to do whatever the experiment required of him'.

Compliance to social influence is thus a very powerful phenomenon in its own right. In order to exhibit compliant behaviour a subject does not have to be a swindler, a gullible fool or a psychopath, but an ordinary person who responds to social expectations and obligations.

Compliance and hypnosis

It is not difficult to generalize these findings to the hypnosis situation. When confronted by a hypnotist saying 'your eyes are closing' or 'your arm is moving down' it may be acutely embarrassing for some subjects not to obey the instructions. Such disobedience could indicate that the subject is a 'bad' one, or that the hypnotist is a poor practitioner.

Hunt (1979) related the hypnosis situation directly to Milgram's analysis of obedience, and mentions Nelson's (1965) remark that in stage hypnosis it is more embarrassing for a volunteer to refuse to co-operate than to agree to go along with the show. Hunt (1979) points out how every obedience situation has strain and binding factors. Binding factors include the desire to 'look good' and the fear of embarrassment if the goal of the encounter is not achieved.

Strain factors include finding the task itself trivial, embarrassing or counter to expectations. If the strain factors are sufficient and outweigh the binding factors, then the subject will stop responding. In her own demonstration, Hunt (1979) showed that if one member of a pair of hypnotic subjects refused to carry out a suggestion (thus questioning the authority of the hypnotist) this significantly reduced the responsiveness of the other member.

The motivation to comply may come only partly from the desire to please an authority figure. A subject's initial responsiveness may stem from a genuine attempt to 'have a go' and to try to experience 'hypnosis'. This would result in a social commitment, irrespective of the prestige of the hypnotist (Wagstaff 1981a).

There are a number of classic anecdotal examples from the literature of people exhibiting compliance in the hypnosis situation (see, for example, Sarbin and Coe 1972, Kidder 1973, Wagstaff 1981a), and the results of a number of experimental investigations accord with the compliance hypothesis. For example, if subjects are led to believe that a certain response (catelepsy of the dominant hand) is a characteristic of hypnosis (which it is not) they will tend to show this response (Orne 1959). Altering the label of an identical situation by calling it either 'hypnosis' or a test of 'gullibility' can also affect responsiveness (Barber 1969). Such studies indicate that responsiveness can be affected by subjects' expectations as to what is desired of them, and what is socially acceptable in the particular experimental context. The influence of compliance presents a very parsimonious way of interpreting a variety of other results. For instance, if subjects who have been given an induction procedure are given suggestions for deafness and are asked, 'Can you hear me?' some will answer, 'No, I can't hear you' (Barber, Spanos and Chaves 1974). In a classic case a subject's amazing display of apparent uniocular blindness was partly attributable to her practising being blind at home with a friend (Pattie 1935). In further examples age-regressed subjects have shown responses under the erroneous impression that children would display them, i.e. they thought that children would display such responses, when in fact the appropriate age group would not (Gidro-Frank and Bowersbuch 1948, Barber 1969, Walker, Garratt and Wallace 1976, Wagstaff 1981a).

There have been many experimental attempts to dismiss compliance as a source of hypnotic responding, but two paradigms deserve particular attention. According to Orne (1970) if compliance is involved in hypnosis then hypnotically susceptible subjects should be more susceptible to compliance in general. To investigate this hypothesis he divided subjects into high and low susceptibility and then asked them if they would send a stack of postcards back to the experimenter – the rationale being that if the high susceptible subjects were generally more compliant they should return more postcards. In fact, there was no significant difference between the groups; if anything, the low-susceptibility subjects posted back more cards. The main problem with this paradigm is that it may be confounded by a powerful effect found in other social psychological research. If subjects are made to feel they have ruined an experiment (for instance, by thinking they have blown up the apparatus) they are more likely to comply with a future request (Wallance and Sadalla 1966). There may thus be a valid case for suggesting that by not responding to the hypnotic suggestions the insusceptible subjects felt they had ruined the experiment or disappointed the hypnotist. One way of 'making up' might be to mail back the cards.

Another paradigm that has been used to dismiss the influence of compliance involves the use of 'honesty reports' (Bowers 1967, 1983). According to Bowers, if compliance operates, then motivating subjects to be honest in their reports should decrease subjective reports of hypnotic phenomena. However, he suggests that hypnotic subjects are not affected by demands for honesty in their reports of hypnotic hallucinations. Other research also indicates that honesty demands have little influence on hypnotic reports (Kihlstrom *et al.* 1980). Unfortunately, the proposal that honesty demands will overcome compliance is over-optimistic. In a classic study by Levy (1967) subjects were involved in a verbal learning task, the success of which depended on their being unaware of the reinforcement contingencies. Levy arranged it so that before the experiment an accomplice informed the subjects of the contingencies. Not one subject spontaneously volunteered his or her knowledge to the experimenter during the experimenter. On questioning only one of sixteen subjects reported truthfully that he had been informed; 75 per cent denied any prior knowledge of the experiment, and significantly more questions were required to elicit reports of awareness from this informed group than from a group who had not been informed. Relating these findings to hypnosis, Sarbin and Coe concluded: 'If subjects operate under self-instructions to lie in a verbal learning experiment there is no reason to believe that the same kinds of self-instructions may not be activated in the hypnotic setting, (1972: 134).

Although compliance seems implicated in many studies, few have tried to assess its presence by direct attempts to remove the pressures for compliance. One attempt was made by Wagstaff (1977a), who demonstrated that reports of post-hypnotic amnesia could be eliminated by providing instructions that allowed subjects to admit to 'role-playing', rather than being in a 'state' or 'trance'. The most important finding in this study was that amnesia was eliminated when compliance was removed, yet interestingly a few subjects still reported feeling 'hypnotized'. This could indicate that some subjects had such a strong investment in the 'role' of appearing 'hypnotized' that they assumed they were still supposed to report 'being hypnotized', or some honestly believed they were 'hypnotized' (or possibly both).

The evidence reviewed so far may be seen to suggest that compliance could play a significant role in hypnotic responding; however, some subjects may genuinely believe themselves to be, or have been, in a condition or state of 'hypnosis'. How could this come about?

Hypnosis and belief

According to a traditional 'state' view of hypnosis, people will label themselves as 'hypnotized' because they have fallen into a unique state. An alternative view is that the insight can be gained by looking at some of the more general principles that govern the ways in which people label their experiences and behaviours.

In the face of ambiguous information there is evidence that we tend to rely on external factors to label our experiences (Bem 1965, 1972). Also perceptions of ambiguous internal states, such as pleasure and fear, can be manipulated by giving subjects fake feedback about their physiological condition (Valins 1966, Valins and Ray 1967). If such an analysis is applied to the hypnosis situation, then hypnotic subjects given an induction procedure and suggestions may find their experiences ambiguous; how they label such experiences will then depend on external factors (such as whether they are told, 'You are hypnotized') and expectations (whether, for example, being relaxed but aware is a sufficient criterion for being 'hypnotized').

A number of features of the hypnotic situation may evoke sensations that, although not psychologically unusual, may be ambiguous to naive subjects. Several experiences that subjects may interpret as evidence for being 'hypnotized', such as changes in size, giddiness, changes in the distance of the hypnotist's voice, changes in temperature, feelings of floating and detachment, sleepiness, are readily experienced by individuals who have been instructed to close their eyes and trained to relax (Barber, Spanos and Chaves 1974, Edmonston 1977). Although relaxation may form a major source of sensations that subjects label as hypnosis (Edmonston 1977, 1981, Fellows, Chapter 3 above), the two are not to be equated. Even when relaxation is not present, then as long as a situation is defined as hypnosis, subjects may continue to show a high level of responsivenesss to suggestions (Barber 1969, Banyai and Hilgard 1976, Malott 1984). These findings accord with the proposal that subjects will report their experiences as evidence for 'hypnosis' if these experiences tally with their beliefs as to what is to be expected from 'hypnosis' (Wagstaff 1981a, 1985b). It just so happens that the general conception of hypnosis is one of relaxation and sleepiness, and as most induction procedures employ relaxation techniques the resulting experiences may concur with expectations and enter the self-attributional process. Relaxation experiences, however, are not a prerequisite for reports of feeling 'hypnotized'; if subjects are told they are not necesssary, or believe such, then they will rely on other cues.

A number of investigators have drawn attention to some perfectly 'normal' psychological phenomena often employed in the hypnotic situation, which because of their ambiguous status can subsequently be used by subjects as evidence of 'being hypnotized' (Skemp 1972, Kidder 1973) – for example, eye fixation, gravity and imagery. Indeed, subjects do not need to be submitted to an induction procedure in order to respond to most of the suggestions and to determine hypnotic responsiveness (Barber 1969, Barber, Spanos and Chaves 1974). Further support for this proposal comes from evidence indicating that, *if given a choice*, most subjects will prefer to describe themselves as 'absorbed' rather than 'hypnotized', which they use only when they are given no alternative scheme for classifying their experiences (Spanos 1982).

The interaction of compliance and belief

Although compliance may be a major motivating force in hypnotic responding, it has obvious disadvantages to its perpetrator. The compliant subject may feel deceitful, the self-image may be threatened, and even intense personal disappointment may be experienced. If given a choice, therefore, between *believing* something has happened and experiencing the *pretence* that something has happened, there will be strong internal pressures to accept the former. It can be argued that the motivation to believe something has happened or is happening will be particularly strong in the clinical context where 'pretence' would offer little relief from medical problems. There is evidence, from social-psychological studies of cognitive dissonance theory, indicating that people can be strongly motivated to reduce discrepancies between private attitudes or beliefs and overt behaviour, by changing their attitudes and beliefs. There is no obvious reason why such a mechanism should not operate in the hypnosis situation (Wagstaff 1981a). In this way hypnotic subjects would be motivated to try to make hypnotic suggestions 'work' within the limitations of the hypnosis context; i.e. if possible the subject will attempt to carry out the suggestions so that the resulting responses are both publicly and privately acceptable. The interaction between compliance and belief may therefore be seen as a three-stage process (Wagstaff 1983a) by which, when confronted by any suggestion or set of suggestions, subjects

(1) decide what the hypnotist 'really' wants;
(2) attempt to employ cognitive strategies to produce congruent actions and experiences;
(3) if (2) fails, resort to behavioural compliance.

This process may vary between individuals, according to their capacities to adopt the 'normal' cognitive strategies mentioned under (2), their expectations as to what is appropriate and their susceptibility to social influence. Some may stop at (2) and fail to respond; others may ignore (2) and go straight to (3). For future reference this three-stage process will be termed the ESC process (expectation, strategy, compliance). According to this formulation, compliance will operate to its fullest when the social pressures and susceptibility to them are greatest, and when cognitive strategies have failed to produce appropriate (or 'believable') subjective and overt behavioural responses.

The ESC process may be illustrated by reference to the phenomenon of hypnotic amnesia. In the standard paradigm for hypnotic amnesia the subject will be given a range of suggestions, or some other stimulus material, and will be told, 'now you cannot remember' what has happened or what has been learned. Typically, if subjects respond positively to the suggestion, they will remember nothing (total amnesia) or a few items (partial amnesia) until told 'now you can remember'. The instructions will be given during the hypnotic procedure, although they may suggest that the amnesia will not occur until the procedure has terminated (post-hypnotic amnesia). According to the traditional 'state' approach to hypnosis these instructions result in an amnesic block, which prevents subjects from remembering, no matter how hard they try (Kihlstrom 1978, Bowers 1983). Thus Kihlstrom argues: 'the hypnotized amnesia subject appears to be trying about as hard as he can to recall the forgotten material ... There is some impediment in retrieval that prevents him from easily and efficiently recollecting any more of the available memories' (1978: 75). One difficulty with this approach is that it does little to explain the phenomenon. Kihlstrom, a leading advocate of this view, comments that we simply do not yet know enough about memory, amnesia and hypnosis. If the ESC formulation is applied, however, another explanation is possible. Thus when told they 'cannot remember' – stage (1) – subjects may either behaviourally comply, by pretending they cannot remember – stage (3) – or try to adopt a strategy that will enable them to convince the experimenter, and in some cases *themselves*, that they actually cannot remember – stage (2). If they do neither of these, then they will not respond at all and will be termed 'insusceptible'. If the strategies in (2) fail they may either 'give up' or revert to (3) (pure compliance).

According to Spanos and his associates the chief cognitive strategy for achieving amnesia is that of 'inattention' (Spanos 1982). Their experiments reveal that when subjects are instructed to treat the amnesia suggestion as a request to attend away from the target material, amnesia is significantly increased, but when the challenge to remember is to be interpreted as a challenge to recall actively (i.e. refocus attention) amnesia is drastically reduced. They also found that the disorganization of recall in partial anmesia, thought to be a defining characteristic or hypnotic anmesia (Evans and Kihlstrom 1973), could also be replicated in subjects given strategies to focus attention away from the recall task (Spanos and D'Eon 1980).

However, a challenge to the inattention hypothesis comes from studies indicating that some highly susceptible subjects continue to remain 'amnesic' in spite of instructions to try actively to remember and to be honest (Kihlstrom *et al.* 1980). According to Spanos and his associates (Spanos 1982) these results occurred because the subjects involved ignored the instructions to recall actively. This interpretation is directly in line with stages (1) and (2) of the ESC formulation; i.e. these highly committed subjects decided that what was 'really' expected of them was the maintainance of appearing amnesic – some subjects maintain what they feel is implicit in the social context.

There are, however, other problems for the inattention hypothesis, when subjects are required to forget very simple and obvious items such as their names, or when they show *total* amnesia (the latter occurs for some subjects in virtually all studies of post-hypnotic amnesia). It seems doubtful that even the most absorbing inattention strategy would enable people to forget *everything* that occurred only a few minutes previously, or to forget their own names. The problem is well illustrated by Smith:

> If someone were to say to you, 'Stop thinking of the word hippopotamus for thirty seconds and I'll give you a thousand dollars', you would never collect your

money. You would know, if you had ever played this mind game, that it is impossible not think of the word hippopotamus when told not to, because you really have been instructed to orient to it in a devious way. (1978: 77)

In such cases the most viable alternative to a 'state' theory of an unconscious 'amnesic block' is not inattention but simple behavioural compliance; i.e. the subject deliberately withholds material that is available (Wagstaff 1981a).

In order to breach amnesia totally, therefore, one needs a manipulation that will eliminate compliant-role behaviour as well as the elimination of cognitive strategies maintained to convey the impression that hypnotic amnesia is taking place. The study by Wagstaff (1977a) mentioned earlier was effective in this exercise; giving subjects an opportunity to say they were 'role-playing' rather than 'hypnotized' eliminated all reports of post-hypnotic amnesia.

*Spanos, Chapter 5 below, also discusses how amnesia may be breached –
P.L.N.N.*

To summarize, the experimental literature on hypnotic amnesia is supportive of the view that hypnotic responsiveness results from a willingness and/or response to pressure, to play the role of a 'hypnotized' person. The role is determined by personal preconceptions and the social context, as defined by the hypnotist and the hypnotic situation. The way this is manifested involves (1) working out what is explicitly or implicitly demanded by the hypnotic situation, (2) employing strategies so as to maintain a correspondence between external demands and private experience, i.e. to maximize concordant beliefs, and (3) reverting to behavioural compliance if (2) is not effective or is impossible to apply, or if strategies involved in (2), such as inattention or visualization, are deemed to be illegitimate in the context (for instance, some subjects may not think it 'legitimate' for a 'hypnotized' subject to be deliberately trying to bring about effects). It is now necessary to see how well this socio-cognitive view can be applied to other hypnotic phenomena.

Physiological correlates

If the compliance/belief of the ESC socio-cognitive formulation is valid, then one would not predict there to be any unique correlate of a hypnotic 'state'; i.e. all physiological correlates should be reproducible by subjects instructed to engage in the 'normal' cognitive activities such as relaxation, imagination and eye-closure that a hypnotic subject might perform. Indeed it does seem that, when controls for such factors are applied, there is no accepted, reliable, discrete set of physiological indicators that correlate with 'being hypnotized'. Subjects who are said to be 'hypnotized' cannot be reliably differentiated on a variety of physiological measures including EEG, electroculogram, electromyogram, cortical potentials, skin resistance, palmar potentials, respiration rate, blood pressure, peripheral blood flow, blood clotting time, skin temperature and oral temperature (Barber 1970, Sarbin and Slagle 1972,

Wagstaff 1981a). A failure to find correlates of a hypnotic state does not mean that responses to physiological measures do not *change* with hypnotic induction, but that equivalent changes can occur if subjects are given instructions for relaxation and eye-closure, or to imagine various effects.

Transcendent feats

Since the beginnings of hypnosis it has been reported that hypnotized individuals can transcend 'normal capacities', and a number of experimental studies have appeared to support such notions. Frequently, however, either the studies failed to supply appropriate motivating instructions to their control groups (if present at all), or the within-subjects design was used, i.e. subjects acted as their own non-hypnotic controls. This latter design is inappropriate in hypnosis experiments, as the evidence suggests that subjects tend to suppress their performance in the 'waking' control condition, in order to give a spurious boost to their performance in the hypnotic condition (Wagstaff 1981a). The literature on this topic is enormous; more comprehensive reviews are given by Barber (1969), Barber, Spanos and Chaves (1974) and Wagstaff (1981a, 1982f). However, the following examples may be used to illustrate the general findings. In a very comprehensive review of the literature concerning hypnotic performance and muscular strength and endurance, psychomotor behaviour and athletic performance, Morgan concludes that 'a review of the experimental literature does not justify the view that performance in the hypnotic and post-hypnotic states will necessarily surpass performance in the motivated waking state' (1972: 193).

A review of the literature on hypnotically suggested deafness reveals that, when sophisticated techniques such as delayed auditory feedback are used, there is no evidence that 'hypnotic deafness' resembles actual physiological deafness, or cannot be reproduced in non-hypnotic conditions (Wagstaff 1981a).

Whilst some investigators have reported that a deeply hypnotized subject may display 'alpha-blocking', a physiological correlate of organic blindness, a similar response can result if subjects deliberately unfocus their eyes (Barber, Spanos and Chaves 1974). Furthermore, claims that hypnotic subjects can be made colour-blind become less spectacular when it is realized that non-hypnotic control subjects simply asked to act 'as if' colour-blind give similar responses (Barber 1969). Also, suggestions for the improvement of eyesight are equally effective regardless of whether they are accompanied by hypnotic induction (Barber, Spanos and Chaves 1974, Wagstaff 1983d).

Studies of reports of hypnotically suggested negative visual hallucinations, i.e. the selective elimination of parts of the visual input, are equivocal. Although there is evidence that hypnotic subjects may actively *try* to eliminate material (Gray, Bowers and Fenz 1970), there is no definitive proof that they succeed in doing so (Underwood 1960, Wagstaff 1981a). Attempts to corroborate reports of hypnotically suggested positive hallucinations using techniques such as delayed auditory feedback and pupillary contractions have proved negative, and studies employing coloured after-images indicate that subjects report what they think they *ought* to see, rather than what would occur if a positive hallucination of a colour had actually occurred (Wagstaff 1981a). Whilst it has been shown that some hypnotic subjects may display optokinetic nystagmus (eye movement reflexively induced by watching a moving object) when asked to hallucinate a rotating drum, equivalent responses can be evoked from 'waking' subjects asked to visualize the same image (Barber 1969, 1972). More will be said on the subject of hallucinations later.

A number of reports have indicated that if subjects are given hypnotic suggestions to dream on a suggested topic before going to bed, then when they are woken up at various times there is a tendency for them to have been dreaming on the topic. However, these studies suffer from important methodological inadequacies (Barber, Spanos and Chaves 1974, Wagstaff 1976, 1981a). Stoyva (1965) reported that hypnotic subjects showed a decrease in REM production following a post-hypnotic dream suggestion; however, Wagstaff, Hearne and Jackson (1980) found that REM production was equally present in subjects who were not given a hypnotic induction procedure.*

Some studies have indicated that learning and memory can be improved by the administration of hypnotic induction procedures, but reviews of the literature indicate that, when proper methodological controls are applied, there is no evidence that hypnotic procedures will facilitate memory to a greater extent than non-hypnotic procedures (Barber 1969, Wagstaff and Ovenden 1979, Wagstaff 1981a, 1981c, 1982d–g, 1983c, 1984, 1985c, Wagstaff, Traverse and Milner 1982, Smith 1983, Wagstaff and Maguire 1983, Wagstaff and Sykes 1984).

A similar story emerges for studies of hypnotic age regression. Claims have been made that hypnotic procedures can reinstate perceptual abilities characteristic of childhood (Parrish, Lundy and Leibowitz 1969, Walker, Garratt and Wallace, 1976), but others have failed to replicate these findings (Spanos 1982, Wagstaff 1984). Other studies involving the production of neonatal behaviour (Raikov 1982) childlike transitional object relations (Nash, Johnson and Tipton 1979) and other allegedly convincing performances of age regression (for example, Reiff and Scheerer 1959) have been criticized for methodological inadequacies (O'Connell, Shor and Orne 1970, Wagstaff 1981a, 1984).

In summary, there seems little reason to qualify the statement made by Orne that 'studies with simulating subjects as well as other recent research . . . have demonstrated that hypnosis does not magically increase capacities beyond those available in a motivated waking condition' (1971: 206). The efficacy of hypnotic procedures for decreasing pain and treating other clinical phenomena will be considered shortly.

---

* *REM, or rapid eye movement, is exhibited by sleepers, when dreaming; its incidence declines after a period of dreaming. – P.L.N.N.*

Non-transcendent properties of hypnosis

In view of the failure to find transcendent properties of hypnosis a number of investigators have looked for evidence that hypnotic subjects behave in a unique way. Many of these studies have employed the real–simulator design, comparing 'real' hypnotic subjects with simulators instructed to 'fool' the hypnotist (Orne 1971). This ingenious design has a number of advantages; it enables one to assess the extent to which hypnotic behaviours lie within 'normal' limits by providing controls for motivation, and also enables one to assess whether overt behaviours and subjective reports *could* be the result of simulation or compliance. Problems occur, however, when differences between the 'reals' and simulators emerge, because there are some fundamental differences between the groups. Firstly, simulators tend to be selected because they are not susceptible to hypnotic suggestions (so, according to the state theorists, they do not themselves 'fall into hypnosis'). This presents difficulties because non-susceptible subjects may differ from susceptible subjects in their attitudes to and preconceptions about hypnosis (Wagstaff, 1981a, 1981b). Secondly, 'reals' and simulators operate under different instructions. Many of the real subjects, if applying the ESC process, will attempt to experience the suggestions by applying cognitive strategies such as inattention, visualization and imagination and will be motivated to convince *themselves* as well as the hypnotist that they are 'hypnotized'. On the other hand, simulators will not be motivated to convince themselves, and some may not attempt to experience the effects. Thus when differences between 'reals' and simulators emerge this does not necessarily provide evidence for a unique 'state' of hypnosis, unless it can be shown that such differences are *not* due to population differences or to the application of 'normal' cognitive strategies (Wagstaff 1983a).

A number of studies have entered the literature showing differences between 'reals' and simulators. The important question for this chapter is, are the results compatible with a socio-cognitive view?

In one study hypnotic subjects showed a post-hypnotic response, after the experiment had ceased, more often than simulators (Orne, Sheehan and Evans 1968). However, these results are explicable in a number of ways in accordance with the view advanced in this chapter. The simulators were not susceptible and may have had different attitudes; but more importantly, the simulators had no investment in keeping up the response after the experiment, since everyone involved before and after the experiment knew it was legitimate for them to simulate (Wagstaff 1981a).

In another classic example Evans and Orne (1971) found that real subjects would continue responding longer than simulators when the hypnotist left in the middle of the hypnotic procedure. Again there was a problem because the simulators were not susceptible; however, Barber (1972) has argued that the simulating group was inappropriate, and there is evidence to show that a group simply told to relax would behave in the same way as the hypnotic subjects. Sarbin and Coe (1972) have also argued that the different instructions to the groups created different expectations as to the appropriate role. The hypnotic subjects were relaxed and comfortable, so there was no need for them to abandon the role; by contrast the simulators were only alert to cues so as not to give themselves away, so when the hypnotist left they abandoned the role.

Another, sometimes apparent difference between 'reals' and simulators is that simulators respond on average as if *more* 'hypnotized' than 'reals' (the overplay effect). One contributing factor to this effect is that low-susceptibility subjects may have extreme and unrealistic expectations about hypnosis; for example, they may fear losing control (Wagstaff 1979, 1981a). It is thus possible that the high responsiveness of some simulators simply reflects their conception of how a 'good' hypnotic subject should behave; they clearly manifest in their behaviour the preconception that good hypnotic subjects respond to most if not all suggestions. However, a more likely explanation is simply that simulators act under direct instructions to be 'good' subjects, whereas 'reals' operate under self-instructions and may choose not to play out the role completely. Nevertheless, simulators cannot be distinguished from 'reals' on the basis of the overplay effect alone, as this extreme behaviour of some simulators is indistinguishable from that of some extremely responsive real subjects (Orne 1959, 1971).

The limitations of the real–simulator design are also emphasized in studies of 'trance-logic' (Orne 1959). In these studies some 'real' subjects appear to tolerate logical incongruities such as carefully walking round a chair which is supposed to be 'invisible' to them. They also accurately describe scenes on the far side of a hallucinated object, as if it seemed transparent. Simulators allegedly do not respond in this way. However, Johnson, Maher and Barber (1972) found evidence that non-hypnotic subjects gave the same kind of trance-logical reports as hypnotic subjects. These findings fit well with the overplay effect and the ESC formulation. Simulators will not report transparency because they report *complete* hallucinations that blot out the background, just like many 'good' hypnotic subjects. When some hypnotic subjects report transparency it is as if they are simply *imagining* an image. Thus when instructed to 'see' an image some hypnotic subjects may try hard to carry out the suggestion by imagining it. To some of these the resulting 'normal' cognitive response is sufficient to comply with the role of being 'hypnotized', and it is reported as transparent. To others the normal process of imagination does not produce what they conceive of as being sufficient, so they either report they have seen nothing or comply and pretend they have seen a complete non-transparent image (Wagstaff 1981a). The notion that when subjects say they have 'seen' a hallucination they really mean they have 'imagined' it (Wagstaff 1981a) is supported by data from Spanos and his associates indicating that, if given the option, subjects will prefer to say that suggested hallucinations were 'imagined' rather than 'seen'. Rare cases where subjects report that they have 'seen' rather than 'imagined' suggested hallucinations occur as often in non-hypnotic task-motivated conditions as in hypnotic ones (Spanos 1982). Together these results indicate that, although differences may sometimes emerge between simulators and 'real' subjects, when appropriate controls are applied for population differences and cognitive strategies that may be differentially used by the two groups, then there is no conclusive evidence for uniquely hypnotic behaviours.

Hypnosis and pain

The fact that treatments labelled as hypnotic appear to be useful in the alleviation of clinical pain is well documented (Wadden and Anderton 1982, Hilgard and Hilgard 1984). The essential question again, however, is whether one needs to invoke a special process of 'hypnosis' to explain the effects, or whether other psychological processes are adequate. A socio-cognitive view would draw attention to the following points (for reviews see Barber, Spanos and Chaves 1974, Chaves and Barber 1976, Wagstaff 1981a).

(1) There is a small proportion of the general population who appear to be able to tolerate surgery without chemical anaesthetics. Contrary to some popular reports, hypnosis in surgery is comparatively rare, and only a small proportion of patients are selected for hypnotic surgery.
(2) Clinical pain may be alleviated if fear and anxiety are removed. Much is done by way of pre-operative preparation to remove fear and anxiety from patients about to be operated on using hypnosis. Also if the patient believes the treatment will be effective, this can in itself remove anxiety and consequently lessen pain.
(3) Hypnotic procedures usually involve a variety of non-unique techniques such as suggestive imagery, relaxation and distraction, which, in the absence of hypnosis, may be potent pain-relievers.
(4) Many parts of the body are less sensitive to pain than is commonly realized; for example, the following are insensitive to *incision*: subcutaneous tissue, bone, brain, lungs, surface of heart, stomach, uterus, spleen, liver and kidney. Rarely is hypnosis used alone; it is usually accompanied by a local anaesthetic, which will act on areas that are sensitive to incision (for example, the skin).
(5) Some patients low on susceptibility as determined by other criteria receive as much pain relief following hypnotic treatments as those high on susceptibility. This would suggest that the effectiveness of the treatment is not necessarily a consequence of a unique hypnotic element.
(6) There are some reports of a superior outcome with hypnosis (Wadden and Anderton 1982); these may be due to the particular placebo characteristics of the hypnotic situation (to be discussed in the next section).

The whole area of hypnosis and clinical pain is confused. In the clinical situation it is extremely difficult to control for factors such as the placebo effect, anxiety, fear, distraction, the doctor–patient relationship, suggestions *per se* and base-line levels of pain, so that the influence of hypnotic induction can be assessed. A number of investigators have accordingly turned to laboratory studies of hypnotic analgesia. Unfortunately, laboratory studies of pain bring their own problems, because laboratory pain may be less distressing than clinical pain, and pain reports in the laboratory may be open to greater influence from demand-characteristic artifacts (Wagstaff 1981a).

A number of studies indicate that suggestions given without hypnotic induction are as effective as hypnotic suggestions for analgesia (Evans and Paul 1970, Spanos, Barber and Lang 1974), and attempts to find physiological correlates of hypnotic analgesia have been inconclusive (Wagstaff 1981a). Moreover, simulators can successfully imitate the responses of hypnotically susceptible subjects given suggestions for pain relief (Hilgard *et al* 1978), except that they tend to overplay their role and do not maintain their reports of analgesia when 'honesty demands' are made. However, as has been pointed out, the latter findings are compatible with a socio-cognitive view; i.e. (1) 'honesty demands' will be differentially interpreted by simulators who can legitimately admit to pain experienced, (2) the simulating role explicitly demands a 'good' hypnotic performance, and (3) simulators will not necessarily apply voluntary cognitive strategies such as distraction and imagery in order to attempt to reduce pain sensations.

The latter point is supported by the finding of Spanos *et al.* (1984) that 'real' subjects frequently did not use pain-coping strategies unless the experimental situation gave them permission to do so. These data are also consistent with the view that when, in hypnosis situations, low-susceptibility subjects do not appear to manifest the same pain reduction as high-susceptibility subjects, this is not necessarily because the high-susceptibility subjects have achieved a greater depth of 'trance' allowing them to experience less pain, or that they possess greater coping skills, but instead low-susceptibility subjects do not define the hypnosis situation as one in which they should exercise voluntary coping strategies. Further support for this view is indicated by the finding that low susceptibles are as successful at reducing pain in non-hypnotic contexts as the high-susceptibles, but the performance of low susceptibles deteriorates in the hypnotic context. That is, the low susceptibles are as successful as the high susceptibles at applying coping strategies in non-hypnotic situations, but when given hypnotic induction they neglect to use the strategies or use them less efficiently (Spanos, Kennedy and Gwynn 1984).

Other clinical uses of hypnosis

Hypnosis has been applied in many other clinical contexts besides the alleviation of pain. A socio-cognitive view does not argue that hypnotic techniques are of no value in clinical contexts, but that the explanation of their effectiveness does not necessitate the introduction of a unique hypnotic process.

The clinical use of hypnosis has been reviewed comprehensively by Wadden and Anderton (1982). The main conclusions are that hypnosis can be effective in the treatment of insomnia, obesity, mild phobias, smoking, dental stress and alcoholism. The success can be attributed to a variety of factors that are not unique to the hypnotic situation – for example, social support, covert modelling and relaxation. There do appear to be some reports, however, that hypnosis may sometimes provide a superior outcome in the treatment of chronic pain, warts and asthma. According to Bowers and Kelly (1979) and Wadden and Anderton (1982) the main characteristic of these latter disorders is that they are not self-initiated. This is significant in that placebos appear to be most effective in the alleviation of non-voluntary chronic illness, especially pain, to the extent that some individuals achieve as much pain relief from placebos as from morphine (Evans 1974). It may, therefore, be postulated that when hypnotic induction appears to 'add' something to therapy, it is a placebo effect; i.e. what it 'adds' is a ritual that culminates in some patients *believing* that the treatments will be effective. Indeed, hypnotic induction has all the ingredients of a good placebo (Barber 1981, Wagstaff 1985d). This explanation would appear to be the most parsimonious, as other attempts to assess any unique contribution of hypnotic induction have been inconclusive. For example, some have argued that hypnosis adds features such as 'intense concentration and receptivity', although there is no conclusive evidence that hypnosis increases concentration, relaxation or the clarity of visual imagery (Wadden and Anderton 1982).

That 'belief in efficacy' is the key ingredient of any superior outcome for hypnosis is also supported by previously mentioned findings that a significant number of low-susceptibility subjects respond equally well to hypnotic treatments (Wagstaff 1981a, Wadden and Anderton 1982). This suggests that it is not some unique hypnotic skill that is responsible. Such a view is not negated by evidence that hypnotic responding is not related to placebo responding, as placebo responding is not itself transituationally consistent (Buckalew, Ross and Starr 1981); and the classic demonstration reporting that hypnotic responding is different from placebo responding (McGlashan, Evans and Orne 1969) is inconclusive due to methodological problems (Wagstaff 1985d).

Hypnotic susceptibility and hypnotic 'skills'

A number of writers (for example, Bowers 1983) have argued that hypnotic susceptibility is a stable characteristic. This in itself is not incompatible with a socio-cognitive view, because expectations, attitudes and even compliance can possesss some stable characteristics (Wagstaff 1983b). However, in order to define more completely the stable characteristics of hypnotic susceptibility both some state and non-state writers have emphasized the role of absorption in imaginings in hypnotic behaviours (Barber, Spanos and Chaves 1974, Sheehan and Perry 1976). If we view hypnotic susceptibility as a capacity to become absorbed in imaginings, and invoke concepts from attribution theory to account for how individuals may come to believe that their imaginings are attributable to 'hypnosis' (Wagstaff 1981a), then the state and non-state views converge.

However, an analysis of hypnotic responding solely in terms of absorption in imaginings and possible cognitive skills (Sigman, Phillips and Clifford 1985) appears to be inadequate (Wagstaff 1985a), as subjects will readily exhibit responses that run counter to imaginings. Thus if subjects are asked to *imagine* their arms bending, whilst being told their arms are rigid, they will keep their arms rigid (Zamansky 1977, Spanos, Weeks aand de Groh, 1984). Also, attempts to relate hypnotic susceptibility to skills that would have been thought useful in the hypnotic context, such as attention, have been difficult to replicate (Spanos 1982), or leave significant numbers of people low in these skills still able to perform high on scales of hypnotic susceptibility (Graham and Evans 1977, Wagstaff 1985a).

Thus, although there appears to be considerable evidence that hypnotic susceptibility is related to absorption in imaginings, there is 'something missing'. According to the ESC socio-cognitive formulation, disparities will inevitably occur between behaviour, on the one hand, and absorption, imagination or the use of other cognitive strategies, on the other, when the use of such strategies – from stage (2) of the ESC formulation – is made void or is ineffective in producing the desired or expected response. In such cases the subject will be presented with a conflict between what is expected and what is experienced, and stage (3) may come about; i.e. the subject will revert to behavioural compliance, for example by pretending that an arm will not bend by deliberately keeping it stiff (Wagstaff 1981a, 1983a). The results of the studies of Zamansky (1977) and Spanos, Weekes and de Groh (1984) can be explained if it is assumed that subjects apply the simple rule: *when all else fails, revert to compliance*. Thus according to a socio-cognitive view the 'missing ingredient' that accounts for major disparities between the use of cognitive skills and strategies and hypnotic behaviour is compliance (Wagstaff 1983a).

There is, however, an area of grey between the use of cognitive strategies and the manifestation of compliance in the face of ambiguous hypnotic stimuli (Wagstaff 1981a). For example, if subjects deliberately *ignore* instructions to attend to material or to imagine various effects (Spanos 1982), is this compliance? In as much as subjects deliberately ignore instructions that would invalidate their concept of what is 'really' expected, then unless a most elaborate form of self-deception takes place, there is an element of sham in such behaviour and it constitutes compliance. However, if subjects disobey such instructions to convince *themselves*, i.e. evoke concordant *beliefs*, then the distinction is blurred. The ESC formulation, however, can accommodate both categories of subjective experience, but would propose compliance as the more likely explanation in these cases.

According to the socio-cognitive view expressed in this chapter, no single skill or capacity is likely to account for more than a small portion of the variance in hypnotic responding. A number of skill variables may be involved – for example, dramaturgic ability (Sarbin and Coe 1972) as well as the capacity to become absorbed in imaginings (Tellegen and Atkinson 1974).

However, it is important to emphasize the significance of compliance in accounting for differences in hypnotic susceptibility, as sometimes it can equal and even out-perform some of the more popular 'skills' allegedly related to hypnotic susceptibility. Recent results indicate, for instance, *no* relation between hypnotic susceptibility and vividness of mental imagery (Van Dyne and Stava 1981), *no* relationship betwen hypnotic susceptibility and the ability to concentrate and focus attention (Reilley and Rodolfa 1981), yet significant relationships between hypnotic susceptibility and compliance as determined by alumni annual giving (Graham and Green 1981) and the Asch conformity paradigm (Shames 1981). Simulators can also replicate a number of responses assumed to be the result of specialized imaginative activities (Wagstaff 1977b).

Indeed, the relationship between hypnotic susceptibility and cognitive skills or capacities is still unclear. It remains to be established whether (a) hypnotically susceptible subjects possess a range of skills or strategies not available to unsusceptible subjects or (b) unsusceptible subjects are unaware of such skills or strategies or deem them inappropriate to the hypnosis situation; i.e. they do not think deliberate cognitive effects are acceptable in the hypnosis situation (which should be involuntary) and fail to utilize them. The account given by Spanos in Chapter 5 suggests that the latter may sometimes be the case.

To summarize, the existence of stable individual differences in hypnotic responding presents no particular problems to the ESC socio-cognitive formulation. However, where the ESC formulation diverges most from some modern theorizing is in its explanation of what happens when 'normal' cognitive strategies or skills like 'absorption' fail to account for the data (such as when some subjects continue to be 'amnesic' even when instructed to attend, or subjects' responses run counter to their imaginings). The ESC interpretation simply suggests that such results are due to compliance.

Conclusion

The view expressed in this chapter is not that all hypnotic behaviours are 'faked', that hypnosis does not 'work' or that hypnotherapy is useless. It is rather that the processes responsible for hypnotic effects are more readily explicable by reference to familiar psychological processes than to a unique hypnotic process. It is hoped that as our knowledge advances, not only will our understanding of hypnotic phenomena be helped by drawing attention away from the enigma of the hypnotic 'state' or 'trance', but also the useful ingredients of hypnotic procedures – such as relaxation and the use of imaginative suggestions – may be made more acceptable to those in applied contexts at present wary of the mystique of 'hypnosis'. A good example of this direction has been in the application of hypnosis to forensic investigations, which has sparked off a large amount of research to identify non-hypnotic factors that may aid witness recall (Wagstaff 1982c, Geiselman, *et al.* 1985).

It is hoped that, if the recent emphasis on cognitive aspects of hypnotic behaviour and experience continues (for example, Sheehan and McConkey 1982), the 'state' and 'non-state' views will eventually converge until the differences concern purely the use of language, rather than the postulation of different processes. Other theorists have already made considerable progress in reappraising the language applied to hypnosis – for example, Sarbin and Coe (1972, 1979), Barber and Wilson (1977) and Coe and Sarbin (1977); particular attention must be paid to the prolific work of Spanos and his associates, whose strategic-enactment, cognitive-social approach bears many similarities to the socio-cognitive approach described in the present chapter (Spanos 1982, Spanos, Radtke and Bertrand 1985).

Demystifying hypnosis does not have to be a negative enterprise. Research into hypnotic phenomena may continue to provide us with a rich supply of pure and applied knowledge, but gains are likely to be small if encumbered by a reluctance to give up the notion that 'we don't know what hypnosis is'.

References

Aronson, E. (1977) *The Social Animal*. San Francisco: Freeman.

Banyai, E. I. and Hilgard, E. R. (1976) A comparison of active alert hypnotic induction and a traditional relaxation induction. *Journal of Abnormal Psychology*, 85: 218–24.

Barber, T. X. (1969) *Hypnosis: A Scientific Approach*. New York and London: Van Nostrand Reinhold.

(1970) *LSD, Marijuana, Yoga and Hypnosis*. Chicago: Aldine.

(1972) Suggested ('hypnotic') behaviour: the trance paradigm versus an alternative paradigm. In E. Fromm and R. E. Shor (eds.), *Hypnosis: Research Developments and Perspectives*. Chicago: Aldine-Atherton.

(1981) Medicine, suggestive therapy, and healing. In R. J. Kastenbaum *et al.* (eds.), *Old, Sick and Helpless: Where Therapy Begins*. Cambridge, Mass.: Ballinger.

Barber, T. X., Spanos, N. P. and Chaves, J. F. (1974) *Hypnotism: Imagination and Human Potentialities*. New York and Oxford: Pergamon.

Barber, T. X. and Wilson, S. C. (1977) Hypnosis, suggestions and altered states of consciousness: experimental evaluation of the new cognitive-behavioural theory and the traditional trance-state theory of 'hypnosis'. *Annals of the New York Academy of Sciences*, 296: 34–47.

Bem, D. J. (1965) An experimental analysis of self-persuasion. *Journal of Experimental Social Psychology*, 1: 199–218.

(1972) Self-perception Theory. In L. Berkowitz (ed.), *Advances in Experimental Social Psychology*, Vol. 6. New York: Academic Press.

Bowers, K. S. (1967) The effects of demands for honesty on reports of visual and auditory hallucinations. *International Journal of Clinical and Experimental Hypnosis*, 15: 31–6.

(1983) *Hypnosis for the Seriously Curious*. New York: Norton.

Bowers, K. S. and Kelly, P. (1979) Stress, disease, psychotherapy and hypnosis. *Journal of Abnormal Psychology*, 88: 490–505.

Buckalew, L. W., Ross, S. and Starr, B. J. (1981) Nonspecific factors in drug effects: Placebo personality. *Psychological Reports*, 48: 3–8.

Chaves, J. F. and Barber, T. X. (1976) Hypnotic procedures and surgery: a critical analysis with applications to 'acupuncture analgesia'. *American Journal of Clinical Hypnosis*, 18: 217–36.

Coe, W. C. and Sarbin, T. R. (1977) Hypnosis from the standpoint of a contextualist. *Annals of the New York Academy of Sciences*, 296: 2–13.

Edmonston, W. E. (1977) Neutral hypnosis as relaxation. *American Journal of Clinical Hypnosis*, 30: 69–75.

(1981) *Hypnosis and Relaxation: Modern Verification of an Old Equation.* Chichester: Wiley.

Evans, F. J. (1974) The placebo response in pain reduction. In L. V. Di Cara *et al.* (eds.), *Bio-Feedback and Self-Control.* Chicago: Aldine.

Evans, F. J. and Kihlstrom, J. F. (1973) Posthypnotic amnesia as disrupted retrieval. *Journal of Abnormal Psychology*, 82: 317–23.

Evans, F. J. and Orne, M. T. (1971) The disappearing hypnotist: The use of simulating subjects to evaluate how subjects perceive experimental procedures. *International Journal of Clinical and Experimental Hypnosis*, 19: 277–296.

Evans, M. B. and Paul, G. L. (1970) Effects of hypnotically suggested analgesia on physiological and subjective responses to cold stress. *Journal of Consulting and Clinical Psychology*, 35: 362–71.

Frank, D. P. (1944) Experimental studies of personal pressure and resistance: 1. Experimental production of resistance. *Journal of General Psychology*, 30: 23–41.

Frankel, F. H. (1976) *Hypnosis: Trance as a Coping Mechanism.* New York: Plenum.

Geiselman, R. E., Fisher, R. P., MacKinnon, D. P. and Holland, H. L. (1985) Eyewitness memory enhancement in the police interview: cognitive retrieval mnemonics versus hypnosis. *Journal of Applied Psychology*, 70: 401–12.

Gidro-Frank, L. and Bowersbuch, M. K. (1948) A study of plantar response in hypnotic age regression. *Journal of Nervous and Mental Disease*, 107: 443–58.

Gill, M. M. and Brenman, M. (1959) *Hypnosis and Related States.* New York: International Universities Press.

Goffman, E. (1959) *The Presentation of Self in Everyday Life.* New York: Doubleday Anchor.

Graham, C. and Evans, F. J. (1977) Hypnotizability and the deployment of waking attention. *Journal of Abnormal Psychology*, 86: 631–8.

Graham, K. R. and Green, L. D. (1981) Hypnotic susceptibility related to an independent measure of compliance – alumini annual giving, *International Journal of Clinical and Experimental Hypnosis*, 29: 351–4.

Gray, A. L., Bowers, K. S. and Fenz, W. D. (1970) Heart rate in anticipation of and during a negative visual hallucination. *International Journal of Clinical and Experimental Hypnosis*, 18: 41–51.

Hilgard, H. and Hilgard, J. (1984) *Hypnosis in the Relief of Pain*, Oxford: Freeman.

Hilgard, E. R., Hilgard, J. R., Macdonald, H., Morgan, A. H. and Johnson, L. S. (1978) Covert pain in hypnotic analgesia: its reality as tested by the real-simulator *Journal of Abnormal Psychology*, 87: 655–63.

Hilgard, E. R., Macdonald, H., Morgan, A. H. and Johnson, L. S. (1978) The reality of hypnotic analgesia: a comparison of highly hypnotizables with simulators. *Journal of Abnormal Psychology*, 87: 239–46.

Hunt, S. M. (1979) 'Hypnosis as obedience behaviour. *British Journal of Social and Clinical Psychology*, 18: 21–7.

Johnson, P. F., Maher, B. A. and Barber, T. X. (1972) Artifact in the 'essence of hypnosis': an evaluation of trance logic. *Journal of Abnormal Psychology*, 79: 212–20.

Kidder, L. H. (1973) On becoming hypnotised: How sceptics become convinced: A case of attitude change? *American Journal of Clinical Hypnosis*, 16: 1–8.

Kiesler, C. A. and Kiesler, S. B. (1970) *Conformity*. Reading, Mass.: Addison-Wesley.

Kihlstrom, J. F. (1978) Context and cognition in posthypnotic amnesia. *International Journal of Clinical and Experimental Hypnosis*, 26: 246–67.

Kihlstrom, J. F., Evans, F. J., Orne, M. T. and Orne, E. C. (1980) Attempting to breach post-hypnotic amnesia. *Journal of Abnormal Psychology*, 89: 603–16.

Knox, J. V., Morgan, A. H. and Hilgard, E. R. (1974) Pain and suffering in ischemia: the paradox of hypnotically suggested anaesthesia as contradicted by reports from the 'hidden-observer'. *Archives of General Psychiatry*, 30: 840–7.

Levy, L. H. (1967) Awareness of learning and the beneficient subject as expert witness. *Journal of Personality and Social Psychology*, 6: 365–70.

Malott, J. M. (1984) Active-alert hypnosis: replication and extension of previous research. *Journal of Abnormal Psychology*, 93: 246.

Marcuse, F. L. (1976) *Hypnosis: Fact and Fiction*. Harmondsworth: Penguin.

McGlashan, T. H., Evans, F. J. and Orne, M. T. (1969) The nature of hypnotic analgesia and placebo response to experimental pain. *Psychosomatic Medicine*, 31: 227–46.

Milgram, S. (1974) *Obedience to Authority*. London: Tavistock.

Morgan, W. P. (1972) *Ergogenic aids and Muscular Performance*. New York: Academic Press.

Nash, M. R., Johnson, L. S. and Tipton, R. D. (1979) Hypnotic age regression and the occurrence of transitional object relationships. *Journal of Abnormal Psychology*, 88: 547–55.

Nelson, R. A. (1965) *A Complete Course in Stage Hypnotism*. Columbus, Ohio, Nelson.

O'Connell, D. N., Shor, R. E. and Orne, M. (1970) Hypnotic age regression: an empirical and methodological analysis. *Journal of Abnormal and Social Psychiatry*, mono. supp., 76 (3), part 2: 1–32.

Orne, M. T. (1959) The nature of hypnosis: artifact and essence. *Journal of Abnormal and Social Psychology*, 58: 277–99.

—— (1962) On the social psychology of the psychological experiment: with particular reference to demand characteristics and their implications. *American Psychologist*, 17: 776–83.

—— (1966) Hypnosis, motivation and compliance. *American Journal of Psychiatry*, 122: 721–6.

—— (1970) Hypnosis, motivation and the ecological validity of the psychological experiment. In W. J. Arnold and M. M. Page (eds.), *Nebraska Symposium on Motivation*. Lincoln, Nebraska Univ.: Nebraska Press.

—— (1971) The simulation of hypnosis: why, how, and what it means. *International Journal of Clinical and Experimental Hypnosis*, 19: 183–210.

Orne, M. T., Sheehan, P. W. and Evans, F. J. (1968). Occurrence of post-hypnotic behaviour outside the experimental setting. *Journal of Personality and Social Psychology*, 9: 189–96.

Parrish, M., Lundy, R. M. and Leibowitz, H. W. (1969) Effect of hypnotic age regression on the magnitude of the Ponzo and Poggendorff Illusions. *Journal of Abnormal Psychology,* 74: 693–8.

Pattie, F. A. (1935). A report of attempts to produce uniocular blindness of hypnotic suggestion. *British Journal of Medical Psychology*, 15: 230–41.

Raikov, V. L. (1982) Hypnotic age regression to the neonatal period: comparisons with role-playing. *International Journal of Clinical and Experimental Hypnosis*, 30: 108–16.

Reiff, R. and Scheerer, M. (1959) *Memory and Hypnotic Age Regression*. New York: International Universities Press.

Reilley, R. R. and Rodolfa, E. R. (1981) Concentration, attention and hypnosis. *Psychological Reports*, 48: 811–14.

Rock, N., Shipley, T. and Campbell, C. (1969) Hypnosis with untrained non-volunter patients. *International Journal of Clinical and Experimental Hypnosis*, 17: 25–36.

Sarbin, T. R. and Coe, W. C. (1972) *Hypnosis: A Social Psychological Analysis of Influence Communication*. New York: Holt, Rinehart & Winston.

—— (1979) Hypnosis and psychopathology: Replacing old myths with fresh metaphors. *Journal of Abnormal Psychology*, 88: 506–26.

Sarbin, T. R. and Slagle, R. W. (1972) Hypnosis and psychophysiological outcomes. In E. Fromm and R. E. Shor, (eds.), *Hypnosis: Research Developments and Perspectives*. Chicago: Aldine-Atherton.

Shames, M. L. (1981) Hypnotic susceptibility and conformity: on the mediational mechanism of suggestibility. *Psychological Reports*, 49: 563–5.

Sheehan, P. W. and McConkey, K. M. (1982) *Hypnosis and Experience: The Exploration of Phenomena and Process*. Hillsdale, NJ: Lawreance Erlbaum.

Sheehan, P. W. and Perry, C. W. (1976) *Methodologies of Hypnosis: A Critical Appraisal of Contemporary Paradigms of Hypnosis*. Hillsdale, NJ: Laurence Erlbaum.

Sigman, A., Phillips, K. C. and Clifford, B. (1985) Attentional concomitants of hypnotic susceptibility. *British Journal of Experimental and Clinical Hypnosis*, 2: 69–75.

Skemp, R. R. (1972) Hypnosis and hypnotherapy considered as cybernetic processes. *British Journal of Clinical Hypnosis*, 3: 97–107.

Smith, M. C. (1983) Hypnotic memory enhancement of witnesses: Does it work? *Psychological Bulletin*, 94: 387–407.

Smith, M. J. (1978) *Kicking the Fear Habit*. New York: Bantam.

Spanos, N. P. (1982) A social psychological approach to hypnotic behaviour. In G. Weary and H. L. Mirels (eds.), *Integrations of Clinical and Social Psychology*. New York: Oxford University Press.

Spanos, N. P., Barber, T. X. and Lang, G. (1974) Effects of hypnotic induction, suggestions of anaesthesia and demands for honesty on subjective reports of pain. In H. Condon and R. E. Nisbett (eds.), *Thought and Feeling: Cognitive Alteration of Feeling States*. Chicago: Aldine.

Spanos, N. P. and D'Eon, J. L. (1980) Hypnotic amnesia, disorganised recall, and inattention. *Journal of Abnormal Psychology*, 6: 744–50.

Spanos, N. P., Hodgins, D. C., Stam, H. J. and Gwynn, M. (1984) Suffering for science: the effects of implicit social demands on response to experimentally induced pain. *Journal of Personality and Social Psychology*, 46: 1162–72.

Spanos, N. P., Kennedy, S. K. and Gwynn, M. E. (1984) Moderating effects of contextual variables on the relationship between hypnotic susceptibility and suggested analgesia. *Journal of Abnormal Psychology*, 93 (3): 285–294

Spanos, N. P., McNeil, C. Gwynn, M. I. and Stam, H. J. (1984) Effects of suggestion and distraction and reported pain in subjects high and low on hypnotic susceptibility. *Journal of Abnormal Psychology*, 93 (3): 277.

Spanos, N. P., Radtke, H. L. and Bertrand, L. D. (1985). Hypnotic amnesia as a strategic enactment: breaching amnesia in highly susceptible subjects. *Journal of Personality and Social Psychology*, 47: 1155–69.

Spanos, N. P., Weekes, J. R. and de Groh, M. (1984) The 'involuntary' countering of suggested requests: a test of the ideomotor theory hypothesis of hypnotic responsiveness. *British Journal of Experimental and Clinical Hypnosis*, 1: 3–11.

Stoyva, J. M. (1965) Posthypnotically suggested dreams and the sleep cycle. *Archives of General Psychiatry*, 12: 287–94.

Tellegen, A. and Atkinson, G. (1974) Openness to absorbing and self-altering experiences ('absorption'): a trait related to hypnotic susceptibility. *Journal of Abnormal Psychology*, 83: 268–77.

Underwood, H. W. (1960) The validity of hypnotically induced hallucinations. *Journal of Abnormal and Social Psychology*, 61: 39–46.

Valins, S. (1966) Cognitive effects of false heart-rate feedback. *Journal of Personality and Social Psychology*, 4: 400–8.

Valins, S. and Ray, A. A. (1967) Effects of cognitive sensitization of avoidance behaviour. *Journal of Personality and Social Psychology*, 7: 345–50.

Van Dyne, W. T. and Stava, L. J. (1981) Analysis of relationships among hypnotic susceptibility, personality type and vividness of mental imagery. *Psychological Reports*, 48: 23–6.

Wadden, T. and Anderton, C. H. (1982) The clinical use of hypnosis. *Psychological Bulletin*, 91: 215–43.

Wagstaff, G. F. (1976) A note on Mather and Degun's 'A comparative study of hypnosis and relaxation'. *British Journal of Medical Psychology*, 49: 299–300.

(1977a) An experimental study of compliance and post-hypnotic amnesia. *British Journal of Social and Clinical Psychology*, 16: 225–8.

(1977b) Goal-directed fantasy, the experience of nonvolition and compliance. *Social Behaviour and Personality*, 5: 389–93.

(1977c) Post-hypnotic amnesia as disrupted retrieval: a role-playing paradigm. *Quarterly Journal of Experimental Psychology*, 29: 499–504.

(1978) How do I know I'm hypnotized? Paper presented to the BPS, Social Psychology Section, Durham, September.

(1979) The problem of compliance in hypnosis: a social psychological viewpoint. *Bulletin of the British Society of Experimental and Clinical Hypnosis*, 2: 3–5.

(1981a) *Hypnosis, Compliance and Belief*. New York: St Martin's; Brighton: Harvester.

(1981b) Source amnesia and trance logic: artifacts in the essence of hypnosis? *Bulletin of the British Society of Experimental and Clinical Hypnosis*, 4: 3–5.

(1981c) The use of hypnosis in police investigation. *Journal of the Forensic Science Society*, 21: 3–7.

(1982a) A comment on Gibbons' 'Hypnosis as a trance state: the future of a shared delusion'. *Bulletin of the British Society of Experimental and Clinical Hypnosis*, 5: 5–7.

(1982b) Disorganized recall, suggested amnesia and compliance. *Psychological Reports*, 51, 1255–8.

(1982c) Helping a witness remember – a project in forensic psychology. *Police Research Bulletin*, 38: 56–8.

(1982d) Hypnosis and the law: the role of induction in witness recall. *International Journal of Clinical and Experimental Hypnosis*, 30: 225.

(1982e) Hypnosis and recognition of a face. *Perceptual and Motor Skills*, 55: 816–18.

(1982f) Hypnosis and witness recall: a discussion paper. *Journal of the Royal Society of Medicine*, 75: 793–8.

(1982g) Recall of witnesses under hypnosis. *Journal of the Forensic Science Society*, 22: 33–9.

(1983a) A comment on McConkey's Challenging hypnotic affects: the impact of conflicting influences on response to hypnotic suggestions. *British Journal of Experimental and Clinical Hypnosis*, 1: 11–15.

(1983b) A reply to Fellows' and Sheehan's reviews of *Hypnosis, Compliance and Belief Bulletin of the British Society of Experimental and Clinical Hypnosis*, 6: 45–50.

(1983c) Hypnosis and the law: a critical review of some recent proposals. *Criminal Law Review*, March: 152–7.

(1983d) Suggested Improvement of visual acuity: a statistical revaluation. *International Journal of Clinical and Experimental Hypnosis*, 31: 239.

(1984) The enhancement of witness memory by hypnosis: a review and methodological critique of the experimental literature. *British Journal of Experimental and Clinical Hypnosis*, 2, (1): 3–12.

(1985a) A comment on 'Attentional concomitants of hypnotic susceptibility' by A. Sigman, K. C. Philips and B. Clifford. *British Journal of Experimental and Clinical Hypnosis*, (2): 76–80.

(1985b) Discussion commentary on Gibson's 'Experiencing hypnosis versus pretending to be hypnotized'. Observations on hypnosis training workshops. *British Journal of Experimental and Clinical Hypnosis*, 2 (2): 114–17.

(1985c) Hypnosis and the law: the role of induction in witness recall. In D. Waxman, P. C. Misra, M. Gibslon and M. A. Basker (eds.), *Modern Trends in Hypnosis*. New York: Plenum.

(1985d) Is hypnotherapy a placebo? *Proceedings of the First Annual Conference of the British Society of Experimental and Clinical Hypnosis*. Chartham, Kent: BSECH.

Wagstaff, G. F., Hearne, K. M. T. and Jackson, B. (1980) Post-hypnotically suggested dreams and the sleep cycle: an experimental re-evaluation. *IRCS Medical Science*, 8: 240–1.

Wagstaff, G. F. and Maguire, C. (1983) An experimental study of hypnosis, guided memory and witness memory. *Journal of the Forensic Science Society*, 23: 73–8.

Wagstaff, G. F. and Ovenden, M. (1979) Hypnotic time distortion and free-recall learning—an attempted replication. *Psychological Research*, 40: 291–8.

Wagstaff, G. F. and Sykes, C. T. (1984) Hypnosis and the recall of emotionally toned material. *IRCS Medical Science*, 12: 137–8.

Wagstaff, G. F., Traverse, J. and Milner, S. (1982) Hypnosis and eyewitness memory: two experimental analogues. *IRCS Medical Science*, 10: 894–5.

Walker, N. S., Garratt, J. B. and Wallace, B. (1976) Restoration of eidetic imagery via hypnotic age regression: a preliminary report. *Journal of Abnormal Psychology*, 85: 335–7.

Wallance, J. and Sadalla, E. (1966) Behavioural consequences of transgression: 1. The effecs of social recognition. *Jurnal of Experimental Research into Personality*,: 87–94.

Zamansky, H. S. (1977) Suggestion and counter-suggestion in hypnotic behaviour. *Journal of Abnormal Psychology*, 86: 346–51.

HYPNOSIS AND THE MODIFICATION OF HYPNOTIC SUSCEPTIBILITY: A SOCIAL PSYCHOLOGICAL PERSPECTIVE

Nicholas P. Spanos

Like many psychologists, Graham Wagstaff shows a healthy caution in accepting subjective accounts at face value. Nicholas Spanos, who is also a social psychologist, is somewhat more inclined to accept subjects' accounts of hypnosis, as a clue about what is going on. Like Wagstaff however, Spanos argues that there is nothing 'special' about hypnosis. Among other things, Spanos is interested in demonstrating that subjects can be trained to become more responsive to hypnosis, which implies that hypnotizability can be seen as a skill.

Professor Spanos is based in the Department of Psychology, Carleton University, Ottawa, Canada. He and his co-workers have been extremely prolific researchers and publishers in the field of hypnosis.

Preparation of this chapter was supported by grants from the Natural Science and Engineering Research Council of Canada, the Social Science and Humanities Research Council of Canada and the Medical Research Council of Canada. I thank L. D. Bertrand, W. P. Cross, E. P. Menary and L. Robertson for critically reading earlier versions.

The preceding two chapters have presented ample evidence that so-called hypnotic behaviour is not as remarkable as is commonly supposed. However, this point will be further pursued by discussing a few more examples of hypnotic behaviour – examples that have often been cited as support for a 'special-state' explanation of hypnosis. It will be suggested that such a view is unnecessary, since well-known psychological mechanisms can account for the effects of hypnosis very adequately. Yet it has to be recognized that there are large individual differences in hypnotic susceptibility, a fact that is readily accommodated by a state theory. It would simply propose that the less susceptible were unable fully to 'enter the state'. The second section of the chapter addresses this issue, and shows that an appropriate non-state account can also explain the existence of individual differences. The closing section describes attempts to modify subjects' hypnotic susceptibility. Conventional special-state theories are not able to account for the changes that will be described, but mechanisms are proposed that do explain the susceptibility shifts.

Hypnotic responding is strategic

'Good' hypnotic subjects often report that their responses to suggestions occurred involuntarily, and sometimes even give the appearance of struggling unsuccessfully to control their own actions. Special-process theorists usually take subjects at their word and conceptualize hypnotic responding as involving a loss of conscious control over behaviour (Bowers 1976, Hilgard 1977, Kihlstrom and Shor 1978). On the other hand, social psychological theorists such as Wagstaff (Chapter 4 above), contend that hypnotic behaviours are not the involuntary happenings they appear to be. Instead, hypnotic responses are seen as being goal-directed actions that are guided by subjects' attempts to enact the hypnotic role as this is defined for them by the ongoing situation. From this perspective responsive hypnotic subjects convey the impression that their behaviour is involuntary because the communications they receive in the hypnotic situation define such an appearance as appropriate to their role as 'good hypnotic subjects'. Many responsive hypnotic subjects appear to convey the impression of non-volition not only to their external audience (the hypnotist) but to themselves as well. Thus at least some of these subjects come to misinterpret their goal-directed actions as being involuntary happenings (Spanos 1971, Spanos, Rivers and Ross 1977, Sarbin 1984). The strategic nature of hypnotic responding can be illustrated by examining several specific phenomena in some detail.

Countering suggested effects

Some hypnotic suggestions first specify the occurrence of a response (e.g. 'your arm is stiff and rigid') and then challenge subjects to test the effects of the suggestion by attempting to counter the response (e.g. 'try to bend it – you can't'). When challenged in this manner many hypnotic subjects behave as though they are trying to counter the suggested response but are unable to do so (e.g. they fail to bend their stiffened arm).

If hypnotic responding involves a loss of voluntary control over behaviour, then instructions aimed at inducing 'hypnotized' subjects to counter their suggested responses are likely to be relatively ineffective. Alternatively, the social psychological hypothesis holds that such instructions can be either ineffective or effective, depending upon the meanings attached by subjects to response countering. If instructions to counter imply something like 'countering your responses to suggestions means that you are not deeply hypnotized', then subjects who are attempting to self-present as deeply hypnotized should fail to counter. However, if subjects can be convinced by instructions that maintaining (rather than losing) voluntary control is a sign of deep hypnosis, then they should counter suggested responses very easily. Spanos, Cobb and Gorassini (1985) found that highly susceptible hypnotic subjects either countered or failed to counter depending upon which pattern of responding enhanced their self-presentation as "deeply hypnotized." These findings indicate that even very responsive hypnotic subjects retain control over their suggested responses. The subjects often become highly involved in conveying the impression that they have lost behavioural control, because such a self-presentation is demanded by the constraints of the hypnotic situation. Furthermore, as stated earlier, subjects seem to succeed in convincing themselves as well as the hypnotist that their responses really feel involuntary.

Breaching hypnotic amnesia

Wagstaff (Chapter 4) has already discussed the apparent inability of some subjects to recall well known information, following instructions to forget. For special-process theorists the persistence of amnesia in the face of various treatments designed to breach the 'blockage' (e.g., exhortations to report honestly) is interpreted to mean that at least some hypnotically amnesic subjects lose voluntary control over memory retrieval processes and thereby are *unable* to recall efficiently until they receive the 'remember' cue that cancels their amnesia (Hilgard 1977, Kihlstrom *et al.* 1980, McConkey and Sheehan 1981). On the other hand, social psychological formulations of hypnotic amnesia emphasize its goal-directedness and its dependence on subjects' motivations and interpretations of situational demands (Wagstaff 1977, Coe 1978, Spanos and Radtke 1982). According to this perspective the complete recall of target material in the face of typical breaching treatments would violate the role requirements for being deeply hypnotized and would also tend to discredit subjects' previous failures to recall when challenged. For instance, subjects who failed to recall after an initial challenge, but then recalled fully after being exhorted to be honest, would be tacitly acknowledging that they had been dishonest when responding to the initial challenge. Thus because of high investment in the role of being hypnotized many subjects tend to ignore or reinterpret instructions that if followed literally, would compromise their hypnotic self-presentation.

The social psychological perspective would predict that even highly responsive hypnotic subjects could be led to breach amnesia completely, by convincing them that breaching is a sign (rather than a counter-indication) of being very deeply hypnotized. Spanos, Radtke and Bertrand (1984) tested this idea with eight very highly responsive hypnotic subjects who, in previous testing, had consistently described their responses to suggestion as involuntary and repeatedly failed to breach amnesia despite exhortations to be honest. These subjects were told that during hypnosis hidden parts of their mind remained aware of things that they could no longer consciously remember. They were further told that one hidden part remained aware of everything that occurred in the right hemisphere of their brain while a different hidden part remained aware of all that occurred in their left hemisphere. Subjects learned a short list that contained both abstract and concrete words. Half were told that concrete words were stored in the right hemisphere and abstract words were stored in the left. The remaining subjects were given opposite information about the storage location of the words. Subjects were also told that the experimenter could contact and communicate with each of their hidden parts. Following a suggestion to forget, all subjects exhibited high levels of amnesia for the list. However, before cancelling amnesia with the 'remember' cue, the experimenter successively contacted each subject's right and left 'hidden parts'. Every subject recalled all of their 'left hemisphere' words but none of their 'right hemisphere' words when contact was made with their left 'hidden part', and exhibited the opposite pattern of recall when contact was made with their right 'hidden part'.

Thus every one of these very highly responsive hypnotic subjects breached amnesia easily and completely when doing so supported a self-presentation as deeply hypnotized. These finding, along with the findings of Spanos, Cobb and Gorassini (1985) concerning the countering of motor responses, are very straightforward. They indicate clearly that hypnotic subjects do not lose voluntary control over their behaviour. It is inaccurate to describe these subjects as unable to remember, unable to counter response and so on. Instead, highly responsive hypnotic subjects are very skilled both at conveying the impression that they have lost control over their behaviour and at generating the interpretations and subjective experiences that enable them to believe in the impressions that they convey to others.

The hidden observer and hypnotic analgesia

Hilgard (1977, 1979) has formulated an influential special-process theory of hypnotically induced pain reduction (i.e. hypnotic analgesia) that revolves upon the idea of psychological dissociation. According to Hilgard the most important component in hypnotically induced pain reduction involves separation of the pain from conscious awarenesss by an amnesia-like barrier. Supposedly, dissociation is not a conscious process. Instead, the construction of an 'amnesic barrier', between an unconscious cognitive subsystem that experiences high levels of pain and conscious awareness, is something that occurs automatically as a result of hypnotic suggestions for analgesia. The occurrence of dissociation is purportedly restricted to hypnotically responsive subjects.

The evidence most often cited in favour of the dissociation hypothesis comes from a series of 'hidden-observer' experiments conducted by Hilgard and his associates (Hilgard, Morgan and Macdonald 1975, Hilgard, Hilgard *et al.* 1978, Knox, Morgan and Hilgard 1974). Typically, the 'good' hypnotic subjects who participated in these experiments were exposed to pain stimulation on a base-line trial and during this period gave verbal (i.e. overt) ratings of pain intensity. Subjects were afterwards given a hypnotic induction and explicitly instructed that a hidden part of them remained aware of experiences their 'hypnotized part' was unaware of. For example, they were told:

> When I place my hand on your shoulder, I shall be able to talk to a hidden part of you that knows things that are going on in your body, things that are unknown to the part of you to which I am now talking. The part of you to which I am now talking will not know what you are telling me.
> (Knox, Morgan and Hilgard 1974)

Later, these subjects were given a suggestion that their limb was numb and insensitive and they were again exposed to pain stimulation. Subjects were instructed to give overt reports that reflected the intensity of the pain felt by their 'hypnotized part' (i.e. the 'part' that supposedly received and responded to the suggestion) and hidden reports (numbers tapped out in code on a key press) that reflected the intensity of pain felt by their 'hidden part' (i.e. the 'part' that remains aware of sensations despite the suggestion). Many of the subjects exposed to this testing sequence reported relatively low levels of overt pain (from their 'hypnotized part') but relatively high levels of hidden pain.

According to Hilgard (1977, 1979) hypnotically analgesic subjects undergo high levels of hidden pain regardless of whether or not the experimenter gives them instructions for accessing hidden pain. In other words, 'good' hypnotic subjects respond to a suggestion for pain reduction by consciously feeling very little pain. Nevertheless, even though they do not know it, these subjects continue to feel high levels of pain at an unconscious level. These high levels of pain are blocked automatically from conscious awareness by an amnesic barrier. The hypnotist/experimenter can still contact the hidden part of the person and obtain an accurate estimate of the intensity of pain experienced by the hidden part.

For Hilgard hidden pain reports do *not* result from suggestion or from subjects purposefully attempting to gear their behaviour and experiences to the demands of the test situation. Supposedly, explicit hidden-observer instructions like those cited above do not provide subjects with the idea that they have a hidden part or with the idea that hidden reports and overt reports should be different. Instead, these instructions are thought to provide a structured setting that allows the pre-existing hidden pain more easily to come to light. Wagstaff in Chapter 4, has shown that there are very adequate social psychological accounts of coping with pain. There seems to be no need to propose the existence of a special hidden level of conciousness. The available data indicate that hidden reports of pain do not stem from the operation of dissociated cognitive subsystems that are simply tapped into by the experimenter. Instead, responsive hypnotic subjects behave as if they possessed hidden parts with particular characteristics, because the experimental setting defines such behaviour as role-appropriate (Spanos 1983, Spanos and Hewitt, 1980). At a more general level the findings reviewed above provide strong support for the notion that hypnotic responding is goal-directed social behaviour. Hypnotic subjects do not, in any meaningful sense, lose control over their behaviour. On the contrary, it is only by retaining behavioural control and by judiciously guiding their behaviour in terms of changing contextual cues that they are able convincingly to convey the impression that voluntary control has been lost.

Although our discussion indicates that hypnotic responding is goal-directed, subjects nevertheless exhibit wide variability in their responsiveness to test suggestions. For example, suggestions for pain reduction, amnesia and manifesting hidden parts are responded to successfully by only a relatively few subjects. If such responding involves strategic role enactment, then it becomes important to determine the factors that influence the extent to which subjects are willing and able to adopt the hypnotic role.

Measurements and correlates of hypnotic susceptibility

Assessment of susceptibility

Hypnotic susceptibility (or suggestibility) refers to subjects' level of responsiveness to test suggestions. Test suggestions do *not* instruct subjects to enact an overt behaviour. Instead, their wording describes a 'make-believe' or counterfactual situation. This wording further implies that the make-believe situation is to be treated by subjects as if it were really happening and is to lead to the occurrence of a congruent overt response (Spanos 1971, 1982b). For instance, test suggestions invite subjects to convince both themselves and the hypnotist that they are too heavy to stand up from the chair, that their arm is so light that it rises by itself, that they are unable to remember well-learned material and so on. In short, suggestions implicitly invite subjects to suspend the tacit rules usually employed to differentiate imagined events from actual events, to define the ongoing situation in terms of imagined events and to enact behaviours implied by those imagined events (Shor 1959, 1970, Sarbin and Coe 1972, Spanos 1971, 1982b).

A number of scales of hypnotic susceptibility are available for use with experimental subjects. All of them consist of a hypnotic induction procedure followed by a standardized series of test suggestions. All investigators emphasize the importance of subjects' experiential response to test suggestions. Despite this theoretical emphasis, most susceptibility scales in current use assess only behavioural (i.e. objective) responses. However, the Barber Suggestibility Scale (BSS: Barber 1965) and the Carleton University Responsiveness to Suggestion Scale (CURSS: Spanos, Radtke *et al.* 1983c) both assess subjective as well as behavioural aspects of susceptibility. For example, the CURSS yields three susceptibility scores for each subject. The behavioural score is obtained in the same way as are behavioural scores on the HGSHS:A. In addition, the CURSS yields a subjective score that reflects the extent to which subjects generated the experiences called for by the suggestions, and an involuntariness score that reflects the extent to which subjects experienced each response to suggestion as feeling involuntary.

Some investigators (Bowers 1981, Hilgard 1981) have assumed that hypnotic subjects almost always experience their behavioural responses to suggestions as feeling involuntary, and have consequently argued that separate involuntariness scores are redundant and unnecessary. However, work with the CURSS (Spanos, Radtke *et al.* 1983c) and more recently with a modification of the SHSS:C that assesses subjective aspects of response (Spanos, Salas *et al.* 1986), indicates that the behavioural/involuntariness equivalence assumption is incorrect. Subjects frequently describe their behavioural responses to test suggestions as feeling more *voluntary* than involuntary. These findings are of some importance because they indicate that the behavioural scores obtained on susceptibility scales confound different types of response. Thus, for any particular subject, the behavioural score on a susceptibility scale reflects an unknown mixture of responses that feel mostly voluntary and responses that feel mostly involuntary. Empirical work aimed at delineating antecedent variables (e.g. personality factors, imagery skills) that discriminate between subjects who obtain the same behavioural scores but widely different involuntariness scores has recently commenced in the Carleton laboratory. Firm results, however, are not yet available.

Over the years, a great deal of work has attempted to delineate variables that predict subjects' level of responding to these scales (i.e. level of susceptibility). This work has by and large been disappointing, and few stable and replicable predictors of susceptibility have emerged (for review of this large literature see Barber 1969, Hilgard 1975, Dumas 1977, Sarbin and Slagle 1979). Nevertheless, two classes of predictor variables that have offered some promise are measures of attitudes towards hypnosis and measures of imagery/fantasy-proneness. Relationships between these variables and hypnotic responsiveness will be examined next.

Attitudes and hypnotic responding

A large number of studies have reported statistically significant correlations between the favourability of subjects' attitudes towards hypnosis and hypnotic susceptibility (for a review see Spanos, Brett *et al.* in press). These findings are, however, less straightforward than they may initially appear. For instance, some studies found significant correlations between attitudes and susceptibility for both sexes (Derman and London 1965, Spanos and McPeake 1975a), while others found a significant correlation between these variables for one sex but not the other (e.g. Melei and Hilgard 1964). One study employed two different attitude measures (Spanos, McPeake and Churchill 1976). One of these attitude measures correlated significantly with hypnotic susceptibility in both sexes, while the other failed to correlate significantly with susceptibility in either sex. Even when significant correlations between attitudes and susceptibility have been found, the magnitudes of these correlations have been at best moderate and often relatively low.

When evaluating the findings concerning attitudes and hypnosis it is important to keep in mind that most studies in this area employed correlational techniques that assessed *linear* relationship. Statistical procedures that assess linear relationships underestimate the magnitude of non-linear relationships between variables. Thus the finding of a low linear correlation between attitudes and hypnotic susceptibility is ambiguous. On the one hand this finding may indicate that attitudes play only an unimportant and peripheral role in susceptibility; on the other, it might mean that the relationship between attitudes and susceptibility is not linear.

We recently approached this issue by examining the relationship between measures of attitudes towards hypnosis and hypnotic susceptibility in a large sample of subjects (N = 579: Spanos, Brett *et al.* in press). The linear correlations between the attitude and susceptibility measures were usually statistically significant but of relatively low magnitude ($r \simeq .25$). More important, when attitude scores were plotted against susceptibility scores the relationship between these variables was much more fan-shaped than linear. Subjects with negative attitudes towards hypnosis never obtained high susceptibility scores. As attitudes became increasingly positive the number of subjects scoring high in susceptibility also increased. Even when attitudes were highly positive, substantial numbers of subjects continued to score in the low susceptibility range.

The fan-shaped relationship between attitudes and susceptibility obtained by Spanos, Brett *et al.* (in press) may help to explain the low and sometimes non-significant linear correlations obtained between these variables in earlier studies. Many of these studies employed small sample sizes. With small samples even a relatively few subjects who obtain high attitude scores but low susceptibility scores can substantially lower the magnitude of a linear correlation. Small variations in the proportion of such subjects due to chance or to minor differences in sampling procedures between studies could easily determine whether or not a linear correlation between attitudes and susceptibility attained statistical significance.

The findings of the Spanos, Brett *et al.* study suggest that negative attitudes towards hypnosis suppress hypnotic susceptibility, while positive attitudes allow subjects to obtain high susceptibility. However, positive attitudes, in and of themselves, do not appear to engender high levels of susceptibility. In other words, relatively positive attitudes may be a necessary but not sufficient requirement for high susceptibility. Several investigators have suggested that high susceptibility may require relatively high levels of imagery ability (cf. Sheehan 1979). It is to a consideration of this notion that we now turn.

Imaginal activity and hypnotic susceptibility

The test suggestions contained in hypnotic susceptibility scales frequently invite subjects to imagine specific counterfactual scenes (e.g. 'imagine a helium-filled balloon pulling your arm upward'; 'imagine that your arm is in a cast so the elbow cannot bend'; (Weitzenhoffer and Hilgard 1959, Spanos, Radtke *et al.* 1983*c*). A number of investigators have suggested that the ability to imagine vividly and/or to become absorbed in imagining events might be important components of hypnotic susceptibility (Sheehan 1970, Shor 1970, Spanos and Barber 1974, Sheehan 1979, Barber 1984, Tellegen, 1979). Most of the research in this area has focussed on imagery vividness as measured by some modification of the Betts Questionnaire on Mental Imagery (QMI: Sheehan 1967). The large number of studies assessing the relationship between imagery vividness and susceptibility have yielded contradictory results (for reviews see Sheehan 1979, Spanos in press b). Numerous studies have reported linear correlations of low to moderate magnitude between imagery vividness and susceptibility (Shor, Orne and O'Connell 1966, Wagman and Stewart 1974, Spanos, Stam *et al.* 1980, Hilgard, Sheehan *et al.* 1981, Bowers, 1982, Farthing, Venturino and Brown 1983). On the other hand, a number of other studies failed to find a significant linear relationship between these variables (Morgan and Lam 1969, Perry 1973, Spanos, McPeake and Churchill 1976, Van Dyne and Stava 1981). Contradictory findings have been obtained even among studies that used the same hypnotic susceptibility and imagery measures and studies that examined the relationships among these variables separately for the two sexes (Hilgard 1970, Sutcliffe *et al.* 1970, Diamond and Taft 1975). A number of studies have examined how attitudes towards hypnosis and imaginal proclivities may combine to influence hypnotic susceptibility. For instance, Spanos and McPeake (1975b) found that negative information about hypnosis (i.e. 'only the weak-minded are hypnotizable') disrupted the usual positive correlation obtained between absorption in imaginings and susceptibility. Nevertheless, even in combination, attitude and absorption predictors accounted for only a relatively small proportion of the variance in susceptibility scores.

All of the studies described above assessed *linear* relationships between imagery vividness or absorption and hypnotic susceptibility. Several investigators (Hilgard 1970, Sutcliffe *et al.* 1970, Sheehan 1979, Spanos, Brett *et al.* in press) have suggested that imaginal activity variables and hypnotic susceptibility may be non-linearly related. Recently, Spanos, Brett *et al.* (in press) found that the relationship between absorption scores and hypnotic susceptibility was more fan-shaped than linear. People with very low absorption scores never obtained high susceptibility scores and usually obtained low scores. As absorption scores increased, so did the proportion of subjects scoring high in susceptibility. Nevertheless, substantial numbers of high-absorption subjects scored low on hypnotic susceptibility.

Taken together the available data suggest that both attitudes towards hypnosis and imaginal proclivities are related to hypnotic susceptibility in a fan-shaped pattern. People with negative attitudes towards hypnosis and/or with low levels of imaginal ability usually score as low in susceptibility and rarely if ever score as high in susceptibility. On the other hand, people with positive attitudes and/or high levels of absorptive ability and imagery vividness may be found at all levels of susceptibility. These findings suggest that relatively favourable attitudes towards hypnosis and relatively high levels of imagery vividness/absorption may be required if subjects are to obtain high levels of hypnotic susceptibility. However, these factors either alone or in combination are not sufficient for producing high susceptibility. What must be addd to imaginal ability and favourable attitudes in order to produce high levels of susceptibility? An answer to this question will be approached by examining the literature dealing with the modification of hypnotic susceptibility.

The modifiability of hypnotic susceptibility

The test-retest stability of hypnotic susceptibility is reasonably high. In other words, the susceptibility score a subject obtains on an initial test is usually a reasonably good indicator of the score that the same subject obtains on a readministration of the test given a few days to a few weeks later (Barber 1965, Hilgard 1965, Spanos, Radtke *et al.* 1983b, Spanos, Cobb and Gwynn 1984). The occurrence of high test-retest stability for susceptibility is acknowledged by all investigators. Nevertheless, the theoretical interpretation of this stability remains a controversial issue, as does the related issue of the extent to which susceptibility can be enhanced through training.

As indicated earlier, many special-processs theorists believe that hypnotic procedures lead to a temporary 'splitting off' or dissociation between cognitive subsystems that control behaviour and cognitive subsystems that constitute conscious awareness (Bowers 1976, Hilgard 1977, 1979). Many of these theorists further suggest that people differ in their capacity for experiencing dissociation and that individual differences in dissociative capacity are highly stable and resistant to modification. From this perspective hypnotic susceptibility is a stable, trait-like attribute that has as its major underlying determinant subjects' stable capacity for experiencing dissociation (Bowers 1976, Hilgard, 1977). Social psychological variables such as subjects' attitudes and interpretational sets concerning hypnosis are seen as playing only a relatively minor role in susceptibility, by moderating to some degree the expression of dissociative capacity (Bowers 1976, Perry 1977). In short, the dissociative-trait hypothesis accounts for the high test-retest stability of susceptibility by positing the existence of stable individual differences in dissociative capacity. Supposedly, the large majority of people who score low in hypnotic susceptibility are deficient in their capacity for experiencing dissociation. Since this capacity cannot (as far as is known) be acquired through learning, it should be very difficult, if not impossible, to produce any substantial enhancement in the susceptibility of these individuals by modifying their attitudes and interpretations towards hypnosis and hypnotic responding (Hilgard 1975, Bowers 1976).

Unlike special-process theorists, the accounts of hypnotic susceptibility proffered by social psychological theorists emphasize the importance of such factors as cognitive sets concerning how suggestions are to be interpreted, the utilization of appropriate cognitive strategies, and attitudes and expectations about hypnotic responding (Sachs 1971, Sarbin and Coe 1972, Diamond 1974, 1977, 1982, Spanos in press b). From the social psychological perspective, the temporal stability in hypnotic susceptibility occurs because, between testings, subjects are rarely exposed to information that changes their interrelated attitudes and interpretational sets concerning hypnotic responding. Thus this position predicts that the provision of such information should lead to substantial gains in susceptibility even among subjects who initially scored low on this dimension.

Attempts to alter conscious state

A large number of studies have employed systematic training procedures of various types in an attempt to enhance hypnotic susceptibility. One set of such studies provided subjects with training or feedback that was designed to 'deepen' a hypothesized hypnotic state or to enhance subjects' ability to experience alterations in consciusness. To this end subjects were provided with repeated and individualized hypnotic induction procedures. (As, Hilgard and Weitzenhoffer 1963, Cooper *et al.* 1967); personal growth training (Tart 1970); meditation training (Heide, Wadlington and Lundy 1980, Spanos, Gottlieb and Rivers 1980, Spanos, Stam *et al.* 1980); and electroencephalographic (EEG) biofeedback training (London, Cooper and Engstrom 1974). Although the studies that employed these procedures usually produced statistically significant enhancements in susceptibility, these enhancements were usually of only small magnitude (for detailed reviews of these studies see Diamond 1974, 1977, 1982, Perry 1977).

Several studies reported that relaxation induced by electromyographic (EMG) feedback produced large increments in susceptibility (Wickramasekara 1973, Simon and Salzberg 1981). Unfortunately, other studies (Radtke *et al.* 1983, Spanos and Bertrand 1985) were unable to replicate these findings. Moreover, studies that employed alternative procedures for inducing relaxation (e.g. progressive relaxation) found no enhancements or only small enhancements in susceptibility (Leva 1974, Sachs and Morrow 1977, Simon and Salzberg 1981, Radtke *et al.* 1983). In one study (Sanders and Reyher 1969) large increments in susceptibility were obtained by exposing subjects to sensory restriction procedures. This finding, however, has also proven difficult to replicate (Levitt *et al.* 1962, Shor and Cobb 1968, Talone, Diamond and Steadman 1975). Social psychological theorists would argue that these studies failed to obtain large increments in susceptibility because they failed to manipulate the cognitive and social psychological variables most likely to produce such increments (Diamond 1977, Gorassini and Spanos 1986, Spanos in press b).

Studies based on social learning formulations

Numerous attempts have been made to enhance hypnotic susceptibility by employing training procedures loosely derived from cognitive social learning theory, and a number of recent studies reported very large gains on both overt and subjective indexes of susceptibility (Sachs and Anderson 1967, Diamond 1972, Kinney and Sachs 1974, Springer, Sachs and Morrow 1977, Gfeller *et al*. 1985, Cross *et al*. 1985, Robertson *et al*. in press, Gorassini and Spanos 1986, Spanos, de Groh and de Groot in press). For instance, in each of the five recent studies from the Carleton laboratory and in the study by Gfeller *et al*. (1985) at least half of the initially low susceptible subjects who underwent full cognitive skill training scored as high susceptibles on post-testing. An even larger proportion of initially medium susceptible subjects post-tested as high susceptibles (Gfeller *et al*. 1985, Gorassini and Spanos 1986).

The recent studies that demonstrated transformations from low to high susceptibility in half or more of the skill-trained subjects suggest that hypnotic susceptibility is much more maleable than trait theory allows. Nevertheless, a number of important issues remain to be addressed. For example, what are the components of cognitive skill training that produce large susceptibility increments? Why do some subjects remain low in susceptibility despite training? How generalizable are training effects to novel suggestions, on which subjects have not received training? Can training-induced increments in susceptibility be explained away as the result of inadequate base-line testing or deliberate faking? These issues will be addressed below.

Effective components in skill training

The actual 'training packages' employed in modification studies based on social learning principles have varied substantially. In some experiments each treatment group was exposed to only a single social learning variable (e.g. Gur 1974, Reilley *et al*. 1980, Crouse and Kurtz 1984). These single-variable-per-treatment studies invariably produced only small susceptibility increments. For example, Crouse and Kurtz provided subjects with information aimed at *either* enhancing positive attitudes, *or* encouraging focussed attention, *or* providing imagery strategies. No group was exposed to these components in combination, and susceptibility enhancements in all groups were very small.

Modification studies that reported large susceptibility increments always exposed subjects to multi-component treatment packages (e.g. positive information about hypnosis plus reinforcement for appropriate responding plus exposure to successful role models). Nevertheless, not all multi-component studies obtained large susceptibility increments (e.g. Commins, Fullam and Barber 1975, Katz 1979). Work designed to delineate the combinations of variables that induce such gains has only just begun.

THE CARLETON SKILL TRAINING PACKAGE

Six of the modification studies that produced very large susceptibility increments all employed the same cognitive skills training package. This training package was initially employed by Gorassini and Spanos (1986) and involves three relatively distinct components. The first component includes information aimed at rectifying misconceptions about hypnosis and at producing positive attitudes and motivations towards hypnotic responding. The second component emphasizes the importance of becoming absorbed in imagining 'make-believe' situations that are consistent with the aims of the suggestions. For example, subjects might be given a suggestion for arm lightness and informed that they can make their arm feel light by becoming absorbed in the fantasy that their arm had been transformed into a helium-filled balloon that is rising upwards. The third component includes detailed information about how to interpret specific types of suggestions coupled with practice at responding to such suggestions. The information contained in the treatment package is conveyed to subjects in two ways. First, the experimenter provides subjects with direct and explicit information and with feedback concerning practice responses. Second, subjects are exposed to a videotaped model who successfully responds to a series of suggestions and verbalizes appropriate suggestion-related imaginings as she responds. In a later portion of the videotape subjects see the model being interviewed about her experiences. During the interview the model reiterates her interpretation of suggested communications and the cognitive strategies that she had employed to respond successfully.

Explit information about how to interpret test suggestions was built into this treatment package because the communications contained in suggestions are often ambiguous (Spanos 1982b). For example, the wording of most suggestions implies that suggested effects will happen by themselves without subjects' active participation (e.g. 'your arm is rising higher and higher'; 'the words will be gone, gone completely from your mind'. Spanos (1982b) hypothesized that many low-susceptible subjects tend to interpret test suggestions literally and, thereby, simply wait passively for the suggested effects to 'just happen by themselves'. When nothing happens these subjects are often disappointed that the hypnosis 'didn't work'. Highly susceptible subjects, on the other hand, respond to suggestions as tacit requests to enact the behaviours called for while interpreting their enactments as involuntary occurrences. According to this hypothesis absorption in suggestion related imagery does not in any direct or automatic way cause suggested responses. Nevertheless, involvement in such imagery often aids subjects to experience (i.e. to interpret) their responses to suggestions as feeling involuntary.

On the basis of these ideas the Carleton skill training package emphasizes that responses to suggestions never 'just happen'; they must be enacted. Subjects are further informed that they can make their enacted responses feel involuntary by becoming highly absorbed in fantasy stituations that imply involuntariness (e.g. 'imagine that the arm is hollow and pumped up with air'). Some suggestions challenge subjects to try to overcome suggested effects (e.g. 'try to remember the words'; 'try to bend your arm'). Subjects are informed that such challenges are not to be interpreted as requests to terminate absorption in the fantasy situation. Instead, the challenge is to be incorporated into the fantasy (e.g. 'when challenged to bend your arm imagine that a vice holds the elbow so tightly that no amount of effort can break it'). In short, this treatment package emphasizes the importance of an active interpretational set towards suggestions.

ANALYSIS OF TREATMENT COMPONENTS

Spanos, Robertson *et al.* (in press) suggested that one reason for the highly variable outcomes obtained in studies that use multi-component treatment packages may have been differences in the degree to which these packages emphasized interpretational set information. Spanos, Robertson *et al.* (in press) exposed one group of low-susceptible subjects to the full three-component training package described above. A second group of low susceptibles received two of the three components of that treatment package. These subjects received positive information about hypnosis and information about absorption in imagery. However, they received no information about how to interpret suggestions.

Subjects who received the full three-component package showed large susceptibility gains on both the CURSS and on a modification of the SHSS:C. These subjects showed impressive gains on subjective as well as on behavioural dimensions of susceptibility, and more than half of them scored in the high susceptibility range on *both* susceptibility scale post-tests. Subjects who received the partial treatment package (sans interpretation component) showed only small susceptibility gains, and their post-test scores usually failed to differ significantly from those of control subjects, who were post-tested without intervening treatment. Importantly, subjects in both the complete and partial training groups showed large and equivalent increments in positive attitudes towards hypnosis.

Trait theorists sometimes suggest that the susceptibility increments that occur in modification studies are likely to be very small and when they occur will result from interventions that relieve subjects' transient anxieties, familiarize them with hypnotic procedures and so on. The results of the Spanos, Robertson *et al.* (in press) study contradict these ideas in two ways. First, the susceptibility gains observed in the complete skill training group were very large. Second, subjects exposed to the partial treatment package, aimed at changing attitudes but not interpretational sets, achieved much smaller susceptibility gains than those who received the complete training package. These findings contradict the notions that training gains in susceptibility must be small or that such gains can be accounted for simply in terms of attitude change, fear reduction, practice with suggestions, etc.

Gorassini and Spanos (1986) found that interpretational set information was somewhat more effective when presented both by a videotaped model and by the experimenter than when presented by the experimenter alone. These investigators also tested a group of subjects who, in place of cognitive skill training, practised responding to hypnotic procedures and test suggestions. These subjects were informed that practice would improve their hypnotic performance but were given no information aimed at changing attitudes and interpretational sets. Practice alone was much less effective than cognitive skill training at enhancing susceptibility.

Most of the subjects in Spanos, Robertson *et al.*'s (in press) partial training treatment and also many of those in Gorassini and Spanos's 'practice-alone' group probably wished to co-operate, to please the experimenter and to respond appropriately. However, for the majority of these subjects the appropriate co-operative response was simply to imagine along with the suggestions while waiting for the responses to occur automatically. For subjects who received complete skill training, co-operating implied enacting responses while simultaneously carrying out imaginings that helped to define the enactments as feeling involuntary. In short, co-operating with test demands is most probably a requirement of high susceptibility. However, the achievement off high susceptibility also requires that subjects know *how* to co-operate effectively.

Individual differences in response to skill training

Although cognitive skill training produces substantaial increments in suscepti-bility, some subjects remain low in susceptibility despite exposure to such training. To investigate this issue Spanos, Cross *et al.* (1985) exposed sixty low-susceptible subjects to the full three-component Carleton skill training package and then post-tested them on susceptibility. Before skill training, subjects were assessed on imagery vividness and absorption inventories. Before post-testing (but after skill training) their attitudes towards hypnosis were assessed. The extent to which subjects showed susceptibility gains on the post-test was predicted both by their attitudes towards hypnosis and by their pre-test levels of imagery vividness. In other words, subjects who maintained relatively negative attitudes towards hypnosis despite skill training also showed relatively small gains in susceptibility. Relatedly, when attitudes towards hypnosis were statistically controlled, relatively higher pre-test imagery vividness was associated with relatively higher post-test susceptibility.

Taken together the Spanos, Cross *et al.* (1985) and Spanos, Robertson *et al.* (in press) studies indicate that modification training will produce large increments in susceptibility when subjects possess the requisite imaginal skills, when skill training is successful in inculcating positive attitudes, and when such training instils an active interpretational set. All of Spanos, Cross *et al.*'s (1985) subjects were exposed to active interpretational set information. Despite this, those with very low imagery vividness and/or those who retained negative attitudes showed little susceptibility gain. Conversely, in the Spanos, Robertson *et al.* (in press) study inculcation of positive attitudes in the absence of interpretational set information was associated with very little gain on susceptibility measures.

The findings of the Spanos, Cross *et al.* (1985) and Spanos, Robertson *et al.* (in press) studies may help to explain why both attitudes towards hypnosis and imagery vividness are related to susceptibility in fan-shaped patterns.

Recall that these fan-shaped patterns occurred because subjects with negative attitudes and/or low imagery vividness were never high in susceptibility, whereas those with positive attitudes and/or high imagery vividness were represented at all susceptibility levels. The association of low susceptibility with negative attitudes and low imagery vividness is consistent with Spanos, Cross *et al.*'s (1985) finding that low scores on these predictors were associated with relatively little or no gain in susceptibility following skills training. Relatedly, Spanos, Robertson *et al.* (in press) found that favourable attitudes were associated with either low susceptibility or high susceptibility, depending upon subjects' implicit interpretational sets towards test suggestions. Perhaps subjects in earlier correlational studies, who did not hold an active interpretational set, obtained relatively low susceptibility scores despite favourable attitudes and adequate imagery levels. Alternatively, those with favourable attitudes, adequate imagery levels *and* an active interpretational set obtained relatively high susceptibility scores.

The generalizability of skill training

Learning a skill implies more than the ability to perform the specific behaviours taught during training. For example, children who memorize the answers to a specific set of arithmetic problems by rote have not learned the skill of adding. Evidence of skill learning requires that the children correctly add sets of numbers to which they did not previously know the answers. By the same token, evidence that hypnotic susceptibility can be modified requires that skill-trained subjects respond successfully to a wide range of suggestions and to suggestions that differ from those on which they were trained. Evidence of this type has been consistently reported in modification studies that obtained large susceptibility gains. For example, numerous studies that employed two different susceptibility scales as post-tests reported large susceptibility gains on both post-test scales (Sachs and Anderson 1967, Diamond 1972, Kinney and Sachs 1974, Spanos, Robertson *et al.* in press Gorassini and Spanos, 1986). The subjects in these studies could not have obtained large susceptibility increments on both post-tests without responding successfully to a much wider range of test items than those to which they had been exposed in their training sessions.

Several studies (Sachs and Anderson 1967, Gorassini and Spanos 1986) have reported detailed analyses of post-test susceptibility responding. For example, Sachs and Anderson pretested subjects on both the HGSHS:A and the SHSS:C susceptibility scales, and afterwards exposed them to a series of training sessions aimed at helping them vividly to experience the subjective and behavioural effects called for by a series of practice suggestions. All of the practice suggestions were taken from the HGSHS:A. Subjects were post-tested twice on the HGSHS:A and once on the SHSS:C and showed large pre-to-post-test gains on both scales. Sachs and Anderson also examined subjects' responses to the specific SHSS:C suggestions that least resembled the

HGSHS:A suggestions used during the training sessions. Subjects showed substantial gains on the behavioural and subjective aspects of these unpractised suggestions. Gorassini and Spanos (1986) conducted separate analyses on those SHSS:C post-test suggestions that differed from both the practice suggestions used during skill training and the suggestions used to assess base-line susceptibility. Skill-trained subjects obtained much higher scores on the behavioural and subjective aspects of these novel suggestions than did untrained control subjects.

TEMPORAL STABILITY

A good deal of data now suggest that large suceptibility gains are relatively stable over intervals that range from a few days to a month after skill training. For instance, Kinney and Sachs (1974) post-tested subjects both immediately and a month after modification training. The two post-tests involved different susceptibility scales. Subjects who had undergone training had much higher susceptibility scores than controls on the delayed post-test as well as on the initial post-test. In three studies from the Carleton laboratory subjects received an initial post-test three to seven days after cognitive skill training and a second post-test one to three weeks after the first (Spanos, Robertson *et al.* in press, 1985, Gorassini and Spanos 1986). The two post-tests always involved different susceptibility scales. In all three studies skill-trained subjects (who had tested as low susceptibles before training) attained much higher behavioural and subjective scores on both post-tests than untrained controls. Furthermore, the correlations between susceptibility scores on the two post-tests were higher than the correlations between susceptibility pre-test scores and scores on either post-test (Spanos, Robertson *et al.* 1985, Gorassini and Spanos 1986). The stability of training-induced susceptibility gains over periods longer than a month has yet to be investigated and constitutes an important area for further research.

The stability of base-line susceptibility

Several investigators (Shor, Orne and O'Connell 1966, Shor and Cobb 1968, Bowers 1976, Perry 1977) have argued that initial scores on tests of hypnotic susceptibility are influenced by the novelty of the hypnotic test situation and by relatively transient fears and apprehensions. For these reasons initial susceptibility testing supposedly tends to underestimate subjects' 'true' level of hypnotic susceptibility. For example, Perry suggested that 'Such factors as fear of being controlled by the hypnotist, inability to let oneself go, fear of having an unpleasant experience may inhibit many subjects, until they have experienced hypnotic phenomena at least once and found them safe' (1977: 129). The implication of these considerations is that any susceptibility gains found in modification studies that employed only a single base-line test are largely artifactual. Thus Bowers argued that 'Any –training-induced— gains reported with initially naive subjects are apt to be cheap – that is, the result of an artifically low pretest baseline' (1976: 84).

In sum, the concerns voiced by Bowers and Perry strongly imply that initial susceptibility scores are artifically low, highly labile and very likely to increase with repeated testing. Interestingly, these same investigators (Bowers 1976, 1981, Perry, 1977) have also argued that hypnotic susceptibility scales are reliable and valid indexes, and that susceptibility is a stable and difficult-to-modify trait. Both of these views cannot be true. Either susceptibility scales given under standardized laboratory testing conditions are reliable or they are not. They cannot be reliable for the purposes of some arguments and unreliable for the purposes of others. As we shall see, the available data suggest that initial susceptibility scores are a good deal less labile than the above quotes from Bowers (1976) and Perry (1977) suggest. The large gains in susceptibility produced by cognitive skill training cannot be explained away in terms of the initial unreliability of base-line susceptibility scores.

RELIABILITY IN HYPNOTICALLY NAIVE SUBJECTS

As indicated in an earlier section, when training procedures are not administered, and when retesting occurs within a few weeks of initial testing, subjects usually obtain similar hypnotic susceptibility scores on the two tests. For example, Spanos, Radtke *et al.* (1983a) tested hypnotically naive subjects twice on the CURSS. Although the two testings were separated by as long as three months, 73 per cent of the subjects obtained a behavioural score on the second test administration that was within one point of their behavioural score on the first test. Furthermore, when susceptibility scores did change they tended to become lower rather than higher. Thus 8.5 per cent of these subjects obtained behavioural score increases of more than one point, while 18.4 per cent showed decreases of more than one point. Two studies (Barber and Calverley 1966b, Barber, Ascher and Mavroides 1971) administered susceptibility scales more than twice to the same subjects without making attempts to modify susceptibility. Barber and Calverley (1966b) readministered the BSS in eight separate sessions. Subjects showed a small but steady decline in susceptibility scores across the sessions. In summary, the available data do not support the notion that initial susceptibility scores are artificially low or likely to increase with a second administration of an equivalent test.

REPEATED BASE-LINES AND SKILL TRAINING INCREMENTS

Five studies that used cognitive skill training of one sort or another to produce large gains in susceptibility also employed more than one base-line susceptibility test (Sachs and Anderson 1967, Diamond 1972, Kinney and Sachs 1974, Springer, Sachs and Morrow 1977, Spanos, Robertson *et al.* 1985). Obviously, the large susceptibility gains obtained in these studies cannot be accounted for in terms of artifically low initial base-line scores. The importance of repeated base-line testing was explicitly investigated by Spanos, Robertson *et al.* (1985). In that study all subjects were selected on the basis of low initial behavioural scores on the CURSS. Half of these subjects were then given the HGSHS:A as a second base-line test and were retained only if their HGSHS:A scores were also low. Half of the subjects in each base-line condition were administered cognitive skill training and were later post-tested on the CURSS and on a modification of the SHSS:C. The remaining subjects served as controls and were post-tested without intervening treatment. Subjects who underwent skill training showed very large susceptibility gains on both post-tests, while controls maintained low scores on both post-tests. The number of base-line tests subjects received had no influence on the magnitude of their post-test scores. These results clearly contradict the notion that initial base-line susceptibility is unstable and artificially low.

Plateau susceptibility

According to the notion of plateau susceptibility some variable number of hypnotic training sessions is required before subjects reach a stable susceptibility 'plateau' beyond which further training is unlikely to add further improvement. A number of investigators (Bowers 1976, Shor and Cobb 1968, Perry 1977) have suggested that subjects' plateau level of susceptibility should be the base-line against which increments in susceptibility due to modification training are measured. The concept of plateau susceptibility is based on the theoretical position that hypnotic responding reflects differences in level of hypnotic or trance 'depth'. The upper level of depth that an individual can achieve is relatively fixed (i.e. the plateau level). However, non-hypnotic factors such as attitudes and expectations concerning hypnosis, unconscious fears and defences concerning loss of control can interfere with subjects' attainment of their plateau level.

Although the concept of plateau susceptibility is sometimes equated with the stability of susceptibility over test administrations, this equation can be misleading. Supposedly, repeated susceptibility testing does not guarantee the attainment of plateau responding. The hypnotist must instead work intensively with subjects attempting to change misconceptions, provide tailored hypnotic inductions and optimal practice, relieve unconscious fears and so on. Plateau susceptibility is purportedly achieved when such interventions lead to stable levels of susceptibility that the hypnotist believes are unlikely to change with continued individualized practice and training (Shor, Orne and O'Connell 1962). Supposedly, attempts to enhance 'true' susceptibility should begin only after plateau susceptibility has been established in this manner.

Although much emphasis has been placed on the notion of plateau susceptibility, the available data suggest that individualized hypnotic training aimed at facilitating optimal manifestations of 'hypnotic depth' has little effect on hypnotic susceptibility. Thus As Hilgard and Weitzenhoffer (1963) and Cooper *et al.* (1967) found that individualized hypnotic training produced only small increments in susceptibility; and Shor, Orne and O'Connell (1962) found that initial susceptibility scores and plateau-susceptibility scores were correlated $r = .83$.

Theoretical limitations with the plateau-susceptibility notion become evident when an attempt is made to apply it to the results of cognitive skill training studies (e.g., Gorassini and Spanos, 1986). Fifty per cent of initially low-susceptible skill-trained subjects but no initially low-susceptible control subjects consistently achieve post-test susceptibility scores in the high susceptibility range. Does this mean that skill-trained subjects were brought to plateau while the controls, despite repeated testings on different susceptibility scales, continued to function much below plateau? Acceptance of this interpretation means that existing susceptibility scales are grossly invalid and consistently underestimate subjects' 'real' susceptibility. This interpretation further suggests that earlier investigators who found only small increments between initial scores and plateau scores were mistaken in their beliefs that their subjects had reached plateau. If the investigators who developed the plateau-susceptibility concept (e.g. Shor, Orne and O'Connell 1966, Shor and Cobb 1968) were unable to determine plateau levels in their own subjects accurately, then the utility of this concept is, to say the least, questionable. An alternative interpretation is that cognitive-skill-trained subjects showed large increments beyond their plateau levels. In other words, these subjects showed substantial increments in their 'depth' of hypnosis. The problem here is that the notion of 'hypnotic depth' with its implications of passive and involuntary responding seems misleading and unnecessary as an explanation for susceptibility enhancements produced by changing subjects' attitudes, strategies and interpretational sets towards situational task demands.

The problem of compliance

As Wagstaff has explained in Chapter 4, above, compliance occurs when there is a discrepancy between privately held beliefs and opinions, and the public espousal of those beliefs and opinions (Kiesler and Kiesler 1970, Wagstaff 1981). For instance, a liberal Democrat may voice pro-Replican sentiments that he does not really believe in the presence of a staunchly conservative boss. In such a case the Democrat is engaged in compliance. On the other hand a liberal Democrat who, under the influence of his boss, changes his opinions and beliefs and becomes a staunch Republican is engaging in conformity but not in compliance. There are a great many social situations in which compliance is expected and where non-compliance is considered boorish, insensitive or in some other way socially inappropriate. For example, crowing gleefully at the funeral of a disliked department head would, to most people, be considered bad form. The more appropriate response would be to comply with social convention by conveying an impression of sorrowful respect despite one's private loathing for the deceased.

From a social psychological perspective the difference between 'genuine' hypnotic behaviour and faked behaviour is the difference between conformity and compliance. 'Genuine' subjects conform by privately defining their overt responses in terms of the manifest interpretations conveyed by the suggestions. In other words, these subjects bring about the subjective experiences called for by the suggestions (e.g. they experience their rising arm as light and as going up by itself; they feel that they are unable to recall the test items covered by an amnesia suggestion). Faking or compliant subjects are those who carry out the overt responses required by the suggestions without subjectively experiencing the effects called for. The issue of compliance is particularly important in hypnosis research because hypnotic situations create strong demands for the production of 'appropriate' overt responses to suggestions, and because hypnotic responses are almost always very easy to fake (Orne 1959, Wagstaff 1979, 1981 and Chapter 4, above). On the other hand, hypnotic test situations also contain strong implicit demands *against* compliance. Most subjects define psychological experiments as serious endeavours aimed at discovering the truth about behavioural phenomena (Adair and Spinner 1981). As indicated earlier, test suggestions do not instruct subjects to voluntarily carry out overt responses. On the contrary, their wording tacitly implies that responses that feel voluntary are to be considered ingenuine. In short, test suggestions implicitly instruct subjects to conform by generating experiences that will enable them to define their behaviours as happening involuntarily. To the extent that subjects wish to avoid defining themselves as behaving dishonestly during a serious scientific endeavour, they must conform rather than comply with hypnotic test demands.

Investigators who adopt a cognitive-behavioural perspective usually interpret susceptibility gains induced by skill training as meaning that subjects have learned the skills and interpretations required for producing subjectively convincing displays of hypnotic behaviour (Sachs 1971, Diamond 1977, Spanos, Robertson *et al.* in press). Others (e.g. Perry 1977), however, have cautioned that such gains may stem from behavioural compliance in the absence of the subjective experiences called for by the suggestions.

COMPLIANCE AND SOCIAL PRESSURE

In the area of modification research, as in other areas of hypnosis research, the compliance issue is complex and by no means easy to resolve (Wagstaff 1981, 1983). A number of findings suggest that a pure compliance hypothesis is unable to account adequately for the findings of modification studies. For example, in many skill training studies (e.g. Gorassini and Spanos 1986) the experimenters who conducted the post-tests were not the same people who trained the subjects and were, in fact, unaware of subjects' treatment group at the time of post-testing. Such precautions do not rule out compliance; but they do suggest that the large susceptibility gains produced by skill training did not result from experimenter bias on the part of those conducting the post-tests or from pressure on the part of the subjects to 'shine' in the presence of the experimenter who trained them.

More compelling evidence against the compliance hypothesis was obtained by

Spanos, Robertson *et al.* (in press). In that study subjects in both the partial and complete skill-training treatments were exposed to strong demands to enhance hypnotic performance. For example, subjects in both groups were repeatedly informed that their training was designed to enhance susceptibility, that such training had worked for others and that hypnosis involved the learning of useful skills. Furthermore, subjects in both groups could have easily faked high levels of responding on the post-tests if that had been their intent. Nevertheless, large susceptibility gains occurred only among the skill-trained subjects supplied with interpretational set information. These considerations suggest that differences in interpretational set rather than faking accounted for the post-test susceptibility differences found between subjects in the complete and partial skill-training treatments. Related findings were obtained by Gorassini and Spanos (1986). In that study, subjects given the opportunity to practise hypnotic suggestions, and explicitly informed that such practice would improve their performance, showed no significant gains in susceptibility. Skill-trained subjects, on the other hand, showed very large susceptibility gains.

Also relevant here are Shor and Cobb's (1968) findings. These investigators exposed subjects to strong and prolonged demands aimed at motivating co-operation and optimal performance. The presssure generated by these demands was so intense that some of the subjects reported 'an intense pressure for achievement and an impending sense of failure as the end of the summer approached' (1968: 179). Despite such pressure Shor and Cobb's subjects showed much smaller susceptibility gains than the skill-trained subjects described above, who were exposed to much less intense and much less prolonged pressure. Taken together, these findings suggest that hypnotic subjects, like hypnotic experimenters, are often acutely sensitive to issues of compliance. It appears that many low-susceptible subjects actively resist complying with even very strong and persistent tasks demands when they have not learned how to create the subjective effects that will enable them to conform to task demands.

Natural highs, created highs and simulators

Another approach relevant to the issue of compliance involves comparing the performance of three groups of subjects: skill-trained subjects, subjects who obtain equivalent levels of susceptibility without training, and subjects explicitly instructed to fake behaving like a deeply hypnotized person. For example, Gorassini and Spanos (1986) compared skill-trained subjects who scored as high susceptibles on post-testing (i.e. created highs) with untrained (i.e. natural) high susceptibles. These subjects reported equivalent levels of subjective responding to suggestions and were also equally likely to define their responses to suggestions as feeling involuntary. Spanos, de Groh and de Groot (in press) obtained similar findings and also reported that skill-trained and natural subjects who exhibited recall deficits when given a novel amnesia task were equally likely to define their forgetting as feeling involuntary. Further,

Gfeller *et al.* (1985) found that created highs and natural highs showed equivalent levels of response to several novel and difficult suggestions that are not included on standard susceptibility scales. Both of these groups showed higher levels of responding to the novel items than did low susceptibles who had not undergone skill training.

The Spanos, Robertson *et al.* (in press) study included a group of low susceptibles who were explicitly instructed to fake responding like excellent hypnotic subjects (i.e. simulators: Orne 1959, 1979). Simulators did not undergo modification training. However, immediately before each post-test they were instructed to fake responding both overtly and on all subjective experience questionnaires in the way that they believed excellent hypnotic subjects would respond.

Numerous studies (reviewed by Orne 1979, Spanos in press a) indicate that simulators tend to overplay the hypnotic role. When given difficult test suggestions, simulators often exhibit higher levels of overt responding and give higher subjective experience ratings than do actual high-susceptible hypnotic subjects. Consistent with these findings Spanos, Robertson *et al.* found that simulators exhibited significantly higher levels of overt and subjective response to suggestions than did skill-trained subjects. In short, simulators explicitly instructed to *comply* with suggested demands did not respond in the same manner as skill-trained subjects on tests of hypnotic susceptibility.

High-susceptible subjects typically exhibit a discrepancy between their behavioural score on susceptibility scales and the score that indicates the degree to which their behaviours felt involuntary. Two studies (Gorassini and Spanos (1986), Spanos, de Groh and de Groot in press) found that skill-trained subjects and untrained subjects who were matched on behavioural scores exhibited discrepancies of equal magnitude between behavioural and involuntariness scores. In the Spanos, Robertson *et al.* (in press) study most of the skill-trained subjects but only one simulator exhibited the behavioural/involuntariness discrepancy that characterizes the performance of natural high susceptibles. Relatedly, Gfeller *et al.* (1985) tested subjects on three tasks that, in previous research, successfully discriminated between the performance of natural highs and simulators. For example, one of these tasks instructs subjects to see (i.e. hallucinate) an object that is not present. Natural highs tend to describe their hallucinated image as transparent, whereas simulators usually describe it as solid (for a review of real/simulator differences see Spanos in press a). As indicated above, Gfeller *et al.* found that natural highs and created highs responded similarly to one another on all of these tasks.

As emphasized by Wagstaff (Chapter 4, above), hypnotic situations include strong pressures towards conformance. For a variety of reasons, however, many subjects who wish to co-operate with the proceedings fail to generate the subjective experiences called for by the suggestions. Some of these subjects comply with suggested demands by enacting the overt responses called for in the absence of the appropriate subjective experience (Wagstaff 1983). Compliance effects of this kind may well account for a small part of the susceptibility increments seen in modification studies just as they undoubtedly account for part of what constitutes high susceptibility in hypnotic testing contexts that do not involve modification training. Nevertheless, the available data suggest that the large susceptibility gains induced by skill traiining reflect conformance to a greater extent than they reflect pure compliance. Thus subjects who were exposed to strong pressures for enhanced susceptibility, and who could have easily complied if they wished to do so, exhibited remarkably *small* susceptibility increments unless they were taught *how* to conform (i.e. how to interpret task demands in a manner that allowed for the enactment of 'subjectively compelling' suggested responses).

Taken together, the available data support the proposition that hypnotic susceptibility is much more modifiable than trait theorists believe it to be. Individual differences in susceptibility appear to be related not only to subjects' levels of imagery/fantasy-proneness, attitudes towards hypnosis and willingness to co-operate with task demands, but also to their implicit interpretations of those task demands. Cognitive skill procedures that modify negative attitudes and unhelpful interpretational sets produce large enhancements in susceptibility. These enhancements generalize across different standardized susceptibility scales, and to novel and difficult test items that are not included on standardized scales. Moreover, the large susceptibility increments induced by skill training cannot be accounted for in terms of inadequate or unreliable base-line testing, experimenter bias or compliance effects.

Hypnotic susceptibility and specific task performance

The available data provide strong evidence against the trait notion that hypnotic susceptibility reflects a largely unmodifiable capacity for psychological dissociation. Nevertheless, the data on skill training discussed thus far might still be interpreted within a modified dissociation perspective. The modified perspective would acknowledge that dissociative capacity was more modifiable than initially presumed, but that cognitive skill training produced large susceptibility gains by enhancing subjects' dissociative capacities. From this perspective the generalization of cognitive skill training to novel suggested tasks would simply reflect the stability and pervasiveness of subjects' newly acquired dissociative capacities.

In this modified form, the dissociation hypothesis holds that low-susceptible subjects must undergo some procedure for boosting dissociative capacity before they can show gains on novel suggested tasks. For example, recall Hilgard's (1979) hypothesis that large reductions in pain following an analgesia suggestion are restricted to people with high levels of dissociative capacity. On the basis of the modified dissociation hypothesis one might expect that low susceptibles, who after skill training become 'created highs', would report large suggestion-induced pain reductions even though they had not been specifically trained in how to reduce pain. Importantly, however, this hypothesis also holds that low susceptibles who had not first undergone some procedure for boosting dissociative capacity would remain unable to exhibit large pain reductions.

Unlike the dissociation hypothesis in either its original or modified forms, a social psychological perspective suggests that correlations between hypnotic susceptibility scores and performance on novel suggested tasks result not from some generalized capacity, but instead from similarities in the attitudes and interpretational sets elicited by the two testing situations. This idea suggests that correlations between hypnotic susceptibility and performance on novel suggested tasks (e.g. suggested analgesia) can be easily disrupted. For instance, it should be possible to modify the task-specific attitudes and interpretations of low susceptibles. Under these circumstances low and high susceptibles should perform equally well on specific suggested tasks even though the low susceptibles had not first undergone some procedure aimed at enhancing their general level of susceptibility. In the last few years a number of studies on suggested-pain reduction have provided data relevant to these ideas.

Numerous studies (Evans and Paul 1970, Hilgard and Hilgard 1975, Spanos, Radtke-Bodorik *et al.* 1979, Spanos, Stam and Brazil 1981) have found significant correlations between initial levels of hypnotic susceptibility and degree of suggestion-induced pain reduction. These findings are, of course, consistent with the view that both susceptibility scale performance and analgesia test performance reflect degrees of dissociative capacity. However, these findings are also consistent with a social psychological perspective.

According to our social psychological hypothesis suggestion-induced reductions in experimentally produced pain result from subjects' use of cognitive strategies. Thus subjects reduce pain by employing imaginal or other strategies that either divert attention away from the noxious stimulation or that lead to a reinterpretation of the noxious stimulation as being less distressing than it initially appeared (Spanos 1982a, Turk, Meichenbaum and Genest 1983). According to this hypothesis both high- and low-susceptible subjects have the ability to employ cognitive strategies for pain reduction. However, low susceptibles come to see themselves as unwilling and/or unable to respond optimally to suggestions associated with hypnosis. They consequently report little or no pain reduction when given suggestions for analgesia. Analgesia suggestions are usually worded in the same passive manner as the suggestions on hypnotic susceptibility scales (e.g. 'your arm is growing numb and insensitive'). It is therefore not surprising that subjects develop similar interpretational sets and similar performance patterns in both test situations. As indicated earlier, people who obtain low scores on standardized susceptibility scales often hold relatively negative attitudes and expectations about hypnosis. Furthermore, poor performance on an initial susceptibility test is likely to confirm the view that these subjects hold of themselves as unresponsive to suggestions. For reasons such as these low susceptibles, who connect the analgesia test situation with their prior hypnotic susceptibility test performance, are likely to develop negative expectancies concerning their response to the analgesia test situation. As a result they are unlikely to initiate and sustain the cognitive strategies that reduce pain. These ideas indicate that the frequently replicated relationship between hypnotic susceptibility and suggested analgesia is context-specific and will tend to break down when the two testing situations are not implicitly or explictly defined as related to one another. Two studies provide data that are pertinent to this hypothesis.

Spanos, Kennedy and Gwynn (1984) and Spanos, Voorneveld and Gwynn (1984) tested the idea that attitudes and expectations about hypnosis held by high- and low-susceptible subjects influence their degree of pain reduction in an analgesia test situation. Spanos, Kennedy and Gwynn (1984) pre-tested subjects on susceptibility and in a separate session instructed them to do everything that they could to reduce the pain produced by noxious stimulation (immersion of a hand in ice-water). Subjects to one group received these analgesia instructions only after they had been administered an hypnotic induction procedure. In this group high susceptibles reported more pain reduction than medium susceptibles, who in turn reported more pain reduction than low susceptibles. High, medium and low susceptibles in a second group received analgesia instructions without a prior hypnotic induction. Importantly, the low susceptibles in this group reported (a) significantly larger pain reductions than the low susceptibles given hypnosis plus instruction and (b) pain reductions as large as those shown by the high susceptibles given hypnosis plus instruction. The only difference between the two groups of low susceptibles in this study was the exposure of those in one group to a hypnotic induction procedure that implicitly defined the analgesia situation as related to subjects' poor performance during their earlier hypnotic susceptibility test session. Thus the large pain reductions shown by the non-hypnotic low susceptibles given analgesia instructions cannot be attributed to procedures that somehow boosted the dissociative capacities of these subjects to the levels found in the high-susceptible hypnotic subjects.

In a related study Spanos, Voorneveld and Gwynn (1984) first tested both high and low susceptibles for hypnotic analgesia. As in numerous earlier studies the high susceptibles exhibited much greater pain reductions than the low susceptibles. In the next part of the study the hypnotic procedures were terminated, and the low susceptibles were informed that independent-minded people like themselves often performed poorly during hypnosis because they are not gullible. These subjects were further informed that they possessed the natural ability to control their own mind and, without hypnosis to interfere, they could employ these natural abilities to reduce their pain. After being given these instructions the low susceptibles reduced their pain significantly more than they had during hypnotic analgesia. In fact, they showed as much pain reduction following the 'natural-ability' instructions as did high susceptibles given hypnotic analgesia suggestions.

Taken together, the findings of these two studies indicate that the commonly obtained relationship between hypnotic susceptibility and degree of suggested analgesia is much more context-dependent than either the original or the modified dissociation hypotheses can allow. Importantly, the low susceptibles in these studies exhibited large pain reductions in the absence of any training designed to enhance susceptibility or boost dissociative capacity. It is difficult to see how these findings can be reconciled with the notions that high levels of suggested analgesia require either special dissociatives capacities or high levels of hypnotic susceptibility. On the other hand, these findings emphasize the social psychological nature of the analgesia test situation and the importance of subjects' attitudes and interpretations in determining the extent of cognitive coping and the degree of pain reduction that occurs.

Overview and conclusions

Attempts to account for individual differences in hypnotic responsiveness have usually begun with the assumption that hypnotic procedures induce an altered state of consciousness. Typically, the degree to which subjects enter into this hypothetical state is described as varying along a dimension of depth. From this perspective suggestion phenomena are occurrencs or happenings that are elicited more or less automatically by the words of the hypnotist. Suggested phenomena are dependent upon non-conscious or dissociated cognitive processes that are facilitated by hypnotic induction procedures. Thus 'hypnotized' subjects are passive observers rather than initiators of their own behaviour. These subjects have lost conscious control over the dissociated cognitive subsystems that govern their responses to suggestions. People differ in the maximum level of depth that they are able to attain and therefore in the number and difficulty level of the suggestions they are able to pass. These individual differences in responsiveness to suggestions (i.e. susceptibility) reflect stable differences in cognitive capacity (e.g. individual differences in dissociative capacity). The stability and relative non-modifiability of this capacity allow hypnotic susceptibility to be described accurately as a stable trait.

The research reviewed in this chapter strongly indicates that this traditional special-process approach towards hypnosis and hypnotic susceptibility is based on a fundamental misconception concerning the nature of hypnotic responding. The approach assumed that hypnotic responses are involuntary happenings, and much of the early research on the modification of hypnotic susceptibility was implicitly based on this premise. The research was aimed at enhancing susceptibility by employing procedures that investigators believed might alter trance capacity (e.g. tailored inductions, sensory restriction, EEG feedback). These diverse procedures consistently produced only small gains in susceptibility and thereby reinforced the notion that susceptibility was a largely unmodifiable trait. Notions like 'stable dissociative capacity' were invented by special-process theorists to account for both the presumed automaticity and the presumed unmodifiability of hypnotic responding.

As I hope to have demonstrated, hypnotic behaviour is, first and foremost, social behaviour. Like other complex social enactments hypnotic responding is strategic rather than automatic. Hypnotic subjects retain rather than lose conscious control over their behaviour. These subjects guide their enactments in terms of their understandings concerning the requirements of the test situation and the social impressions they wish their enactments to convey. From this perspective, individual differences in hypnotic susceptibility reflect individual differences in attitudes, motivations and interpretations concerning hypnosis and the hypnotic situation, and individual differences in the imaginal abilities required to experience suggested effects. Skill-training procedures based on this social psychological perspective have proven much more successful at enhancing susceptibility than have procedures based on special-process formulations. Whatever else may be said about hypnotic susceptibility, it is *not* unmodifiable.

Many facets of hypnotic responding remain only partially understood. The work reviewed in this chapter suggests that a more complete understanding of such responding is most likely to be gained from research programmes that view hypnotic phenomena as goal-directed social enactments.

References

Adair, J. G. and Spinner, B. (1981) Subjects' access to cognitive processes: Demand characteristics and verbal report. *Journal for the Theory of Social Behaviour*, 11: 31–52.

As, A., Hilgard, E. R. and Weitzenhoffer, A. M. (1963) An attempt at experimental modification of hypnotizability through repeated individualized hypnotic experience. *Scandinavian Journal of Psychology*, 4: 81–9.

Balthazard, C. G. and Woodey, E. Z. (1985) The 'stuff' of hypnotic performance: a review of psychometric approaches. *Psychological Bulletin*, 98: 283–96.

Barber, T. X. (1965) Measuring 'hypnotic-like' suggestibility with and without 'hypnotic induction'; psychometric properties, norms, and variables influencing response to the Barber Suggestibility Scale (BSS). *Psychological Reports*, 16 (Monograph Supplement 3-V16): 809–44.

(1969) *Hypnosis: A Scientific Approach*. New York: Van Nostrand Reinhold.

(1979) Suggested ('hypnotic') behaviour: the trance paradigm versus an alternative paradigm. In E. Fromm and R. E. Shor (eds.), *Hypnosis: Developments in Research and New Perspectives*. Chicago: Aldine-Atherton.

(1984) Changing 'unchangeable' bodily processes by (hypnotic) suggestions: a new look at hypnosis, cognitions, imaginings and the mind-body problem. In A. A. Sheikh (ed.), *Imagination and Healing*. New York: Baywood.

Barber, T. X., Ascher, M. M. and Mavroides, M. (1971) Effects of practice on hypnotic suggestibility: a re-evaluation of Hull's postulates. *American Journal of Clinical Hypnosis*, 14: 48–53.

Barber, T. X. and Calverley, D. S. (1964a) An experimental study of 'hypnotic' (auditory and visual) hallucinations. *Journal of Abnormal and Social Psychology*, 63: 13–20.

(1964b) Effect of E's tone of voice on 'hypnotic-like' suggestibility. *Psychological Reports*, 15: 139–44.

(1964c) Experimental studies in 'hypnotic' behaviour: suggested deafness evaluated by delayed auditory feedback. *British Journal of Psychology*, 55: 439–446.

(1964d) Toward a theory of 'hypnotic' behaviour: an experimental study of 'hypnotic time distortion'. *Archives of General Psychiatry*, 10: 209–16.

(1964e) Toward a theory of 'hypnotic' behaviour: Enhancement of strength and endurance. *Canadian Journal of Psychology*, 18: 156–67.

(1966a) Effects on recall of hypnotic induction, motivational suggestions, and suggested regression: a methodological and experimental analysis. *Journal of Abnormal Psychology*, 71: 169–80.

(1966b) Towards a theory of hypnotic behaviour: experimental evaluation of Hull's postulate that hypnotic susceptibility is a habit phenomenon. *Journal of Personality*, 34: 416–33.

Barber, T. X. and Hahn, K. W. Jr (1962) Physiological and subjective responses to pain producing stimulation under hypnotically suggested and waking-imagined 'analgesia'. *Journal of Abnormal and Social Psychology*, 65: 411–18.

Barber, T. X. and Ham, M. W. (1974) *Hypnotic Phenomena*. Morristown, NJ: General Learning Press.

Barber, T. X., Spanos, N. P. and Chaves, J. F. (1974) *Hypnosis, Imagination and Human Potentialities*. New York: Pergamon.

Barber, T. X. and Wilson, S. C. (1977) Hypnosis, suggestions, and altered states of consciousness: experimental evaluation of the new cognitive-behavioural theory and the traditional trance-state theory of 'hypnosis'. *Annals of the New York Academy of Sciences*, 296: 34–47.

Botto, R. W., Fisher, S. and Soucy, G. P. (1977) The effects of a good and poor model on hypnotic susceptibility in a low demand situation. *International Journal of Clinical and Experimental Hypnosis*, 25: 175–83.

Bowers, K. S. (1976) *Hypnosis for the Seriously Curious*. Monterey, Calif.: Brooks/Cole.

(1981) Do the Stanford Scales tap the classic suggestion effect? *International Journal of Clinical and Experimental Hypnosis*, 29: 42–53.

Bowers, P. (1982) The classic suggestion effect: relationships with scales of hypnotizability, effortless experiencing, and imagery vividness. *International Journal of Clinical and Experimental Hypnosis*, 30: 270–9.

Coe, W. C. (1976), Effects of hypnotist susceptibility and sex on the administration of standard hypnotic susceptibility scales. *International Journal of Clinical and Experimental Hypnosis*, 24: 281–6.

Coe, W. C. (1978) The credibility of post hypnotic amnesia: A contextualist's view. *International Journal of Clinical and Experimental Hypnosis*, 26, 281–86.

Coe, W. C. and Sarbin, T. R. (1971) An alternative interpretation to the multiple composition of hypnotic scales: a single role-relevant skill. *Journal of Personality and Social Psychology*, 18: 1–8.

Commins, J., Fullam, F. and Barber, T. X. (1975) Effects of experimenter modeling, demands for honesty, and initial levels of suggestibility on response to hypnotic suggestions. *Journal of Consulting and Clinical Psychology*, 43: 668–75.

Cooper, L. M., Branford, S. A., Schubot, E. and Tart, C. T. (1967) A further attempt to modify hypnotic susceptibility through repeated individualized experience. *International Journal of Clinical and Experimental Hypnosis*, 15: 118–24.

Crouse, E. and Kurtz, R. (1984) Enhancing hypnotic susceptibility: the efficacy of four training procedures. *American Journal of Clinical Hypnosis*, 27: 122–35.

de Groh, M., Cross, W. P. and Spanos, N. P. (1985) Attitudes and imagery in the prediction of hypnotic suggestibility. Unpublished manuscript, Carleton University, Ottawa.

Derman, D. and London, P. (1965) Correlates of hypnotic susceptibility. *Journal of Consulting and Clinical Psychology*, 29: 537–45.

Diamond, M. J. (1972) The use of observationally presented information to modify hypnotic susceptibility. *Journal of Abnormal Psychology*, 79: 174–80.

(1974) Modification of hypnotizability: a review. *Psychological Bulletin*, 81: 180–98.

(1977) Hypnotizability is modifiable. *International Journal of Clinical and Experimental Hypnosis*, 25: 147–65.

(1982). Modifying hypnotic experience by means of indirect hypnosis and hypnotic skill training: an update. *Research Communications in Psychology, Psychiatry and Behaviour*, 7: 233–9.

Diamond, M. J., Steadman, C., Harada, D. and Rosenthal, J. (1975) The use of direct instructions to modify hypnotic performance: the effects of programmed learning procedures. *Journal of Abnormal Psychology*, 84: 109–13.

Diamond, M. J. and Taft, R. (1975) The role played by ego permissiveness and imagery in hypnotic responsivity. *International Journal of Clinical and Experimental Hypnosis*, 23: 130–8.

Dubreuil, D. L., Spanos, N. P. and Bertrand, L. D. (1982) Does hypnotic amnesia dissipate with time? *Imagination, Cognition and Personality*, 2: 103–13.

Dumas, R. (1977) EEG alpha-hypnotizability correlations: a review. *Psychophyisology*, 14: 431–8.

Edmonston, W. E. Jr and Erbeck, J. R. (1967) Hypnotic time distortion: a note. *American Journal of Clinical Hypnosis*, 10: 79–80.

Evans, M. B. and Paul, G. L. (1970) Effects of hypnotically suggested analgesia on physiological and subjective response to cold stress. *Journal of Consulting and Clinical Psychology*, 35: 362–71.

Farthing, G. W., Venturino, M. and Brown, S. W. (1983) Relationship between two different types of imagery vividness questionnaire items and three hypnotic susceptibility scale factors. *International Journal of Clinical and Experimental Hypnos*, 31: 8–13.

Gfeller, J., Lynn, S., Pribble, W. and Kvinge, D. (1985) Enhancing hypnotic susceptibility: interpersonal and rapport factors. Paper presented at the Annual Convention of the American Psychological Association, Los Angeles.

Gorassini, D. R. and Spanos, N. P. (1986) A cognitive skills approach to the successful modification of hypnotic susceptibility. *Journal of Personality and Social Psychology*, 50, 1004–1012.

Gregory, J. and Diamond, M. J. (1973) Increasing hypnotic susceptibility by means of positive expectancies and written instructions. *Journal of Abnormal Psychology*, 82: 363–7.

Gur, R. C. (1974) An attention-controlled operant procedure for enhancing hypnotic susceptibility. *Journal of Abnormal Psychology*, 83: 644–50.

Ham, M. W. and Spanos, N. P. (1974) Suggested auditory and visual hallucinations in task-motivated and hypnotic subjects. *American Journal of Clinical Hypnosis*, 17: 94–101.

Havens, R. A. (1977) Using modeling and information to modify hypnotizability. *International Journal of Clinical and Experimental Hypnosis*, 25: 167–74.

Heide, F. J., Wadlington, W. L. and Lundy, R. M. (1980) Hypnotic responsivity as a predictor of outcome in meditation. *International Journal of Clinical and Experimental Hypnosis*, 28: 358–66.

Hilgard, E. R. (1965) *Hypnotic Susceptibility*. New York: Harcourt.

(1975) Hypnosis. *Annual Review of Psychology*, 26: 19–44.

(1977) *Divided Consciousness*. New York: Wiley.

(1979) Divided consciousness in hypnosis: the implications of the hidden observer. In E. Fromm and R. E. Shor (eds.), *Hypnosis: Developments in Research and New Perspectives* (2nd edn). New York: Aldine.

(1981). Hypnotic susceptibility scales under attack: an examination of Weitzenhoffer's criticisms. *International Journal of Clinical and Experimental Hypnosis*, 29: 24–41.

Hilgard, E. R. and Hilgard, J. R. (1975) *Hypnosis in the relief of pain*. Los Angeles, CA: William Kaufman.

Hilgard, E. R., Hilgard, J. R., Macdonald, H., Morgan, A. H. and Johnson, L. S. (1978) Covert pain in hypnotic analgesia: its reality as tested by the real-simulator model. *Journal of Abnormal Psychology*, 87: 655–63.

Hilgard, E. R., Morgan, A. H. and Macdonald, H. (1975) Pain and dissociation in the cold pressor test: a study of hypnotic analgesia with 'hidden reports' through automatic key-pressing and automatic talking. *Journal of Abnormal Psychology*, 84: 280–9.

Hilgard, E. R., Sheehan, P. W., Monteiro, K. P. and Macdonald, H. (1981) Factorial structure of the Creative Imagination Scale as a measure of hypnotic responsiveness: an international comparative study. *International Journal of Clinical and Experimental Hypnosis*, 29: 66–76.

Hilgard, E. R., Weitzenhoffer, A. M., Landes, J. and Moore, R. K. (1961) The distribution of susceptibility to hypnosis in a student population: a study using the Stanford Hypnotic Susceptibility Scale. *Psychological Monographs: General and Applied*, 75: 1–22.

Hilgard, J. R. (1970) *Personality and Hypnosis*. Chicago: University of Chicago Press.

(1974) Imaginative involvement: some characteristics of the highly hypnotizable and the non-hypnotizable. *International Journal of Clinical and Experimental Hypnosis*, 22: 138–56.

Jones, B. and Spanos, N. P. (1982) Suggestions for altered auditory sensitivity, the negative subject effect and hypnotic susceptibility: a signal detection analysis. *Journal of Personality and Social Psychology*, 43: 637–47.

Katz, N. W. (1979) Comparative efficacy of behavioural training plus relaxation and a sleep/trance hypnotic induction in increasing hypnotic susceptibility. *Journal of Consulting and Clinical Psychology*, 43: 119–27.

Kiesler, C. A. and Kiesler, S. B. (1970) *Conformity*. reading, Mass.: Addison-Wesley.

Kihlstrom, J. F. (1978) Context and cognition in posthypnotic amnesia. *International Journal of Clinical and Experimental Hypnosis*, 26: 246–67.

Kihlstrom, J. F., Evans, F. J., Orne, M. T. and Orne, E. C. (1980) Attempting to breach posthypnotic amnesia. *Jurnal of Abnormal Psychology*, 89: 603–12.

Kihlstrom, J. F. and Shor, R. E. (1978) Recall and recognition during posthypnotic amnesia. *International Journal of Clinical and Experimental Hypnosis*, 26: 330–49.

Kinney, J. M. and Sachs, L. B. (1974) Increasing hypnotic susceptibility. *Journal of Abnormal Psychology*, 83: 145–50.

Kirsch, I., Council, J. R. and Mobayed, C. 1984 Imagery versus response expectancy as determinants of hypnotic behaviour. Unpublished manuscript, University of Connecticut.

Knox, V. J., Morgan, A. H. and Hilgard, E. R. (1974) Pain and suffering in ischemia: the paradox of hypnotically suggested anesthesia as contradicted by reports from the 'hidden observer'. *Archives off General Psychiatry*, 30: 840–7.

Leva, R. A. (1974) Modification of hypnotic susceptibility through audio-tape relaxation training: preliminary report. *Perceptual and Motor Skills*, 39: 872–4.

Levitt, E. E., Brady, J. P., Ottinger, D. and Hinesley, R. (1962) Effects of sensory restriction on hypnotizability. *Archives of General Psychiatry*, 7: 343–5.

London, P., Cooper, L. M. and Engstrom, D. R. (1974) Increasing hypnotic susceptibility by brain wave feedback. *Journal of Abnormal Psychology*, 83: 554–60.

London, P. and Fuhrer, M. (1961) Hypnosis, motivation and performance. *Journal of Personality*, 29: 321–33.

Lynn, S. J., Nash, M. R., Rhue, J. W., Frauman, D. C. and Sweeney, C. A. (1984) Nonvolition, expectancies, and hypnotic rapport. *Journal of Abnormal Psychology*, 93: 295–303.

McConkey, K. M. and Sheehan, P. W. (1981) The impact of videotape playback of hypnotic events on posthypnotic amnesia. *Journal of Abnormal Psychology*, 90: 46–54.

Melei, J. and Hilgard, E. R. (1964) Attitudes toward hypnosis, self-predictions and hypnotic susceptibility. *International Journal of Clinical and Experimental Hypnosis*, 12: 99–108.

Morgan, A. H. and Lam, D. (1969) *The Relationship of the Betts Vividness of Imagery Questionnaire and Hypnotic Susceptibility: Failure to Replicate*. Hawthorne House Research Memorandum, No. 103.

Orne, M. T. (1959) The nature of hypnosis: artifact and essence. *Journal of Abnormal and Social Psychology*, 58: 277–99.

(1979) On the simulating subject as a quasi-control group in hypnosis research: what, why and how. In E. Fromm and R. e. Shor (eds.), *Hypnosis: Developments in Research and New Perspectives*. New York: Aldine.

Perry, C. W. (1973) Imagery, fantasy and hypnotic susceptibility: a multi-dimensional approach. *Journal of Personality and Social Psychology*, 26: 217–21.

(1977) Is hypnotizability modifiable? *International Journal of Clinical and Experimental Hypnosis*, 25: 125–46.

Radtke, H. L., Spanos, N. P., Armstrong, L. A., Dillman, N. and Boisvenue, M. E. (1983) Effects of electromyographic feedback and progresssive relaxation on hypnotic susceptibility: disconfirming results. *International Journal of Clinical and Experimental Hypnosis*, 31: 98–106.

Reillery, R. R., Parisher, D. W., Carona, A. and Dobrovolsky, N. W. (1980) Modifying hypnotic susceptibility by practice and instruction. *International Journal of Clinical and Experimental Hypnosis*, 28: 39–45.

Sachs, L. B. (1971) Construing hypnosis as modifiable behaviour. In A. Jacobs and L. B. Sachs (eds.), *Psychology of Private Events*. New York: Academic Press.

Sachs, L. B. and Anderson, W. L. (1967) Modification of hypnotic susceptibility. *International Journal of Clinical and Experimental Hypnosis*, 15: 172–80.

Salzberg, H. C. and DePiano, F. A. (1980) Hypnotizability and task-motivating suggestions: a further look. *International Journal of Clinical and Experimental Hypnosis*, 28: 261–71.

Sanders, R. S. Jr and Reyher, J. (1969) Sensory deprivation and the enhancement of hypnotic susceptibility. *Journal of Abnormal Psychology*, 74: 375–81.

Sarbin, T. R. (1950) Contributions to role-taking theory: 1. Hypnotic behaviour. *Psychological Review*, 57: 255–70.

(1984) Nonvolition in hypnosis: a semiotic analysis. *Psychological Record*, 34: 537–49.

Sarbin, T. R. and Coe, W. C. (1972) *Hypnotic Behaviour: The Psychology of Influence Communication*. New York: Holt.

(1979) Hypnosis and psychopathology: replacing old myths with fresh matephors. *Journal of Abnormal Psychology*, 88: 506–26.

Sarbin, T. R. and Slagle, R. W. (1979) Hypnosis and psychophysiological outcomes. In E. Fromm and R. E. Shor (eds.), *Hypnosis: Developments in Research and New Perspectives.*

Sheehan, P. W. (1967) A shortened version of the Betts Questionnaire upon Mental Imagery. *Journal of Clinical Psychology*, 23: 386–9.

(1979) Hypnosis and the processes of imagination. In E. From and R. E. Shor (eds.), *Hypnosis: Developments in Research and New Perspectives.* New York: Aldine.

Shor, E. R. (1959) Hypnosis and the concept of the generalized reality orientation. *American Journal of Psychotherapy*, 13: 582–602.

(1970) The three factor theory of hypnosis as applied to the book reading fantasy. *International Journal of Clinical and Experimental Hypnosis.* 18: 89–98.

Shor, R. E. and Cobb, J. C. (1968) An exploratory study of hypnotic training using the concept of plateau responsiveness as a referent. *American Journal of Clinical Hypnosis*, 10: 178–97.

Shor, R. E. and Orne, E. C. (1962) *Harvard Group Scale of Hypnotic Susceptibility: Form A.* Palo Alto, Calif.: Consulting Psychologists Press.

Shor, R. E., Orne, M. T. and O'Connell, D. N. (1962) Validation and cross-validation of a scale of self-reported personal experiences which predicts hypnotizability. *Journal of Psychology*, 53: 55–75.

(1966) Psychological correlates of plateau hypnotizability in a special volunteer sample. *Journal of Personality and Social Psychology*, 3: 80–95.

Simon, J. M. and Salzberg, H. (1981) Electromyographic feedback and taped relaxation instructions to modify hypnotic susceptibility and amnesia. *American Journal of Clinical Hypnosis*, 24: 14–21.

Spanos, N. P. (1971) Goal-directed fantasy and the performance of hypnotic test suggestions. *Psychiatry*, 34: 86–96.

(1982a) A social psychological approach to hypnotic behaviour. In G. Weary and H. L. Mirels (eds.), *Integrations of Clinical and Social Psychology*, New York: Oxford University Press.

(1982b) Hypnotic behaviour: a cognitive and social psychological perspective. *Research Communications in Psychology, Psychiatry, and Behaviour*, 7: 199–213.

(1983) The hidden observer as an experimental creation. *Journal of Personality and Social Psychology*, 44: 170–6.

(in press a) Hypnotic behaviour: a social psychological interpretation of amnesia, analgesia and trance logic. *Behavioural and Brain Sciences.*

(in press b) Hypnosis, nonvolitional responding and multiple personality: a social psychological perspective. In B. Maher and W. Maher (eds.), *Progress in experimental Personality Research*, 14, New York: Academic Press.

Spanos, N. P. and Barber, T. X. (1968) 'Hypnotic' experiences as inferred from subjective reports: auditory and visual hallucinations. *Journal of Experimental Research in Personality*, 3: 136–50.

(1974) Toward a convergence in hypnosis research. *American Psychologist*, 29: 500–11.

Spanos, N. P., Barber, T. X. and Lang, G. (1974) Cognition and self-control: cognitive control of painful sensory input. In H. London and R. E. Nisbett (eds.), *Thought and Feeling: Cognitive Alteration of Feeling States.* Chicago: Aldine.

Spanos, N. P. and Bertrand, L. D. (1985) EMG biofeedback, attained relaxation and hypnotic susceptibility: is there a relationship? *American Journal of Clinical Hypnosis*, 27: 219–25.

Spanos, N. P., Brett, P. J., Menary, E. P. and Cross, W. P. (in press) A measure of attitudes toward hypnosis: relationships with absorption and hypnotic susceptibility. *American Journal of Clinical Hypnosis*.

Spanos, N. P., Cobb, P. and Gorassini, D. (1985) Failing to resist hypnotic suggestions: a strategy for self-presenting as deeply hypnotized. *Psychiatry*, 48: 282–93.

Spanos, N. P., Cobb, P. and Gwynn, M. I. (1984) The Carleton University Responsiveness to Suggestion Scale: stability and reliability under conditions of individual administration. *Psychological Reports*, 54: 123–8.

Spanos, N. P., Cross, W. P. and De Groh, M. (1985) Measuring resistance to hypnosis and its relationship to hypnotic susceptibility. Unpublished manuscript, Carleton University, Ottawa.

Spanos, N. P., Cross, W. P., Menary, E. P., Brett, P. J. and de Groh, M. (1985) Attitudinal and imaginal ability predictors of social cognitive-skill training enhancements in hypnotic susceptibility. Unpublished manuscript, Carleton University, Ottawa.

Spanos, N. P., de Groh, M. and de Groot, H. P. (in press) Skill training for enhancing hypnotic susceptibility and word list amnesia. *British Journal of Experimental and Clinical Hypnosis*.

Spanos, N. P., de Groot, H. P., Tiller, D. K., Weekes, J. R. and Bertrand, L. D. (1985) Trance logic duality and hidden observer responding in hypnotic, imagination control, and simulating subjects: a social psychological analysis. *Journal of Abnormal Psychology*, 94: 611–23.

Spanos, N. P. and Gorassini, D. R. (1984) Structure of hypnotic test suggestions and attributions of responding involuntarily. *Journal of Personality and Social Psychology*, 46: 688–96.

Spanos, N. P., Gottlieb, J. and Rivers, S. M. (1980) The effects of short term meditation training on hypnotic responsivity. *Psychological Record*, 30: 343–8.

Spanos, N. P. Gwynn, M. I. and Stam, H. J. (1983) Instructional demands and rating of overt and hidden pain during hypnotic analgesia. *Journal of Abnormal Psychology*, 92: 479–88.

Spanos, N. P., Ham, M. W. and Barber, T. X. (1973) Suggested ('hypnotic') visual hallucinations: experimental and phenomenological data. *Journal of Abnormal Psychology*, 81: 96–106.

Spanos, N. P. and Hewitt, E. C. (1980) The hidden observer in hypnotic analgesia: discovery or experimental creation? *Journal of Personality and Social Psychology*, 39: 1201–14.

Spanos, N. P., Jones, B. and Malfara, A. (1982) Hypnotic deafness: now you hear it – now you still hear it. *Journal of Abnormal Psychology*, 91: 75–7.

Spanos, N. P., Kennedy, S. K. and Gwynn, M. I. (1984) The moderating effect of contextual variables on the relationship between hypnotic susceptibility and suggested analgesia. *Journal of Abnormal Psychology*, 93: 282–94.

Spanos, N. P. and McPeake, J. D. (1975a) Involvement in everyday imaginative activities, attitudes toward hypnosis, and hypnotic susceptibility. *Journal of Personality and Social Psychology*, 31: 594–8.

—— (1975b) The interaction of attitudes toward hypnosis and involvement in everyday imaginative activities on hypnotic suggestibility. *American Journal of Clinical Hypnosis*, 17: 247–52.

(1977) Cognitive strategies, goal-directed fantasy and response to suggestion in hypnotic subjects. *American Journal of Clinical Hypnosis*, 20: 114–23.

Spanos, N. P., McPeake, J. D. and Churchill, N. (1976) Relationships between imaginative ability variables and the Barber Suggestibility Scale. *American Journal of Clinical Hypnosis*, 19: 39–46.

Spanos, N. P. and Radtke, H. L. (1982) Hypnotic amnesia as a strategic enactment: a cognitive social-psychological perspective. *Research Communications in Psychology, Psychiatry and Behaviour*, 7: 215–31.

Spanos, N. P., Radtke, H. L. and Bertrand, L. D. (1984) Hypnotic amnesia as a strategic enactment: the successful breaching of hypnotic amnesia in high susceptible subjects. *Journal of Personality and Social Psychology*, 47: 1155–69.

Spanos, N. P., Radtke, H. L., Hodgins, D. C., Bertrand, L. D., Stam, H. J. and Dubreuil, D. L. (1983a) The Carleton University Responsiveness to Suggestions Scale: stability, reliability, and relationships with expectancies and hypnotic experiences. *Psychological Reports*, 53: 555–63.

Spanos, N. P., Radtke, H. L., Hodgins, D. C., Bertrand, L. D., Stam, H. L. and Moretti, P. (1983b). The Carleton University Responsiveness to Suggestion Scale: relationships with other measures of susceptibility, expectancies and absorption. *Psychological Reports*, 53: 723–34.

Spanos, N. P., Radtke, H. L., Hodgins, D. C., Bertrand, L. D. & Stam, H. J. (1983c) The Carleton University Responsiveness to Suggestion Scale: normative data and psychometric properties. *Psychological Reports*, 53: 523–35.

Spanos, N. P., Radtke-Bodorik, H. L., Ferguson, J. D. and Jones, B. (1979) The effects of hypnotic susceptibility, suggestions for analgesia and the utilization of cognitive strategies on the reduction of pain. *Journal of Abnormal Psychology*, 88: 282–92.

Spanos, N. P., Rivers, S. M. and Gottlieb, J. (1978) Hypnotic responsivity, meditation and laterality of eye movements. *Journal of Abnormal Psychology*, 87: 566–9.

Spanos, N. P. Rivers, S. M. and Ross, S. (1977) Experienced involuntariness and response to hypnotic suggestions. *Annals of the New York Academy of Sciences*, 296: 208–21.

Spanos, N. P., Robertson, L. A., Menary, E. P. and Brett, P. J. (in press) A component analysis of cognitive skill training for the enhancement of hypnotic susceptibility. *Journal of Abnormal Psychology*.

Spanos, N. P., Robertson, L. A., Menary, E. P., Brett, P. J. and Smith, J. (1985) Effects of repeated baseline testing on cognitive skill training induced increments in hypnotic susceptibility. Unpublished manuscript, Carleton University, Ottawa.

Spanos, N. P., Salas, J., Menary, E. P. and Brett, P. J. (1986) A comparison of overt and subjective responses to the Carleton University Responsiveness to Suggestion Scale and the Stanford Hypnotic Susceptibility Scale under conditions of group administration. *Psychological Reports*, 58, 847–856.

Spanos, N. P., Spillane, J. and McPeake, J. D. (1976) Cognitive strategies and response to suggestions in hypnotic and task-motivated subjects. *American Journal of Clinical Hypnosis*, 18: 252–62.

Spanos, N. P., Stam, H. J. and Brazil, K. (1981) The effects of suggestion and distraction on coping ideation and reported pain. *Journal of Mental Imagery*, 5: 75–89.

Spanos, N. P., Stam, H. J., Rivers, S. M. and Radtke, H. L. (1980). Meditation, expectation and performance on indices of nonanalytic attending. *International Journal of Clinical and Experimental Hypnosis*, 28: 244–51.

Spanos, N. P., Voorneveld, P. W. and Gwynn, M. I. (1984) The mediating effects of expectation on hypnotic and nonhypnotic pain reduction. Unpublished manuscript, Carleton University, Ottawa.

Spanos, N. P., Weekes, J. R. and de Groh, M. (1984) The 'involuntary' countering of suggested requests: a test of the ideomotor hypothesis. *British Journal of Experimental and Clinical Hypnosis*, 1: 3–11.

Springer, C. J., Sachs, L. B. and Morrow, J. E. (1977) Group methods of increasing hypnotic susceptibility. *International Journal of Clinical and Experimental Hypnosis*, 25: 184–91.

Starker, S. (1974) Effects of hypnotic induction upon visual imagery. *Journal of Nervous and Mental Disease*, 159: 433–7.

Sutcliffe, J. P., Perry, C. W. and Sheehan, P. W. (1970) The relation of some aspects of imagery and fantasy to hypnotizability. *Journal of Abnormal Psychology*, 76: 279–87.

Talone, J. M., Diamond, M. J. and Steadman, C. (1975) Modifying hypnotic performance by means of brief sensory experiences. *International Journal of Clinical and Experimental Hypnosis*, 25: 184–91.

Tart, C. T. (1970) Increases in hypnotizability resulting from a prolonged program for enhancing personal growth. *Journal of Abnormal Psychology*, 75: 260–6.

Tellegen, A. (1979) On measures and conceptions of hypnosis. *American Journal of Clinical Hypnosis*, 21: 219–36.

Tellegen, A. and Atkinson, G. (1976) Complexity and measurement of hypnotic susceptibility: a comment on Coe and Sarbin's alternative interpretation. *Journal of Personality and Social Psychology*, 33: 142–8.

Turk, D. C., Meichenbaum, D. and Genest, M. (1983) *Pain and Behavioural Medicine: a Cognitive Behavioural Perspective*, New York: Guildford.

Van Dyne, W. T. and Stava, L. J. (1981) Analysis of relationships among hypnotic susceptibility, personality type and vividness of mental imagery. *Psychological Reports*, 48: 23–6.

Wagman, R. and Stewart, C. G. (1974) Visual imagery and hypnotic susceptibility. *Perceptual and Motor Skills*, 38: 815–22.

Wagstaff, G. F. (1977) An experimental study of compliance and posthypnotic amnesia. *British Journal of Social and Clinical Psychology*, 16, 225–228.

Wagstaff, G. F. (1979) The problem of compliance in hypnosis: a social psychological viewpoint. *Bulletin of the British Society of Experimental and Clinical Hypnosis*, 2: 3–5.

(1981) *Hypnosis, Compliance and Belief*. New York: St Martin's Press.

(1983) A comment on McConkey's 'Challenging hypnotic effects: the impact of conflicting influences on response to hypnotic suggestion'. *British Journal of Experimental and Clinical Hypnosis*, 1: 11–15.

Wagstaff, G. F. and Ovenden, M. (1979) Hypnotic time distortion and free recall learning – an attempted replication. *Psychological Research*, 40: 291–8.

Weitzenhoffer, A. M. and Hilgard, E. R. (1959) *Stanford Hypnotic Susceptibility Scale: Forms A and B*. Palo Alto, Calif.: Consulting Psychologists Press.

(1962) *Stanford Hypnotic Susceptibility Scale: Form C*. Palo Alto, Calif.: Consulting Psychologists Press.

Wickramasekara, I. (1973) Effects of electromyographic feedback on hypnotic susceptibility: more preliminary data. *Journal of Abnormal Psychology*, 82: 74–7.

Yanser, R. J. and Johnson, H. J. (1981) Absorption and attitude toward hypnosis: a moderator analysis. *International Journal of Clinical and Experimental Hypnosis*, 29: 375–82.

HYPNOSIS AND SIGNAL DETECTION: AN INFORMATION-PROCESSING ACCOUNT

Peter L. N. Naish

The preceding chapters have shown that explanations of hypnosis are probably best sought in the mechanisms already well known to psychology. The last two accounts have used the processes familiar to social psychology but also referred to a cognitive element. In Chapter 6 Peter Naish returns to the cognitive theme, injecting more ideas from the psychology of perception. He pursues the Spanos line of taking note of subjects' descriptions of hypnotic experiences, and goes so far as to take such descriptions as a basis for his account of hypnotic behaviour.

Dr Naish works in the University of Oxford, Department of Experimental Psychology.

Much of this book has been concerned with showing that there is nothing very magical about hypnosis. Nor are people who have experienced a hypnotic induction made able to perform behaviour outside their normal repertoire. However, to watch the behaviour of a 'good' hypnotic subject can be an impressive experience. Orne (e.g. 1959) has suggested that, when all that is common to 'normal' behaviour has been stripped away from the hypnotic performance, there remains an essence of hypnosis – that which really has to be explained. There is not universal agreement that an underlying essence exists (see Wagstaff, Chapter 4, above), but in the absence of an 'essence' an explanation is still required. Even if it is accepted that everything a so-called hypnotized subject does could be done by a simulator, it is nevertheless pertinent to ask why the person should behave in this way. An explanation would serve to cut the circularity of definition referred to by Barber (e.g. 1969). He has complained that traditionally a person's behaviour has been explained as resulting from the hypnosis, yet the hypnotic condition is assumed to be present only because of the behaviour it is supposed to be explaining. If an independent explanation of the behaviour could be furnished, then it would effectively also be an explanation of hypnosis.

Hypnotic behaviour

It was stated above that the so-called hypnotized person can produce behaviour that, although not exceptional, nevertheless impresses. How can behaviour be unexceptional yet impressive? It must be because the subject's activities are unexpected; one does not normally expect a person to 'see' people who are not there, or to feel a non-existent fly on the face. Nor is it generally expected for a person to let a 'light' arm go floating up above the head, or to become 'unaware' of the existence of the number seven. Although we can all behave in this way if we wish, we generally seem to reserve such antics for the hypnotic situation. Why should this be so? A naive answer would be that the hypnosis caused the behaviour, but this will not do, for it is far from clear that hypnosis can actually *cause* anything. It was pointed out in Chapters 1 and 2 that 'magnetism' seemed to cause Mesmer's patients to have crises. In fact the crises were the clear results of the patients' expectations. Hypnosis, the modern counterpart of mesmerism, frequently employs a relaxation style of induction, and the result is that the recipients do absolutely nothing, except look relaxed. The reason why subjects sometimes go on to enact the more bizarre types of behaviour is simply because the hypnotist asks them to. It seems that the hypnotist's behaviour is more bizarre than the subjects'! There is, of course, method in the hypnotist's madness, for he or she needs to know whether the subject has become hypnotized (whatever that may mean). As hypnosis on its own leaves no mark, the success of the induction procedure has to be judged by requesting the subject to perform rather unlikely feats. A successful performance is taken to imply a successful induction.

Reasons for hypnotic behaviour

The above account seems, on the face of it, to describe a very illogical state of affairs. Modern theorists are in general agreement that a hypnotic induction cannot engender otherwise impossible behaviour. Nevetheless, having carried out such an induction, the researcher is likely to ask the subjects to do some of the very things that they could have done anyway, to determine their susceptibility to hypnosis. Since it is accepted that we could all 'pass the test' we should all register as maximally susceptible. In fact there is considerable variability between subjects, in the extent to which the critical behaviours are performed. Thus hypnotic susceptibility is not strictly speaking judged on *ability* to perform a certain task, but on whether or not the task *is* performed.

A possible reason for embarking upon improbable behaviour in the hypnosis situation is simply that the subject welcomes the excuse. This may well be the case in a clinical setting, when a patient is asked to discuss some personal and rather embarrassing topic. The patient would like to talk about the matter, but normally finds the embarrassment too great. Hypnosis offers the ideal opportunity to circumvent this difficulty, since the patient can in effect say to the therapist, 'You cannot blame me for mentioning such things, because you have hypnotized me and made me do it'. However, this kind of explanation cannot be applied convincingly to the sort of behaviour requested during susceptibility assessment. It is hard to believe that the average hypnosis subject always wanted to pretend that there was a fly tickling his or her face, but had hitherto been too embarrassed to do so.

Since the kind of task given to assess susceptibility is rather trivial, it becomes pertinent to ask why subjects sometimes do *not* carry out the required behaviour, rather than concentrating on the fact that they sometimes do. It is as if an unspoken agreement is established between experimenter and subjects. Because the subjects know that the responses are to serve as a measure of hypnosis, they will undertake not to perform the tasks unless hypnotized. The hypnotist does not normally phrase the test instructions as direct requests for the desired behaviour. Thus rather than saying, 'Please behave as if there is a fly on your face', the more subtle 'You can feel a fly on your face' is used. Such a statement may or may not elicit behaviour such as wrinkling the face, or brushing with the hand. The implication of the therapist's choice of words, together with the apparent experimenter – subject agreement, is that the subject will produce the behaviour only when he or she has the appropriate precipitating experience. In the example being used here, the subject will show signs of being irritated by a fly only if a tickling sensation is actually experienced.

Subjective data

The conclusion reached above is important, for the remainder of this chapter is argued upon the premise that outward hypnotic behaviour is a reflection of internal experience. If this is correct, then the behaviour should no longer be seen as bizarre – it is the precipitating experience that is inappropriate. Thus it is not strange that someone should brush away a troublesome fly, but it is odd that the irritation should be experienced in the absence of a real fly. The shift of interest from behaviour to personal experience is not an explanation of hypnosis; it merely changes the area that must be examined if an explanation is to be offered. Unfortunately, the shift is to an area which is even more difficult to investigate; for while overt behaviour can at least be witnessed by an experimenter, subjective experiences can only be guessed at, or gleaned from the subjects' own accounts. It has been pointed out (Naish 1985b) that this kind of subjective information is a risky source of data for an experimental psychologist. Subjective data are inevitably unverifiable in the full scientific sense, so an experimenter is forced to take the subject's word for what happened. Even when the soul of veracity, it is quite normal to find that a subject experiences difficulty in giving effective and accurate accounts of internal events. However, following a period in which psychologists strenuously rejected anything that smacked of subjectivity, many cognitive psychologists are now prepared to supplement objective data by asking their subjects to describe internal thoughts.

In the context of hypnosis, there are those who consider it to be more parsimonious to discount subjective reports. For example, Wagstaff (1981a) does not look to subjectively reported misperceptions as the true cause of 'hypnotic' behaviour. Rather, he considers subjects to produce the reponses in order to be compliant to the social pressures inherent in the hypnosis situation. Something of a difficulty for this explanation is that the putative drive to comply inspires very few subjects to carry out all the tests in a susceptibility assessment. It seems reasonable to ask why a subject should comply for some things but not others. Wagstaff addresses this issue in Chapter 4, above. The subjects themselves offer an attractive, although unverifiable, explanation for their non-uniformity of response. As has already been suggested, the behavioural reponses occur only following appropriate internal experiences. This author has often heard subjects complain with disappointment that whereas one suggestion gave very real sensations another just did not 'work'. It is not unprecedented that this sort of testimony should be taken more or less at face value. For example, Bowers (1976) states that, for the deeply hypnotized, events are experienced as happening to them. Even Wagstaff (1981b) accepts that the reports of some hypnotic subjects may have a genuine element, and in his chapter in this book he suggests that subjects may attempt to use cognitive strategies to generate the 'hypnotic' effects, before resorting to compliant behaviour.

Clearly hypnosis subjects might make claims about their experiences for a variety of reasons, and with varying degrees of accuracy. However, it does not seem impossible that, at least some of the time, these claims are a true reflection of the subjects' perceptions. That assumption is adopted in this chapter, so attention must now be turned to the question of how it can be possible for a person to have an experience in the absence of the usual precipitating stimuli.

Perception and misperception

To summarize the discussion so far, it has been suggested that, although subjective reports should be treated with caution, subjects' descriptions of their hypnotic experiences can be useful indicators of what is going on. These reports suggest that a hypnotic procedure is not a direct precursor to inappropriate behaviour, but that it can lead to perceptions that are not congruent with reality. It is the misperceiving that then gives rise to the apparently misplaced behaviour, although the behaviour would be appropriate, were the perception correct.

To those not familiar with the psychology of perception, it must seem obvious that our experiences of the world are veridical representations of our surroundings; if we see something it is because it is there, and moreover it is as it looks. However, any elementary textbook of perception will indicate that this is not strictly true, and it is easily demonstrated that our conscious

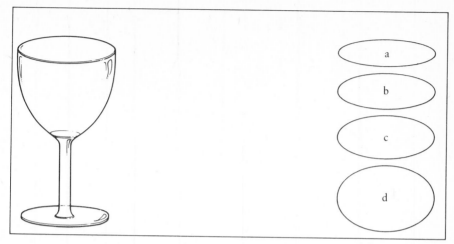

Figure 6.1 Which of the ellipses on the right would fit the top of the wineglass, as drawn on the left?

experiences are not dictated solely by the pattern of stimulation at the sense organs. Two examples will serve to illustrate this point. First, inspect Figure 6.1 and try to judge which of the four ellipses on the right has been used to represent the top of the wineglass on the left. People's judgements in this task differ, but most are agreed that the glass rim looks 'fatter' than ellipse (a) and probably more like (b) or even (c). In fact (a) is the correct answer. The broadening effect is a result of the drawing being interpreted as representing a three-dimensional object, with the elliptical top acting as a perspective view of what is in reality a circle. Our knowledge of the world changes the perception of the physical drawing on the paper, to seem more like what we know the real shape to be. This example has been given to demonstrate that what we perceive may not necessarily be an accurate representation of what is really there. However, it might be argued that in the case of the wineglass the misperception is actually a *better* representation of reality, since glasses do have circular rims. Moreover, as with other visual illusions, it is the picture itself that causes a wrong judgement to be made.

This is a far cry from the hypnotic situation, in which perceptions seem to become distorted in response to the spoken word. Nevertheless, it will also be demonstrated that perceptual changes can be brought about by a few words. Unless the reader has seen Figure 6.2 before, it is unlikely that he or she will be able to make much of it, other than a series of irregular blobs. If after a few moments' examination the figure still looks like nothing much, then use the two words 'Moo' and 'Milk' as clues, and look again. If still in doubt, then reference should be made to Figure 6.3. Once the appropriate way of perceiving this stimulus has been discovered, the picture becomes so clear that it seems almost to have been better drawn. Of course, it consists of the same blobs, and what has changed is the viewer's way of 'seeing' them.

The above example is a clear indication that our perceptions can be greatly

Figure 6.2   The effect of knowledge upon perception. Find the hidden object.

influenced by expectations, and that they are based upon, rather than determined by, the actual stimulus. However, the key words here are obviously
'based upon'; and, returning to the fly example, one is bound to ask what
underlying stimulation could be used as a basis for perceiving the irritation of
a non-existent fly. Although the examples given lend support to the claim that
a conscious perception might be based very loosely upon the initiating
stimulus, it has not been demonstrated that a perception could be conjured
from no stimulus at all. However, contemporary psychology does recognize a
mechanism by which such an event can take place.

Signal detection theory

Good acounts of this theory may be found in Swets, Tanner and Birdsall
(1961) or Green and Swets (1966). For present purposes a brief, qualitative
description will be presented.

It is clear that, for every unique sensation we are able to experience, there
must be a corresponding unique pattern of neural activity (see, for example,
Barlow 1985). It would seem to follow that the absence of a particular
sensation necessarily implies that there is no corresponding activity in the
appropriate cells. That deduction is incorrect, however, because neurons do
not remain dormant until information has to be signalled. In fact there is
always some neural activity, its intensity rising and falling randomly. This
haphazard 'babble in the brain' is rather appropriately referred to as 'noise'.

When the brain responds to a genuine event, the noise is supplemented with a 'signal', but the change is only quantitative. This means that there is no qualitative way of distinguishing between neural activity based upon real events and that resulting from noise. The difference is that signals usually give rise to more intense activity than when there is noise alone. Even signals incorporate the same element of randomness as noise, so that a real event may sometimes cause activity that is as weak as noise usually is. On the other hand, since noise is by definition variable, there will be some occasions when the random background activity becomes as intense as that usually associated with a signal.

The situation can be summarized in graphical form, as shown in Figure 6.4. One axis represents the range of levels of neural activity that might be found with noise alone or in the presence of a signal. The other axis shows the probability that a particular level of activity will occur. The most probable level of activity when there is no signal is $\bar{N}$, corresponding with the highest point on the 'noise' curve. This curve gets lower for activity that is either more or less than $\bar{N}$, indicating that it is less likely that these more extreme levels will be encountered. A similar picture exists for signal activity, with the most likely level being represented by $\bar{S}$. It was explained above that noise can sometimes be intense, and signals can occasionally be represented by low activity levels, to the extent that each can encroach into the other's usual domain. This is represented in the diagram by the overlap of the two curves. This situation poses a problem for our perceptual mechanisms. Although a rule such as 'strong activity = event; weak activity = nothing (only noise)' is likely to give the right answer quite often, the overlap implies that we must also inevitably make some mistakes. We seem to set a criterion point, as at C on the diagram. If the activity exceeds this value, then it is deemed to represent a signal; if it is less, then it is rejected as noise. However, it can be seen that the criterion line cuts across both curves, so that noise can sometimes be to the right of the line, and signal to the left. This means that noise will sometimes exceed the criterion and be accepted as a genuine signal (a false alarm), and a signal might on occasion cause activity falling below the criterion, to remain ignored (a miss). Unfortunately, these two kinds of error cannot be eliminated, although the chances of making one can be reduced by paying the cost of increasing the frequency of the other. If, for example, we wished to avoid responding to too many false alarms, the criterion could be moved well to the right. The region of the graph labelled 'false alarm' would then become very small. On the other hand, the area labelled 'miss' would have become relatively large, indicating that many real events would fail to initiate a response.

The processes described are taking place all the time, for all the events we are able to perceive, although the vetting procedure seems, in general, to precede the point at which a conscious perception is generated. Thus if neural activity exceeds the criterion for a particular event, then that event is perceived; if the criterion is not passed, then no perception results. Although we are largely unaware of these processes, we are at least able to exercise some

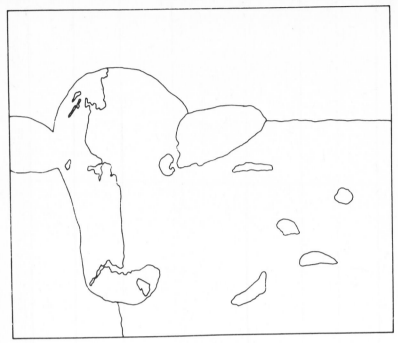

Figure 6.3   A clearer representation of Figure 6.2.

control over the criterion point. For example, an anxious mother is likely to set her criterion particularly low for the sound of the baby crying. On the graph this means moving C to the left, so that 'miss' becomes small, although 'false alarm' becomes large. As a result it is unlikely that the baby will ever cry without the mother noticing. On the other hand, the parent is likely often to put her head round the door, thinking that she heard something, only to find that all is peaceful.

There is one more parameter represented in Figure 6.4, which has not been mentioned. It is the distance between the peaks of the two curves, and is labelled 'discriminability'. Many of life's events lead to such intense neural activity that the overlap with the noise-only situation is very small. In such a situation the event is highly discriminable and there is little likelihood of suffering from a false alarm or a miss. Other events are not so easily discriminated from the background, so the corresponding graphical representations would show the two curves closer together and with more overlap. By way of example, we would be unlikely to experience difficulty in deciding whether a nearby canon had fired, but when waiting for pins to drop we might 'hear' some that were not there and miss others that were.

The foregoing account applies to perceptions of all types. The examples have been to do with hearing, and this, together with the use of the term 'noise' to describe random activity, might give the impression that signal detection theory applies only to listening for sounds. That is not the case, and the theory

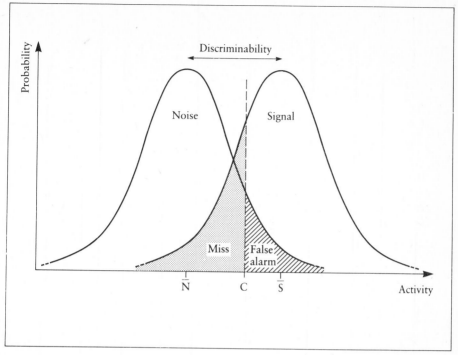

Figure 6.4 A graphical representation of the signal detection problem.

can even be applied to the situation in which the signal to be detected is one of our own memories.

The application of signal detection theory to hypnosis

From the above it can be seen that perceptual errors (misses or false alarms) must become quite frequent if the criterion is shifted to an extreme position. Depending upon the direction of movement, either noise will become accepted as if arising from a real signal, or signals will be rejected as if only noise. As an example of the first case, the acceptance of noise in a particular set of neurons might lead to the sensation that a fly was present on the face. In the alternative situation, ignoring the appropriate set of signals might enable a patient to tolerate the dentist's activities without discomfort. These two examples of possible misperceptions are typical of the kind of sensation (or lack of sensation) said to be brought about during hypnosis. It is suggested, therefore, that hypnotic experiences are mediated by an extreme shifting of the subject's perceptual criteria.

It seems irrefutable that a person would experience strange misperceptions if he or she made large shifts in perception criteria. However, the fact that such an assertion can be made does not prove that the process takes place. There is, after all, a world of difference between a person making the occasional perceptual error (as we all do) and a hypnosis subject who will claim to be having unusual experiences, persisting over a relatively extended period of time. Recalling the example of the anxious mother, it would be surprising indeed if she were to open the door, gaze at the peaceful baby and still believe that she could hear it crying. That, however, is just the sort of experience a hypnosis subject might claim to have. If we are going to accept such a claim as being a true reflection of internal experience, it is necessary to show how a perception so divorced from reality could become established in this way. This problem has two parts; there is a need first to explain the misperception, then to account for its persistence, in the face of all the contrary evidence.

As has been explained, our perceptual processes are, in principle, well able to generate quite gross misperceptions. Some might wish to argue that this ability is surely not generally encountered, but to be found only in certain of the mentally disturbed. That, however, appears not to be the case. An appreciable proportion of the population will admit to having had experiences of an hallucinatory nature (e.g. Bentall and Slade 1985), and it has been suggested that the experiencing of hallucinations lies on a continuum with normal mental states (e.g. Launay and Slade 1981). However, hypnotic experiences are not random and unbidden, but appear to be appropriate to the situation, usually developing in response to the hypnotist's suggestions. This implies an element of control over the situation, and, since the hypnotist can have no direct command over the subject's perceptual processes, it follows that the control must come from within. Control over what we perceive seems to be exercised by the application of expectation. The point has been made above that criterion shifting would engender misperceptions, but no explanation was given as to how the criteria might suddenly shift. An important determinant of criterion setting is expectation, and numerous experiments investigating signal detection parameters (e.g. Naish 1983) have shown that, as subjects are led to expect more events, so they respond to more, even to ones that are not there. In other words, a high expectation leads to a lowering of the criterion position, with a consequent increase in false alarms. Conversely, when an event is not expected the criterion is raised, so reducing the chances of making false alarms, but increasing the incidence of misses.

A clear indication of the complexity of perceptual processes has been given in this chapter, showing that higher-level knowledge can affect the way in which stimuli are perceived. Signal detection processes can impinge upon every level of this long road from sense organ to perception. Treisman (1964) points out that noise could arise not only at the input stage, but also in the judgement process. Clearly, where there is noise there must also be a need for criterion setting. In a complex hierarchy of analysis and decision-making, small shifts in criteria, brought about by expectancy changes, could lead to dramatic changes in the final interpretation of the incoming signal. Indeed, such a system would readily generate a perception, even in the absence of an incoming signal. Another feature of a system of this nature, with its capacity for control from above, is that once a perception has been found to be an adequate representation of the incoming stimuli, then subsequent information is incorporated into the overall picture in a way that will support the established interpretation. An example of such an effect has already been given in the wineglass illusion (Figure 6.1). The overall picture is interpreted as representing a familiar three-dimensional object. Having adopted this view, a lifetime's experience of perspective demands that the rim is perceived as being less elliptical than is really the case. The rim of the glass projects an image on the eye's retina of the same shape and size as ellipse (a), but expectations created by the picture require that the conscious perceptions of the two shapes differ.

The discussion so far has been intended to show not just that misperceptions are a possibility in principle, but that our perceptual systems in fact operate in a way that makes misperceiving relatively easy to trigger. The fact remains, however, that in everyday life we do not often find ourselves experiencing the kind of misperception reported by hypnosis subjects. The explanation for this fact has already been given implicitly, when reference was made to a perception being an adequate representation of the incoming stimuli. It is apparent that we do not make do with any old perceptual interpretation, of just part of the stimulus material. Instead, we endeavour to establish a perception that most effectively incorporates all the relevant facts to which we have access. This process involves reality testing, which is an essential activity if the environment is to be perceived correctly. Earlier it was suggested that a hypnotic subject's ability to maintain a false perception, in the face of conflicting evidence, was a problem still requiring an answer. The answer must be that the hypnotic subject simply does not take any account of information that would undermine the suggested perception. Moreover, many subjects would be able to discount any conflict that did develop between the contrived perception and some of the sensory information, because the mismatch would seem natural to those who expected hypnosis to do 'funny things'. Such circumstances would not prompt them to rethink their perceptions; for, as Gibbons (1982) has pointed out, within the legitimizing context of a 'trance' even the most bizarre sugggestions can be accepted with equanimity. In summary, it is suggested that hypnotic subjects are able to generate and maintain unusual experiences, by first shifting appropriate sets of perception criteria and then failing to engage in normal reality testing.

A hypnosis session as an exercise in misperceiving

To encapsulate the ideas developed so far, a typical hypnotic induction will be described in the perceptual terms used above.

The subject is seated in a comfortable chair, in a warm room. He is told to shut his eyes, to take some long breaths, then to start relaxing all his muscles. Different areas are specifically brought to the subject's attention for relaxation – first the feet, then the legs, the hands, the arms and so on. This treatment, it will be argued, has two effects. First, by shutting his eyes and directing his attention to internal stimuli, such as his breathing and whether the arms are 'floppy' enough, the subject goes some way towards cutting himself off from the kind of stimulation that would usually be monitored for reality testing. Second, this concentration upon internal stimuli, which in more normal situations pass unnoticed, encourages the subject to look inwards for his source of information about events. Meanwhile, the hypnotist continues to speak: 'You feel very relaxed and heavy.' Of course he does! The instructions have all been directed to that end. 'Your breathing has become slow and gentle.' Again, it is bound to have done, because a relaxed person needs less oxygen. However, these truisms help to establish the hypnotist as a reliable source of information for reality testing. The hypnotist then starts to make suggestions for experiences that will not automatically be present. 'So that you can become really relaxed, I want you to feel yourself lying on a warm beach. Notice all the sensations – the pressure of the beach under you, the warmth of the sun.' We can all imagine a pleasant beach scene, but a reasonably susceptible subject can go further than just imagining it. He does feel pressure under him (from the chair) and it is nice and warm, just as if the sun were shining on him. His sensations are more or less congruent with the scene, and he begins to organize his perceptions accordingly. 'You can hear the slow, montonous sound of the waves,' says the hypnotist. This of course would fit the scene, and the hypnotist has said that it will occur. Thus, with this expectation, the subject lowers the appropriate criteria and, sure enough, starts to 'hear' the sea.

It can be seen from the above example how a subject's normal way of perceiving may be subtly shifted to produce erroneous sensations. The principle is the same whether the subject is to be 'at the seaside', to have a 'fly' on his face, or to 'see' someone who is not there. These different experiences are not all equally divorced from reality. It was pointed out that some of the 'beach' sensations would already be reasonably approximated in the real environment. Other sensations have little foundation upon which to build. So it is not surprising that many subjects find some effects easy to generate, while other sensations are not established convincingly.

A commonly used indicator of hypnotic ability is the arm levitation test. If this is to be described in terms of criterion shifts it requires a rather more complicated sequence of events. As might be expected if the process is more complicated, there are many subjects who fail to pass this test, although they claim that their experiences of things like beaches and flies are very real. It is proposed that the processes leading to a raised arm are as follows. The hypnotist tells a subject that one of her arms is going to become light; she is to concentrate on it, paying particular attention to the fingers, where the sensation will begin. 'As the lightness starts to take effect,' the experimenter might say, 'you will feel small movements in your fingers. Soon these will become more noticeable, and you will have the sensation of the fingers and hand wanting to float up, as if there are balloons tied to your fingers. Concentrate on your fingers, notice the movement and try to visualize the balloons tugging upwards.' If and when clear movements become discernible, the hypnosit will suggest that the lightness is spreading into the whole arm, and that it will start to float up towards the ceiling.

What are the effects upon the subject of comments such as these? If the subject does as she is told, she will start by attending to the sensations in her fingers. Noise in the nerves that control the muscles is likely to cause very small movements in them. Paying unaccustomedly close attention to the fingers, the subject is likely to notice the slight movements and to interpret them as evidence that things are already becoming 'a bit different'. We know where our limbs and digits are, even without looking at them, because nerves lead from special receptors in the joints, which indicate position and movement. There are also receptors indicating what our muscles are doing. These are the receptors that, for example, allow us to suit our grip to either holding an egg or cracking a nut. It is proposed that an arm-raising hypnotic subject adjusts sensory criteria in such a way that position information remains highly salient, while signals relating to muscle tension are ignored. Eventually, as the subject monitors the sensation from the fingers, a slight upward twitch is noticed; by chance an upward-pulling muscle becomes triggered momentarily. The subject wanted to feel something of the sort, so the experience was quite rewarding. It is a well-established psychological principle that rewarded behaviour is more likely to be repeated. The application of the principle in this circumstance implies that the upward-lifting muscle fibre is likely to be activated again, perhaps along with others acting in the same direction. The more noticeable movement that this causes is even more rewarding, so the whole process escalates, to start first the fingers, then the hand and arm, moving towards the ceiling. The important aspect of this sequence of events is that the subject is aware of her arm's position but not of the muscle tension that establishes the position. Consequently, the subject will feel that her arm has floated up by itself.

It is hoped that enough has now been presented to show that hypnosis could plausibly be described as a changed way of perceiving. An outline has been given of the kind of process that could mediate the postulated perceptual shifts, and the examples have shown that these processes could indeed account for various well-known 'hypnotic' behaviours. However, to show that a process is in principle feasible is not the same thing as proving that it takes place. It is appropriate now to look for other evidence in support of this account.

Evidence in support of the model

A direct experimental test of the 'misperception model' of hypnosis is not easy to devise, as an example will show. Naish (1985c) reported the results of a test on a single subject: a test designed to assess the viability of this description of hypnosis. A major feature of this model is that subjects are presumed to experience 'hypnotic' perceptions as a result of making large criterion shifts. If a subject could be shown to make large changes of this sort, then the result would seem to offer clear support for the model. Following this reasoning, an experiment was designed that would show how a subject responded to suggestions of perceptual changes. So that the results would be suitable for the calculation of signal detection parameters, a very simple task was given to the subject. She had to listen to a long series of tone bursts, each about one-third of a second in duration, and at a frequency of 1kHz. These sounded like brief bleeps, at a pitch around two octaves above middle C. About 10 per cent of the time, and on a random basis, the bleep would be of a slightly shorter duration. Since the length changed by less than 17 per cent, these short tone bursts were not easily distinguished from the more frequently occurring longer bleeps. Nevertheless, it was the subject's task to indicate each time she noticed a short bleep. As was to be expected in these circumstances, she missed some of the short signal tones, and at other times thought that she had heard one when it had in fact been a long tone burst. From the proportions of these misses and false alarms it was possible to calculate what criterion position the subject was using for her internal dividing line between short and long bleeps. From what has been explained of signal detection theory, it will be appreciated that a bleep would sometimes give rise to a neural response on the 'wrong side' of the criterion. A good account of the way in which both criteria and discriminability measures may be calculated and expressed is given by Welford (1968).

The subject in this signal detection experiment had first been given a typical hypnotic induction, then was requested to listen to the tone bursts for ten minutes, indicating when she noticed a short signal, as explained above. Following this test period, the subject was told that her hearing would become very acute, so that the short tone bursts would stand out very clearly. She was then given a further 10 minutes' exposure to a similar set of stimuli. Again, the numbers of hits, misses and false alarms were recorded, and the subject's criterion position was calculated. It turned out that she had adopted a much more relaxed criterion, reflected in the fact that she missed far fewer short signals but 'heard' many more that were not there. In fact the subject remarked that she had not indicated all the occurrences of the short bursts she had noticed, since she could not believe that there were so many. This is a significant comment, because if accepted as accurate, it indicates that a subject can make adjustments to her way of perceiving, at a stage of analysis before a conscious perception is established. When the result of the analysis reaches a conscious level of awareness it seems real to the subject and, as in this case, may even be surprising to her. In a more normal situation this surprise could be expected to lead to some careful reality testing, since, as Treisman (1964) has indicated, in the course of daily activities it is necessary to keep the number of false perceptions to a minimum. In this hypnosis experiment the subject appears to have shifted her criterion in such a way that, on most occasions, the signal resulting from the short bleeps would be comfortably beyond the dividing line, giving the impression that the bleeps 'stood out clearly'. Obviously this move allowed more 'noise' through. Before the instructions for hearing improvement had been given, the subject's criterion position was, in numerical terms, more than 60 per cent higher (calculated as the change in the signal detection parameter beta). This original more cautious mode of listening was presumably closer to the style that would be adopted outside the hypnosis situation, when false perceptions could be an embarrassment.

This experiment also produced data that underline the fact that hypnosis is not able to unleash 'super powers'. It will be recalled that discriminability can be represented graphically as the degree of separation between the signal and noise curves (Figure 6.4). The instructions to the subject had been that her hearing would become more acute, making the short tone bursts more discriminable. If this had really been possible, it would have been equivalent to asking her to move the signal and noise curves further apart. In signal detection terminology this separation is expressed by the quantity d'. For the subject in this experiment, d' actually became 13 per cent smaller when her hearing was supposed to be improving. In other words, far from making the task easier, the instructions for sharper hearing had actually resulted in a marginally worse ability to distinguish between one sound and another.

At first examination the results of the above experiment seem to offer strong support for the model of hypnosis being presented here. The subject's inappropriate responses were a clear indication that she had shifted her perceptual criterion; she showed every sign of misperceiving, just as the theory would predict. The results certainly were in line with the experimental predictions, although before accepting them as any kind of proof, it would be better to repeat the experiment with more subjects. This would be to ensure that the findings on this occasion were not just a statistical fluke. However, even if replicated, results of this kind can never serve as strong proof that this signal detection description of hypnosis is correct; they can only be treated as being *consistent* with the theory. A medical analogy might make this distinction clearer. Checking for a fever serves only as a weak test for influenza; the absence of a fever may be taken to rule out 'flu', but the presence of a raised temperature is no more than consistent with having this infection. A case of influenza is not *proved* by the existence of a fever, since fevers may result from many other conditions.

Returning to the matter of hypnosis, the problem for the signal detection experiment is that criterion shifting is not uniquely linked to hypnosis, any more than fevers are a unique feature of influenza. As was explained earlier in this chapter, we all change our criteria, to suit the expectations of the moment. In the hypnosis experiment the subject would naturally expect to hear more signals, having been told that her hearing would be more acute. This changed expectation would normally lead to a lowering of the criterion, and sure enough the subject did indisputably relax her criterion. Consequently, all that can truly be said to have been proved is that a 'hypnotized' subject behaved in a 'normal' manner – not the object of the exercise! As the criterion-shifting picture of hypnosis remains unproven, it is necessary to look elsewhere for support for the theory.

Hypnosis and memory enhancement

Although hypnosis is quite widely used in therapeutic settings, the application most likely to catch the headlines in newspapers is for eyewitness memory enhancement. Typically the police have a witness to a crime, who has only a hazy recollection of certain key facts. Having failed to gain the information they require, the police call in a hypnotist to uncover the memories that everyone seems to assume must be lurking below the surface. What would the signal detection approach predict in this situation? The metaphor of sub-merged memories waiting to be exposed suggests a useful analogy for dealing with this question.

Readily available memories are like islands poking above the surface of a lake, while knowledge that cannot currently be recalled can be represented by submerged features. A person might be able to retrieve hitherto unrecalled information, by lowering the appropriate criteria. In terms of the analogy, this would be like starting to drain the lake, when some of the sunken islands would once more break through the surface. However, if the water level fell too far, submerged features that had never been islands would become uncovered. This, in terms of memory, would be equivalent to generating pseudo-memories – 'remembering' noise that never was a real event. Apart from this source of error, another possibility for erroneous recall must be expected in the hypnotic situation. If a subject tends to rely upon the hypnotist as a foundation for reality testing, then any carelessly phrased questions by the hypnotist may be taken up by the witness, as if his or her own thoughts, and regurgitated in the belief that they were personal memories.

The above picture describes the reality very well. Some accounts, unfortunately often anecdotal, have suggested that hypnosis can occasionally facilitate witness recall (see, for example, DePiano and Salzberg 1981), but a growing body of reasearch is providing evidence that 'super memory' is yet another example of a super ability that hypnosis is unable to promote. Warnings of the danger of confabulation have been given for some time (e.g. Orne 1979). Also the specific risk that the questioner may, by the use of leading questions, unwittingly provide the witness with cues has frequently been highlighted (e.g. Putnam 1979, Zelig and Beidleman 1981). These warnings are not always heeded, and Karlin (1983) reports two cases in the United States in which miscarriages of justice were only just averted. In each example a victim of a violent crime, who had no real memory of her assialant, was convinced during unskilled hypnotic questioning that she remembered the attacker's face. In both cases innocent men were arrested on the strength of the victim's description. Fortunately, neither was finally found guilty. Karlin (1983) concludes that hypnosis can lead to a modest increase in the quantity of accurate information, but also to a larger increase in the quantity of inaccurate material produced. Interetingly, Karlin suggests that this may be due to a relaxation of the subject's criteria for what he or she will identify as a memory. Since witnesses to crimes cannot be produced to order, for a carefully controlled study of the efficacy of hypnotic memory enhancement much research has used laboratory-based memory experiments. Here again it would seem that the resuls fit well within the signal detection perspective. For example, Wagstaff, Traverse and Milner (1982) reported that hypnotized subjects produced more false alarms.

Many of the reports quoted in this section use signal detection terms, such as 'false alarm' and 'criteria'. Klatzky and Erdelyi (1985) describe hypnotic memory enhancement as a signal detection problem. However, none of these authors goes on to suggest that hypnosis itself is a phenomenon brought about by unusual signal detection strategies. Clearly the results of these studies do lend support to this view of hypnosis, but, as with the experiment described earlier, the proof is still lacking. The findings of the memory research quoted here show only that hypnotized witnesses relax their criteria, not that the witnesses can be said to be hypnotized *because* they have started to make large criterion shifts. Nevertheless, it is possible to view this research, not just as added support for the hypothesis, but as slightly better support than that given by the 'short bleep' experiment. In the latter, the hypnotized subject was shown only to do what most people do anyway, without any hypnosis; she relaxed her criteria in response to raised expectations. In the memory studies the underlying theme seems to be that hypnotized subjects relax their criteria more than the unhypnotized. If true, the result would be a strong indication that hypnosis has something specifically to do with criterion shifting.

There are researchers (e.g. Barber, Spanos and Chaves 1974) who would claim that any increased tendency to relax criteria during 'hypnotic' questioning is due only to the increased motivation of the witness to produce a 'memory'. This theoretical stance would predict that any means of making the witness highly motivated to recall something would produce similar results. Such a claim must almost certainly be true, since, as has repeatedly been stressed, hypnosis does not produce any unique abilities. However, the strongest conclusion that may reasonably be drawn from such an observation is that hypnosis is still not proved to be a condition of unusual perceiving. To abandon the concept of hypnosis itself merely because similar effects seem to be achieved by other means is believed by this author to be carrying parsimony unnecessarily far.

Other examples of a hypnosis/signal detection link

Memory is not the only area in which the effects of hypnosis can be expressed in signal detection terms. The weakness (from the point of view of proving a signal detection link) in the findings discussed so far is that the criterion effects have been demonstrated only in 'hypnotized' subjects. As has already been pointed out, this kind of association between hypnosis and relaxed criteria does not show what the relationship is between the two. Some studies not concerned with memory have produced results that offer rather stronger support for the signal detection approach. These experiments lend better support because they are predictive in nature. They seek to demonstrate that a subject's responsiveness to hypnosis could be predicted from his or her behaviour outside the hypnosis situation. It is well known that people differ in their susceptibility to hypnosis. If 'being hypnotized' means adopting a particular perceptual style, then presumably the susceptible subjects must more easily or more willingly change their ways of perceiving. Furthermore, if a subject can slip into a diffeent perceiving style easily, it is to be expected that his or her everyday non-hypnotic perceptual strategies will shown signs of that style. This link between non-hypnotic style and hypnotic susceptibility contains a number of 'ifs', but an experiment demonstrating a correlation between style and susceptibility would imply that the postulated link might be real.

Sigman, Phillips and Clifford (1985) described an experiment in which non-hypnotized subjects attempted to report pairs of simultaneously spoken words. Those subjects who, in a separate test, had been rated as more susceptible to hypnosis were able to report more of the words. Naish (1985a) has explained the results in signal detection terms. To recognize two words spoken simultaneously and in the same voice (they had been tape-recorded) is clearly difficult. It is suggested that, to make a response, the subject has to reach a conclusion on the basis of fewer auditory cues than would normally be available during speech perception. Making a positive decision, with less than the normal amount of corroborative evidence, requires the adoption of a lower criterion. Thus these results can be interpreted as showing that, outside hypnosis, the more susceptible subjects take up a less stringent perceptual criterion position than others who are not so susceptible to hypnosis.

Farthing, Brown and Venturino (1982) have demonstrated a similar correlation between susceptibility and criterion setting, in a visual signal detection experiment. Subjects were required to detect a dim flash of light, against a brighter background. It was found that those scoring higher on a hypnotic susceptibility scale adopted a more relaxed criterion. That is, although not 'hypnotized' at the time, the subjects who would have been more susceptible to hypnosis were more likely to say that they had seen the light, even on occasions when it was not there. The researchers pointed out that one explanation for this behaviour was that these more hypnotizable subjects actually experienced the (non-existent) signal, like an hallucination. This reference to hallucinations is interesting, in the light of a report from Bentall and Slade (1985). These workers also used a signal detection study, the task in this case being to detect the presence of a quietly spoken word, within a burst of louder noise. It was found that those subjects who adopted a lower criterion were more likely to report having hallucinatory experiences in everyday life. This result fits quite well within the framework being proposed. If a subject is adept at entering into 'hypnotic' experiences, because of a propensity to adopt relaxed perceptual criteria, then it is likely that the relaxation tendency would also lead to misperception outside the hypnosis situation. Such misperceptions would be classed as hallucinations.

An important aspect of this description of hypnotic perceiving is that the effects are all brought about by criterion shifts, not by changes in the signal or noise levels. Referring back to Figure 6.4, the curves are not presumed to move nearer together, or further apart, to change the discriminability dimension. A study by Sheehan, Smith and Forrest (1982) appears to undermine this position. Theirs was an investigation into possible eyesight enhancement. Two groups of short-sighted subjects were used: the experimental group, who spent some time listening to suggestions that their vision would improve; and, for comparison purposes, a control group, who merely listened to music for the same length of time. Each subject's eyesight was tested before and after the treatment. Whereas the members of the two groups began with comparable disabilities, after treatment the suggestion group seemed to have done better than the music group. The difference was reported to be on the real dimension of visual acuity, with no significant shift in criterion level. Taken at face value, these results seem to imply that hypnosis can, after all, produce a 'super ability', since being able to see better must be considered 'super' for a myopic person. However, there are grounds for rejecting this interpretation of the results. Whatever the nature of the changes manifested by the subjects, they seem not to be attributable to hypnosis. The subjects were tested with a scale usually taken to be a measure of hypnotic responsiveness, but their scores on this test were not found to correlate with the degree of improvement in eyesight. Had the eyesight change been initiated by a hypnotic mechanism, it would have been expected that the more susceptible subjects would have shown the greater improvement. Wagstaff (1983) has highlighted a further reason for interpreting these results with caution. He points out that the Sheehan, Smith and Forrest (1982) data reveal the difference between the suggestion and the music groups of subjects to have been brought about largely by the deterioration in eyesight of the music group, rather than the improvement of the suggestion group. Thus, if any conclusion is to be drawn from the investigation, it is that listening to music is bad for the eyes! The results of this study are not considered to represent a serious challenge to the signal detection approach.

The results of studies cited so far, seeming to show a link between hypnotizability and criterion shifting behaviour, have one thing in common; in each case the more hypnotizable subjects appear to adopt a more relaxed criterion position. This result is consistent with the hypothesis presented in this chapter, but it would also be consistent with the claim that the hypnotically susceptible have a disposition that is permanently acquiescent. If this were the case, such people would indeed be more likely to say, 'Yes I saw it', or 'Yes, I heard it', in signal detection tasks. In so doing they would generate more false alarms and display a more relaxed criterion position than those less disposed to acquiesce. This suggestion is not entirely far fetched, since in one study (Graham and Green 1981) hypnotically susceptible people were shown to be more willing to give to a charity; this could be construed as acquiescent behaviour. This alternative description of the signal detection results is made possible because the different experimental tasks all encouraged the subjects to make positive decisions. A subject responding to such encouragement would automatically demonstrate a lowered criterion position. The results obtained clearly showed that certain subjects adopted a more relaxed criterion, but it is not clear whether that position was adopted because the experiments invited it, or whether it represented a relatively permanent disposition in acquiescent subjects. The criterion-shifting hypothesis requires the former to be the case, but to support this position and to clarify the issue it is necessary to demonstrate that the hypnotically susceptible do shift their criteria, rather than keeping them permanently relaxed. Naish (1983) reported an experiment that addressed this issue.

Criterion shifting and hypnotic susceptibility

The Naish (1983) experiment was in two parts. In the first, a group of subjects participated in an auditory signal detection experiment, very much like that described in the section above, headed 'Evidence in support of the model'. The subjects spent thirty minutes listening for short tone bursts, the time being divided into three ten-minute periods. In the first and last of these periods 10 per cent of the bleeps were short, while the middle third contained 30 per cent of short signals. The subjects were informed what proportion to expect at the start of each ten-minute section. As has been pointed out, people relax their criteria when an event is more likely. Consequently, the subjects in this experiment could be relied upon to lower their criteria for short bleeps during the middle period, when more signals were expected. They would raise them again in the final section, when warned that the signal likelihood had again fallen to 10 per cent. Although it is normal to move the criterion position in such circumstance, the extent of the shift is not the same for all people. Therefore the magnitude of the criterion change was calculated for each individual, using his or her false-alarm and miss rates in the three sections.

Twenty-four hours after the signal detection test the subjects undertook the second part of the experiment. This consisted of a group hypnotic induction procedure, followed by the administration of a group susceptibility test. Naturally, the scores obtained from the test revealed that some subjects were considerably more susceptible than others. If, as has been suggested in this chapter, hypnotic experiences are set in motion by rather extreme shifting of perceptual criteria, then it would follow that the more susceptible subjects employed larger criterion movements during the hypnosis. It might also be expected that those who made large shifts in criteria during this phase of the experiment would also have tended to do so in the signal detection part. In other words, it can be predicted on the basis of the present hypothesis that those subjects who changed their criteria by large amounts in the first part of the experiment would obtain higher susceptibility scores in the second. This predicted correlation between the two scores was indeed obtained, with a numerical value of 0.4 and a probability of occurring by chance of less than 1 per cent. For those unfamiliar with statistical methods, this latter figure implies that there can be reasonable certainty in claiming a link between subjects' behaviours when detecting signals and their hypnotic susceptibility. The value of 0.4 is a measure of the strength of this link. If it were possible to predict precisely how susceptible a person would prove to be solely upon the basis of his or her criterion-shifting score, then the correlation would have been 1.0. On the other hand, if there were no connection between the two types of behaviour, then the correlation would have had a value of zero. The obtained value of 0.4 might therefore be described as 'reasonable but modest'.

The conclusion to be drawn from these results is that those who are more hypnotically susceptible do not just have a permanent tendency to set their criteria low. Rather, they have a greater tendency to move their criteria, as the theory would require. However, since the correlation is less than unity, other factors are clearly involved. In fact plausible explanations for the modest extent of the correlation are not difficult to find, and the figure of 0.4 is not seen as embarrassingly low for the theory. For example, the claimed link between perceptual style and hypnotic susceptibility would lead only to the prediction that large criterion movers *could* have hypnotic experiences. Hypnosis is a voluntary exercise, so people are not obliged to fulfil their potential. In this experiment, many subjects were experiencing hypnosis for the first time, and a number may have been too apprehensive to 'let go' sufficiently to demonstrate the level of susceptibility their criterion-moving behaviour would have allowed. On the other hand, as Wagstaff (1985) has suggested, extreme criterion shifting may tend to be limited to the hypnosis situation. If this were the case, some of the more susceptible subjects need not have 'shown their cards', by making large criterion changes when listening to tone bursts. In summary, the rationale for this experiment was that those with the necessary perceptual style to be susceptible to hypnosis would be likely to show evidence of that style, at least to some extent, outside the hypnosis situation. The correlation that was found, between extent of criterion movement and degree of susceptibility, lends strong support to the claim that the tendency to make large criterion shifts *is* the style of perception required of a 'good' hypnotic subject.

This experiment examined criterion *change*, rather than simply the positions of criteria, and made comparisons between behaviours inside and outside the hypnosis situation. Consequently, it was a particularly appropriate means of testing the criterion-shifting model of hypnosis. A similar technique has since been used by Sigman, Phillips and Clifford (1985), who attempted a partial replication of the above experiment. They also found that the subjects making larger criterion shifts scored higher on a susceptibility scale. A relatively small number of subjects was used in this study, and the effect was not shown to be statistically significant. Nevertheless, the results clearly represent further support for the model. However, in spite of the encouraging nature of these results, it is necessary to conclude this section with a word of warning. The theory proposed claims that hypnotic behaviours are actually brought about by the use of certain perceptual strategies. All that these experiments have shown is that the behaviours and the strategies tend to be exhibited by the same people. This is strong circumstantial evidence, but it does not constitute proof of the theory, since a correlation cannot prove causality.

Summary

An attempt has been made in this chapter to show that the term 'hypnosis' applies to a natural behavioural style, brought about by the unusual deployment of very ordinary perceptual mechanisms. Thus, apart from the changed way of using the perceptual processes, the whole hypnotic event is unremarkable. The behaviour only seems unnatural, because it would not normally be considered appropriate for the circumstances. It is appropriate for the occasion, as the subject perceives it.

The misperceiving, it is suggested, is established by the subject reducing the amount of attention devoted to sources of information that would contradict the desired percept, whilst paying close attention to any confirmatory stimuli. This bias is presumed to be facilitated by making perceptual criterion shifts.

The model of hypnosis being presented here has been shown to give a good account of typical 'hypnotic' behaviour – in particular, explaining the various examples of criterion shifting, in memory and perception. Moreover, viewing the processes of hypnosis in the way that is being advocated establishes a mechanism by which other descriptions of hypnosis may be explained. For example, Sarbin and Coe (1972) and Spanos and Barber (1974) see hypnotized subjects as becoming involved in, and believing in, suggested imaginings. In the terms of this chapter, to become involved in imaginings is to adopt a perceptual style that will make them seem real. Having achieved this, a subject will naturally go on to believe in what appear to be veridical experiences. A compliance perspective (e.g. Wagstaff, 1981a) can also be accommodated within the signal detection framework. A central component of signal detection theory is that criterion setting is influenced by the costs and benefits associated with producing inappropriate and appropriate responses. A compliant subject, in a 'hypnotic' situation, will perceive the production of suggested experiences as being very desirable, whereas not to produce the effects would be seen as an unfortunate failure. Such an extreme view of the costs and benefits of the situation would cause the subject to adopt a similarly extreme criterion position. This in turn would lead to the actual experiencing of the desired effect, probably even to the surprise of the subject. 'Hypnotic' experiences would occur only for those compliant subjects who could also make sufficiently large criterion shifts.

To conceptualize hypnosis in this way forms a bridge between the 'state' and 'non-state' views of the phenomenon. It has been stressed that the basic mental processes in which a 'hypnotized' subject engages are all perfectly normal, and that no unique physiological condition is to be expected. This is exactly what any non-state theorist would maintain. However, it is also suggested that the subject employs his or her usual mental processes in a rather unusual manner, and that a distinct shift occurs in the way the world is perceived. To suggest that there is such a transition does not sound too far removed from the claim that there is a change of state when a person is hypnotized.

The examples given indicate that the approach to hypnosis presented in this chapter has wide applicability, not only as an explanation of 'hypnotic' phenomena, but also by serving as a common denominator to alternative models. It suggests concrete processes around which other approaches may be conceptualized, with the advantage that the proposed mechanisms are all familiar to experimental psychologists. The all-embracing nature of this theory might be taken by some to reflect lack of precision in its formulation; but

Wagstaff (1985) has suggested that, among current models of hypnosis, this one may prove to have a useful unifying role.

References

Barber, T. X. (1969) *Hypnosis: A Scientific Approach*. New York: Van Nostrand Reinhold.

Barber, T. X., Spanos, N. P. and Chaves, J. F. (1974) *Hypnosis, Imagination and Human Potentialities*. New York and Oxford: Pergamon.

Barlow, H. B. (1985) The role of single neurons in the psychology of perception. *Quarterly Journal of Experimental Psychology*, 37A: 121–45.

Bentall, R. P. and Slade, P. D. (1985) Reality testing and auditory hallucinations: a signal detection analysis. *British Journal of Clinical Psychology*, 24: 159–69.

Bowers, K. S. (1976) *Hypnosis for the Seriously Curious*. Monterey, Calif.: Brooks/Cole.

DePiano, F. A. and Salzberg, H. C. (1981) Hypnosis as an aid to recall of meaningful information presented under three types of arousal. *International Journal of Clinical and Experimental Hypnosis*, 29: 383–400.

Farthing, G. W., Brown, S. W. and Venturino, M. (1982) Effects of hypnotizability and mental imagery on signal detection sensitivity and response bias. *International Journal of Clinical and Experimental Hypnosis*, 30: 289–305.

Gibbons, D. E. (1982) Hypnosis as a trance state: the future of a shared delusion. *Bulletin of the British Society of Experimental and Clinical Hypnosis*, 5: 1–4.

Graham, K. R. and Greene, L. D. (1981) Hypnotic susceptibility related to an independent measure of compliance – alumni annual giving: a brief communication. *International Journal of Clinical and Experimental Hypnosis*, 29: 351–4.

Green, D. M. and Swets, J. A. (1966) *Signal Detection Theory and Psychophysics*. New York: Wiley.

Karlin, R. A. (1983) Forensic hypnosis – two case reports. *International Journal of Clinical and Experimental Hypnosis*, 31: 227–34.

Klatzky, R. L. and Erdelyi, M. H. (1985) The response criterion problem in tests of hypnosis and memory. *International Journal of Clinical and Experimental Hypnosis*, 33: 246–57.

Launay, G. and Slade, P. D. (1981) The measurement of hallucinatory predisposition in male and female prisoners. *Personality and Individual Differences*, 2: 221–34.

Naish, P. L. N. (1983) Hypnosis: a signal detection approach. Paper given at January meeting of Experimental Psychology Society, University of London.

(1985a) A comment on Sigman, Phillips and Clifford's 'Attentional concomitants of hypnotic susceptibility'. *British Journal of Experimental and Clinical Hypnosis*, 2: 84–6.

(1985b) The 'trance' described in signal detection terms. *British Journal of Experimental and Clinical Hypnosis*, 2: 133–77.

(1985c) Is a signal detection account of hypnosis supportable? *British Journal of Experimental and Clinical Hypnosis*, 2: 147–50.

Orne, M. T. (1959) Hypnosis: artifact and essence. *Journal of Abnormal Psychology*, 58: 277–99.

(1979) The use and misuse of hypnosis in court. *International Journal of Clinical and Experimental Hypnosis*, 27: 311–39.

Putnam, W. H. (1979) Hypnosis and distortions in eyewitness memory. *International Journal of Clinical and Experimental Hypnosis*, 27: 437–48.

Sarbin, T. R. and Coe, W. C. (1972) *Hypnosis: A Social Psychological Analysis of Influence Communication*. New York: Holt, Rinehart & Winston.

Sheehan, E. P., Smith, H. V. and Forrest, D. W. (1982) A signal detection study of the effects of suggested improvement on the monocular visual acuity of myopes. *International Journal of Clinical and Experimental Hypnosis*, 30: 138–46.

Sigman, A., Phillips, K. C. and Clifford, B. (1985) Attentional concomitants of hypnotic susceptibility. *British Journal of Experimental and Clinical Hypnosis*, 2: 69–75.

Spanos, N. P. and Barber, T. X. (1974) Toward a convergence in hypnosis research. *American Psychologist*, 29: 500–11.

Swets, J. A., Tanner, W. P. and Birdsall, T. G. (1961) Decision processes in perception. *Psychological Review*, 68: 301–40.

Treisman, M. (1964) The effect of one stimulus on the threshold for another: an application of signal detectability theory. *British Journal of Statistical Psychology*, 17: 15–35.

Wagstaff, G. F. (1981a) *Hypnosis, Compliance and Belief*. Brighton: Harvester.

    (1981b) Source amnesia and trance logic: artifacts in the essence of hypnosis? *Bulletin of the British Society of Experimental and Clinical Hypnosis*, 4: 3–5.

    (1983) Suggested improvement of visual acuity: a statistical reevaluation. *International Journal of Clinical and Experimental Hypnosis*, 31: 239–40.

    (1985) A comment on 'Attentional concomitants of hypnotic susceptibility' by Sigman, Phillips and Clifford. *British Journal of Experimental and Clinical Hypnosis*, 2: 76–80.

Wagstaff, G. F., Traverse, J. and Milner, S. (1982) Hypnosis and eyewitness memory – two experimental analogues. *IRCS Medical Science*, 10: 894–5.

Welford, A. T. (1968) *Fundamentals of Skill*. London: Methuen.

Zelig, M. and Beidleman, W. B. (1981) The investigative use of hypnosis: a word of caution. *International Journal of Clinical and Experimental Hypnosis*, 29: 401–12.

AN INDIVIDUAL DIFFERENCES ACCOUNT OF HYPNOSIS

Peter W. Sheehan

In the previous chapter Peter Naish tended to focus upon the differences between 'good' and 'poor' hypnotic subjects, accounting for the difference by relating it to subjects' abilities to deploy just one cognitive skill. The work of Peter Sheehan suggests that this may be an oversimplification. In the next chapter he presents evidence showing that simply to divide people into the susceptible and non-susceptible is to mask interesting differences within the groups. He has found different types of responding in different 'good' subjects, and suggests that they must be employing more than one cognitive strategy.

Professor Sheehan is based in the Psychology Department of the University of Queensland, Australia. He and his collaborators have written a number of influential books and papers on hypnosis.

However one chooses to define hypnosis there is little argument that strong individual differences exist in people's responsiveness to hypnotic test suggestions (Hilgard 1965). Standardized instruments of assessment, such as the Stanford Hypnotic Susceptibility Scales (Forms A, B and C) and the Harvard Group Scale of Hypnotic Susceptibility (Forms A and B), typically present subjects with a variety of graded tasks for them to perform. These tasks range from relatively easy tests such as eye closure, hand lowering and arm levitation through to more difficult tests such as challenge, hallucinations and post-hypnotic suggestions. The data tell us that the scores across these tasks are distributed in regular fashion (Hilgard 1978–9; see also Hilgard *et al.* 1961); relatively few people pass only the simplest of hypnotic tasks (e.g. eye closure), and only few people can perform successfully on tasks as difficult as post-hypnotic suggestions. The different tasks appear to tap varying internal processes. Performance on easy items tends to be explained, for example, in terms of processes such as ideomotor involvement, while performance on the more difficult items appeals to processes such as cognitive-delusory thinking where the person who is hypnotized is said to respond with cognitive distortion as judged by departure from the world of reality. It is arguable whether these different kinds of items reflect related facets of a general factor (Curran and Gibson 1974), but the data they yield form the basis for acknowledging that profound differences clearly exist in people's responsiveness to standard hypnotic suggestions. These differences in response are generally regarded as reflecting essential variation in the ability or skills required to perform given tasks successfully. The term 'hypnotizability' expresses the trait characteristics, or aptitude skills, of individuals that signify their ability to respond successfully to the series of suggested events. Higher levels of trait present are judged to be evident from response on the more difficult items (Hilgard 1965). It is typically assumed, for example, that someone who passes post-hypnotic amnesia suggestions, or suggestions to see an hallucinated object that does not really exist, is manifesting considerable evidence of a marked degree of susceptibility to hypnosis. The attention focussed in the literature on standardized instruments for assessing this trait emphasizes the degree to which individuals of different levels of hypnotizability will vary in their responsiveness across tasks that are graded in difficulty. More recently, however – especially with the movement to develop more phenomenologically valid modes of measuring hypnotic experience (e.g. Shor 1979, Sheehan and McConkey 1982) – there has been a subtle shift in the literature to focus on individual differences among hypnotic subjects themselves in the pattern or style of their responsiveness on tasks that are much more narrowly defined. Particular attention is being paid in this instance to the fine-grained variation in responsiveness to suggestions that exists among subjects who are deeply susceptible to hypnosis. Not all people who hallucinate do so in the same way; not all who are amnesic process the same amnesia suggestions consistently.

The pattern in the variation that results from response to the same hypnotic communications challenges us to search afresh for the processes that best explain the richness of hypnotic experience. Strong intra-group variations in susceptible subjects' responsiveness clearly exist, and this conveys important implications about hypnotic processes. This chapter focusses on such individual differences. The reasons why one very susceptible subject processes a suggestion differently from another who is equally susceptible tells us something important about the nature of hypnotic experience itself. Before looking closely at hypnotic experience in this way, however, we need to examine first the assumptions of a 'hypnotizability' account of hypnotic phenomena to see how well it explains the data.

The relevance of trait

Trait accounts typically argue for internally oriented, structured mechanisms to explain personality functioning. Viewed in this way, hypnotizability is a characteristic of the person that can be expected to create enduring effects observable across a variety of situations in which that trait is relevant. Stability of performance should be evident across different test scales, for example. If the hypnotized person who is susceptible performs well at one time on a particular selection of tasks, then that person can be expected also to perform well at another time on a different sample of (not too dissimilar) tasks. The consistency is not absolute, however. One could not expect that performance will be the same no matter what tasks are used or what situations exist in which the hypnotized person is asked to perform. Rather, hypnotizability viewed as trait argues that consistency in responsiveness is relative. If, for instance, hypnotized individuals A and B perform on the Stanford Hypnotic Susceptibility Scale, Form C, and individual A is judged to be more hypnotizable than individual B, then that ranking should be preserved when the same individuals perform on an independent scale, say, the Stanford Profile Scale of Hypnotic Susceptibility. The trait of hypnotizability that determined A doing better than B in the first situation should produce the same relative ranking when the two individuals perform in the second situation. The specific tasks that appear on the profile scale, however, may influence both A and B in their own right. Task difficulty is much greater on the Profile Scale than the SHSS:C and subjects A and B may be affected quite differently by its peculiar cognitive delusory items.

This issue of the relative consistency of hypnotic performance is one that is assumed by the trait position but rarely formally stipulated by hypnotizability theorists (e.g. Hilgard 1965, Bowers 1976) who espouse the importance of trait. The issue emerges most contentiously in the literature in the debate about whether or not hypnotic responsiveness can be modified. The modifiability debate analyses specifically the impact of special situations in which hypnotizable individuals are placed. The position that hypnotic responsiveness is modifiable (see Diamond 1977) is obviously correct in its assumption that hypnosis does not reflect a durable trait in any absolute sense. On the other hand, few theorists in the field would wish to make the claim that responsiveness to hypnosis can be modified to the point where someone who had no previous ability to pass hypnotic suggestions will change to become a person who is highly responsive to hypnosis and passes with ease suggestions for hallucination, post-hypnotic response and amnesia. Argument is more about the relative consistency of hypnotic test scores. Data suggest that final scores on hypnotic tests correlate positively with original scores, and this supports a trait account. However, levels of hypnotic response can also be altered to some degree by reinforcing the impact of situational influences on the susceptible person's performance. Evidence indicates, for example, that conditions of sensory deprivation (Sanders and Reyher 1969) and drug-induced alterations in cognition and thinking (Levine and Ludwig 1965; see also Bowers 1976) have an effect and can modify the level of hypnotic response. The special training packages described by Spanos (Chapter 5, above) seem also able to produce reasonably large susceptibility changes.

The occurrence of individual differences in responsiveness to hypnotic suggestions is sufficiently regular, and the demonstration of hypnotic effects across different test scales is sufficiently reliable, for us comfortably to conclude that hypnotizability operates in a predictable way. There is some evidence of cross-situational consistency but not to the extent that different test situations have negligible impact or reliably fail to affect subjects' individual test scores. The major sources of the differences that exist appear to lie in the prior expectancies and attitudes that are associated with different test situations

(Sarbin and Coe 1972), the context in which the test items are placed (such as the setting provided by independent test scales) and the extent to which test situations may invoke specific cognitive strategies or modes of information processing that are peculiar to the tasks that subjects are asked to perform. It is person-in-context that shapes hypnotic behaviour and experience, and the significance of the individual differences in hypnotizability that exist is not reduced at all by our recognizing that fact. It also appears that the social features of the hypnotic context, and the cognitive modes of response that this context releases, interact in an active manner with trait characteristics to structure and shape the final detail of hypnotic subjects' response. As Ekehammer (1974) argues, the interaction between these two types of factors (trait and situation) ought to be considered as one that involves mutual, bidirectional influence. Hypnotic responsiveness, for example, should be regarded as a function of both level of hypnotizability and the social-influence character of the specific hypnotic setting in which the hypnotized individual performs. Each interacts with the other to influence actual behaviour and experience.

Discussion of a number of examples from the hypnotic literature serves to illustrate the point. Examples will be taken across the domain of hypnosis to reinforce the basic argument that intra-group differences occur for different hypnotic tasks in a way that implicates distinctive cognitive processes at work for some hypnotic subjects but not for others. Phenomena considered will be analgesia (including hidden observer response), age regression, trance logic, hypnotic rapport and memory distortion. These tap processes relevant to pain sensitivity, dissociation, imaginative involvement, interpersonal attraction and constructive memory. Certain themes thread through the individual differences apparent in analysis of these phenomena and point to relevant constructs pertinent to a model built around an individual differences approach to hypnosis.

Analgesia and hidden observer response

The study of hypnotic analgesia reveals two important components of subject variability in hypnotic responsiveness. The work of Spanos and his associates (see Spanos, Brown *et al.* 1981) has demonstrated strong individual differences in the cognitive strategies subjects use to cope with suggestions of the absence of pain. The work of Hilgard and others (for reviews see Hilgard 1977, 1979) and of Perry and his associates (see Laurence and Perry 1981) has indicated strong evidence of stylistic differences among hypnotic subjects in the nature of their reaction to the effects of analgesia suggestion. Evidence from both sets of studies demonstrates that subjects receiving suggestions for the absence of pain will show a significantly greater tolerance for painful stimuli than subjects who are not given such suggestions. Subjects, however, appear to differ in the ways in which they cope with the pain. Spanos, Radtke-Bodorik *et al.* (1979) observed that distinctive cognitive strategies were reported by subjects given pain reduction suggestions. They found that the subjects who indicated appreciable pain decrements were typically those who did not exaggerate the noxious elements of the situation and who attempted to use specific coping strategies. The authors concluded that their evidence supports the notion that 'high levels of within-treatment variability in reported pain are related to variability in subjects' cognitive activity' (Spanos, Brown *et al.* 1981: 555). Hypnotic susceptibility is obviously related to the degree to which analgesia suggestion is effective in increasing pain tolerance and producing a higher threshold to pain stimulation, but individual differences in cognitive activity may also mediate the same response.

The work of Hilgard, Perry and their associates highlights the fact that, among hypnotic subjects themselves who have a high aptitude for hypnosis, there are strong individual differences in the nature of the experience that is reported. Attention is less here on coping with the pain that is present, than on qualitative features of subjects' reports about their hypnotic experiences. This work centres upon reference procedures for establishing the hidden observer phenomenon, which Spanos described in Chapter 5. Following Hilgard (1977), the hidden observer effect signifies that part of the hypnotized individual is actually experiencing pain during hypnotic analgesia while another part (operating under hypnotic suggestion) denies pain. Typically, the hypnotist makes contact with the experiencing part via instructions to the subject during the hypnotic analgesia item and establishes whether there is a change in pain report. The hidden observer effect is evident when the subject reports a change. The evidence from the literature is consistent in demonstrating that not every susceptible subject reports under hidden observer instruction that pain is, in fact, present. Hypnotic aptitude is necessary for the phenomenon to occur, but it is not sufficient to explain the effect. Approximately 40 to 50 per cent of highly hypnotizable subjects report an increase in experienced pain when the hidden observer is contacted by the hypnotist. The subjects who don't report in this fashion, however, are not less responsive to hypnotic suggestions in other ways and are unable to be discriminated from hidden observer responders in terms of their performance on standard hypnotic test tasks. Discrimination is possible, however, when one examines the fine-grained differences in the nature of the hypnotic experiences that are correlated with hidden observer reports.

Laurence and Perry (1981) highlight this discrimination. In their study, those subjects who responded to the hidden observer item (i.e. those who passed the hypnotic analgesia item but reported pain when that 'other part' of them was contacted) reliably demonstrated dual frameworks of reference. In response to age regression instructions, for example, these subjects typically reported that they felt they were both adult and child, either together or in alternation. This coexistence of distinctly different cognitive frames of reference expresses a reliable individual difference effect that has been observed now across a range of independent studies (Laurence and Perry 1981, Laurence 1983, Nogrady *et al.* 1983). Nogrady *et al.* (1983) label the effect in terms of a cognitive style they called 'cognitive fluidity', and they define it in terms of the ease with which subjects can experience multiple cognitive perspectives. Collectively, results suggest that the hidden observer phenomenon is not one that can be explained purely in terms of the demand characteristics for 'another response'. Its presence in hypnotic analgesia testing reflects an effect that is not typically shown by highly susceptible subjects, although high aptitude for hypnosis is necessary to demonstrate it. One of the special process variables that helps to define its nature is the coexistence of alternative cognitive frames of reference. Analgesic response is relatively predictable knowing the hypnotic aptitude of a subject, but the detail of that subject's response and its accompanying experience is not predictable without appeal to internal processes accounting for the stylistic characteristics of subjects' reactions.

Age regression and trance logic

In age regression a subject is typically instructed to return to some earlier point in time, and the hypnotist guides the subject to experience events of the past in a vivid and richly imaginative way. It is a phenomenon that requires at least a moderate degree of aptitude for hypnosis, but perhaps more importantly it tends to be a testing ground for the observation of important process differences among highly susceptible subjects who can experience age regression with ease. As we have seen, age regression testing demonstrates the tendency for some hypnotic subjects to experience the events of the past and the present at the same time while producing convincing performances of successful age regression response in other ways. An example of this is the age-regressed subject who writes in childlike fashion when asked to indicate his or her name, but who describes the scene unfolding as one that is enjoyed while the subject knows at the same time that he or she is really somewhere else.

Susceptible subjects in age regression sometimes show evidence of trance logic, or tolerance of incongruity. This may occur, for example, when a hypnotic subject is regressed back to childhood and is asked (as a small child) to spell some impossibly difficult sentence for a child of his or her age. A subject who passes the age regression item but who writes correctly a sentence that only an adult could know how to spell is performing paradoxically and demonstrating trance logic. Such a subject combines perceptions that stem from reality with logically contradictory ones that derive from the hypnotist's suggestions or instructions. The same phenomenon is manifested when a subject indicates 'no' to a hypnotist querying whether a loud noise can be heard after the hypnotist has successfully established a negative auditory hallucination response, or when a subject reports seeing two of the one person when confronted with the real person after hallucinating the same identity. In each case, the response that is indicated is seemingly inconsistent, irrational or incongruous. The processes that define trance logic, however, are less than clear (Sheehan 1977). Again, aptitude for hypnosis is not the factor that totally predicts the presence or absence of the phenomenon. Aptitude for hypnosis is necessary to display the effect, but not sufficient to explain it. Appeal must be, as before, to close analysis of the fine-grained experiences reported by susceptible subjects. Data that have been collected (see Sheehan and McConkey 1982) suggest that subjects evidencing trance logic do not see their behaviour as irrational or incongruous when confronted with it in the waking state. What may look to be incongruous or irrational to the independent observer, or to the hypnotist, may not be at all irrational to the experiencing subject. The apparent incongruity of trance logic response may well reflect a particular style of response which is perceived as natural by the experiencing subject either in hypnosis or when the trance logic response is reviewed by the subject out of hypnosis.

Unpublished data from the author's laboratory serve to reinforce the point. In a recent study (Whitehead 1983), subjects were given suggestions to hallucinate a co-experimenter and were then confronted with the real experimenter to test for the occurrence of double hallucination response. Subjects in the study illustrated double hallucination, but (typically) not all real hypnotic subjects produced it, and trance logic behaviour was most apparent when the hallucination was established in a way that did not emphasize its reality and definitive character. Trance logic behaviour was most evident when it was compatible with the fantasy quality of the initial hallucination response. Under the conditions where the hallucination response was firmly detailed and the hypnotist provided subjects with the chance to elaborate their hallucination, the incidence of incongruous behaviour was reduced. These results are less compatible with the notion that trance logic is a defining characteristic of hypnosis than with the notion that it reflects a particular style of response that is characteristic of the behaviour of some deeply responsive subjects but not others.

As in our earlier discussion of analgesia response, certain patterns of coherence or consistency in the data emerge. First, aptitude for hypnosis alone does not define trance logic response among subjects who clearly have the talent to respond hypnotically. Second, individual differences in the cognitive nature of hypnotic response appear to be linked to trance logic behaviour in a meaningful way. To assist in our understanding of what aptitude for hypnosis cannot explain, it seems that other internal processes are required to explain how the experiencing subject works through the demands of the tasks that are posed by the hypnotist.

Hypnotic rapport

Study of the domain of hypnosis that is tapped by the interaction between hypnotist and subjects further helps us understand the essential nature of subject variability in response to hypnosis. This is the area of interpersonal attraction. It is generally acknowledged in the hypnotic literature that rapport is important to help establish deep involvement in the events of hypnosis. If a hypnotist negatively interacts with or alienates a subject, then it is reasonable to expect that hypnotic response will not be optimal, or hypnosis will be experienced less deeply than when care is taken to establish positive rapport. Research has established an objective index of rapport in hypnosis, and a close look at the data indicates again the kind of theme that we have observed in our analysis of hypnotic analgesia and trance logic.

The relevance of interpersonal theorizing to hypnosis has been argued most strongly by theorists who have appealed to the concept of transference (Wolberg 1948, Gill and Brenman 1961, Shor 1962). Shor's concept of 'depth of archaic involvement' (1962: 31), for instance, expresses specifically the degree to which a relationship exists between hypnotist and subject and the extent to which the subject is bound up integrally in that relationship. One dimension of this process is the degree to which a hypnotized subject has a special wish to please the hypnotist and to perform in a way that is compatible with the hypnotist's intent or implied wishes.

Work that has explored the nature of this motivational process within the hypnotic setting revolves upon the concept of 'countering' (Sheehan 1971, 1980). Countering is the phenomenon that occurs when a hypnotic subject has learned outside hypnosis how to respond appropriately while hypnotized, but lays aside this preconception in hypnosis when the hypnotist implies that the earlier acquired expectancy is not in accord with what the hypnotist really wishes. Faced with a conflict between the hypnotist's intent and past knowledge of how to respond successfully, a subject who is in strong rapport with the hypnotist, and especially motivated to please, will solve this conflict in favour of responding in accord with the hypnotist's intent. In the research (Sheehan 1971), hypnotic subjects learned in a lecture demonstration, prior to hypnosis, that they should respond hypnotically in a completely compulsive fashion even when the suggestion in question was about to be removed. In hypnosis, however, when the hypnotist established the same compulsive response as had been seen previously, hypnotic subjects distinctively stopped responding compulsively when the hypnotist told subjects he was about to wake them up. In this way, the hypnotist established implicitly the expectation that he really did not want them to respond compulsively any longer even though the suggestion had not formally been removed. Hypnotic subjects, as opposed to simulating subjects, distinctively resolved their conflict by ceasing to respond compulsively when the hypnotist tested them informally, just prior to waking them up. This phenomenon of countering preconceptions about hypnosis has replicated across a series of studies (Sheehan 1971) and reliably differentiates real and role-playing subjects. Later work (Sheehan 1980) investigated the parameters that defined the phenomenon and analysed the impact on the incidence of countering (going against preconceptions about hypnosis to do what the hypnotist wants) of the hypnotist interacting negatively with subjects. When rapport was manipulated in this way, the incidence of countering was appreciably reduced.

The important aspect of these data for the present argument was that, despite the fact counterers resolved their conflict to follow the hypnotist's intent, thereby implicating a special motivation to please, they passed *fewer* SHSS:C items, on the average, than non-countering subjects. Only in one of ten separate comparisons was there a tendency for this pattern in the data to be reversed. The reliability of the evidence in this respect asserts strongly that it would be incorrect to associate the phenomenon of countering with greater overall behavioural compliance or general conformity of response. The same subjects who detected and responded to the hypnotist's intent not to respond compulsively and stopped responding were not those who responded best to the hypnotist's overt suggestions about how to perform on standard hypnotic test tasks. If subjects who respond as if they are especially attuned to the wishes of the hypnotist are not necessarily those who perform most directly to the requirements of standard test suggestions, then the nature of the experiential involvement of the subjects concerned requires careful scrutiny. It seems plausible to suggest (see Sheehan 1980) that the individual differences that exist in the extent to which highly susceptible subjects will resolve the conflict situation in which they are placed – when strong reasons exist for responding in a way different from what the hypnotist implied – are brought about by susceptible subjects' differing styles of cognition. Countering as an index of involvement with the hypnotist seems compatible, for instance, with an independent mode of cognition that focuses upon subject's taking the initiative and expressing the idiosyncratic character of his or her personal experience of suggestions. This mode of response is implicated, rather than a strictly co-operative mode, since subjects did not really concentrate or depend upon the literal text of the suggestions that were presented. Literal dependence on suggestion would be predicted to yield greater overall compliant response and less personal involvement in the events of the session. Counterers were clearly involved in a personal and deeply committed way, but the style of their response was such that they followed the hypnotist in a way that preserved their independence.

As in our analysis of analgesia and trance logic response, the data on hypnotic rapport that have been examined further assert the inability of the aptitude variable to encompass the range of individual differences that exist among hypnotizable subjects. Despite the fact that real subjects countered appreciably more than simulators, not all highly susceptible subjects counter their preconceptions about hypnosis to favour the hypnotist, and there seems to be special utility in recognizing the variability in commitment to respond that exists among highly susceptible subjects themselves. This variability cannot be attributed soley to differences in aptitude for hypnosis, nor simply to differences in ability associated with related (e.g. imaginative) skills (see Spanos and Barber 1974). Rather, data highlight differences in the level of involvement that hypnotic subjects display and reinforce the need to focus upon cognitive variables and their correlates, not in isolation but in reciprocal interaction with other internal processes such as aptitude for hypnosis, and social-situational factors that define the hypnotic context.

Memory in hypnosis

The issue of whether memory is enhanced in hypnosis or leads to appreciably distorted recall is one that is heavily debated in the literature of the mid-1980s. Theorists in the field assert that hypnotic memory is both reliable and significantly enhanced in its accuracy (e.g. Reiser 1974, Schafer and Rubio 1978), while others claim that hypnotic memory is dependably in error (e.g. Diamond 1980). The evidence basically indicates that there is no uniform effect for accuracy or distortion. Rather, hypnotic memory may be distorted or not depending on the conditions of memory test, whether misleading information has been fed to subjects just prior to recall or well beforehand, and the nature of the stimulus material that is remembered. Where enhancement of memory occurs in hypnosis, for instance, it can be expected to occur for meaningful rather than for nonsense material (for review of the relevant literature see Dhanens and Lundy 1975, DePiano and Salzberg 1981). There is also evidence that misleading suggestions about events that never really happened work more obviously when presented to hypnotic subjects just prior to recall via leading questions (e.g. Putnam 1979, Zelig and Beidleman 1981) than when more subtly fed to subjects before hypnosis is introduced (Sheehan and Tilden 1983). Aptitude for hypnosis does not relate to the degree of distortion that is observed in any simple fashion, and this area, as others we have reviewed, reveals important individual differences in the nature of the response shown by hypnotic subjects themselves. Differences point again to style variation in response that suggests the operation of distinctive hypnotic processes at work.

In a study conducted by Sheehan and Tilden (1984), subjects were pre-screened for high or low susceptibility to hypnosis and tested individually to examine hypnotic memory distortion. Independent groups of subjects were allocated to a design in which hypnotic or simulating subjects were given either misleading or non-misleading information about a series of scenes depicting an apparent robbery. Results showed that real and simulating subjects behaved similarly in being influenced by the misleading information. The information affected recall in both groups, but both groups were comparably distorted. Hypnotic subjects, however, remembered correctly more detail of a peripheral kind about the scenes that they had been shown. They remembered details of environmental surroundings and recalled them more accurately than the role-playing subjects, but hypnotic subjects also distorted more with respect to the same kind of detail. Independent evidence confirms, however, the presence of a negative correlation between accuracy of recall and memory for trivial details (Wells and Leippe 1981). Wells and Leippe demonstrated that witnesses asked to identify a thief, after they had viewed a staged incident, averaged fewer accurate answers on a test of memory that probed for peripheral details than did eyewitnesses who actually identified an innocent person.

The data on the types of detail remembered by subjects suggest the presence of strong individual differences in the way that information about those events was processed. As argued elsewhere (Sheehan and Tilden 1984) and by Wells and Leippe (1981), focus needs to be placed on individual differences in styles of information processing. There appear to be particular skills that characterize the constructive way in which some (but not all) hypnotic subjects organize the input they receive to produce their reported memories of events. Data cross-relate in this respect to the evidence on styles of processing demonstrated with the hidden observer phenomenon, trance logic and hypnotic rapport. Subjects who recalled more peripheral detail (and were more inaccurate with respect to that kind of detail) were not the most responsive to hypnosis. Further, recent evidence has isolated a number of additional and important cognitive strategies that high- (versus low-) hypnotizable subjects employ in their attempts to remember material in hypnosis (Crawford and Allen 1983). Clearly, we need again to look elsewhere for explanation of the ways in which suggestions are processed and the style of response given by particular susceptible subjects.

General discussion

Certain themes thread through the data relating to the phenomena that we have discussed. First, there is the relevance of aptitude for hypnosis to all of the phenomena that have been reviewed. Hypnotic analgesia, trance logic, countering (rapport) and memory distortion are all phenomena associated with high levels of hypnotic susceptibility. This is not to say that the phenomena in question cannot be demonstrated by subjects who are low in hypnotic susceptibility; Spanos's work on analgesia, for instance, was conducted without the introduction of hypnotic instruction, and both high- and low-hypnotizable subjects incorporate misleading information into their memories when presented with false information well before recall. For some phenomena (e.g. trance logic and hidden observer) rather than others (analgesia and memory distortion) aptitude plays more of a necessary part in determining whether the phenomenon will occur, and nearly always aptitude for hypnosis is an important and major facilitating condition. Never, however, does it appear that aptitude for hypnosis is sufficient to account for the phenomena. Aptitude for hypnosis needs to be considered in interaction with other features of subjects' responsiveness such as the style of information processing with which subjects work through the suggestions that are delivered, and the task constraints of the situations in which they are placed.

There appear to be meaningful consistencies in the data with respect to the styles of responding that subjects show. Three major cognitive styles have been isolated in the hypnotic literature and these have been labelled concentrative, independent and constructive (Sheehan and McConkey 1982). The categories are not necessarily exhaustive or independent, but the data indicate that they reflect discrete styles of cognitive processing in hypnosis. The first (concentrative) mode of cognizing is characterized by subjects concentrating on the suggestions of the hypnotist and thinking along in a literal way with the messages contained in the suggestions. The second (independent) mode of cognizing is characterized by subjects assessing the experience suggested by the hypnotist in terms of its personal meaningfulness to them. Subjects illustrate this mode when they do not simply concentrate on the literal messages of the hypnotist but respond, as it were, in independent fashion, in terms of aspects of the situation perceived as most appropriate to them. The third (constructive) mode of cognizing is characterized by subjects considering the communications of the hypnotist from the position of a preparedness or readiness to process incoming information in a schematic way so as to structure events that are happening in accord with what the hypnotist is suggesting. Subjects who illustrate this mode do not simply concentrate on the literal messages of the hypnotist or just interpret suggestions personally; rather, they cognitively react by seeking out ways to synthesize or construct the experience that is being suggested. The data also tell us that the styles that subjects evidence may vary across hypnotic tasks. Low-susceptible subjects tend to demonstrate similar styles of response regardless of the type of hypnotic task that is presented to them, but high-susceptible subjects are more likely to display independent or constructive styles of cognizing (Sheehan and McConkey 1982).

Some of the studies reviewed in this chapter further extend our knowledge of the styles of processing that subjects may show, and the data from them illustrate indications of consistency in the operation of specific modes of processing across different hypnotic tasks. Hidden observer response was linked to age regression response for some subjects – for instance, by the cognitive flexibility with which hidden observer subjects simultaneously held multiple cognitive perspectives in their age regression response. This style is linked to other aspects of hypnotic performance as well. A recent study by Laurence (1982) investigated the falsification of memory in hypnosis. The hypnotist planted a false event in the subject's mind during hypnosis and later tested whether that event was recalled as if it really happened even though no direct suggestion was given that the false memory should persist. Memory was falsified for about half of the highly susceptible sample that was tested, but those subjects who accepted the hypnotist's construction showed duality reports in their testimonies about other aspects of their hypnotic experience. These subjects who were able to accept events that didn't really happen, even though they must have known the events could not have occurred, again demonstrated flexible acceptance of multiple cognitive perspectives. And the same subjects were those who were to experience the hidden observer effect. Evidence suggests that cognitive flexibility is a style that is relatively pervasive, and it would be useful to determine whether this style also characterizes subjects who accept what appears to others as incongruous. Cognitive flexibility is also a style importantly isolated by Crawford and Allen's (1983) work on hypnotic memory and the cognitive strategies adopted by susceptible subjects in hypnosis. Future research may be expected to indicate that concentrative, independent, constructive and flexibility styles hardly exhaust the pattern of regularities in subjects' experience of hypnotic events.

Integral to the concept of style are assumptions about the individuality, variability and complexity of reaction – all of which are evident in our discussion of the phenomena that we have examined. Subjects who showed trance logic, who countered preconceptions about trance and illustrated the hidden observer effect all demonstrated strong idiosyncrasy of response. They organized their experience differently and processed suggestions distinctively, and the idiosyncrasy evident in their response is likely to be missed by the standardized scales of assessment with which we began this chapter. Standard instruments typically focus on the central tendencies of response among hypnotic subjects and ignore the within-group variances that frequently occur among highly susceptible subjects. The variability among hypnotic subjects themselves is sufficient that special techniques of measurement are required to assess it. One technique that has been developed for this purpose is the Experiential Analysis Technique (Sheehan, McConkey and Cross 1978). This technique is a phenomenologically based measurement method that probes subjects' experiences of past hypnotic events in intensive detail. It does so by prompting subjects to recall events just passed and leaves the initiative with the subject to comment on aspects of his or her hypnotic experience that are especially meaningful. The reliability and the validity of the technique are explored in detail elsewhere (Sheehan and McConkey 1982). The relevant point here is that such techniques are essential to analyse the variability and complexity of individual subjects' hypnotic reactions and to highlight the parameters that define an individual differences model of hypnosis.

The complexity of hypnotic response is particularly evident when one considers how trait and skill capacities of the hypnotic subject interact with style of processing and the treatment conditions that hypnotic subjects receive. The notion of 'style' assists in ordering the essential variability of hypnotic responses, but relatively little evidence has until lately emerged to tie qualitative features of information processing to degree of susceptibility to hypnosis. Outside the data already discussed in this chapter, there has been some work on field independence and tolerance for unrealistic experience, as well as other styles (Klein, Gardner and Schlesinger 1962, Roberts 1965, Morgan 1972) but not a great deal. A relationship with hypnotizability has been found for field independence (Morgan 1972), and some relationship exists for sharpening and broad category width (Goldberger and Wachtel 1973), but generally the evidence has been unrewarding (see Bergerone, Cei and Ruggieri 1981). Evidence would suggest that data revealing the precise nature of the interaction between style and aptitude will most appropriately come from intensive study of hypnotic trait–task interactions. As discussed elsewhere (Sheehan and McConkey 1982), the important task is not to ask which source of influence (trait or situation) is more influential or important than the other in understanding hypnosis, but to isolate those conditions where situations are more likely to yield powerful effects and those conditions where person variables such as aptitude and cognitive style are most likely to be influential. We should cease to look for uniformity of response among hypnotic subjects, for such a search is misguided on two counts. First, highly susceptible subjects are far from completely stable in what they do or what they experience if one looks closely at their responses; and second, any assumption of uniformity necessarily underestimates the impact of task constraints on how susceptible subjects will perform.

A model built around an individual differences account of hypnotic responsiveness is one in which the variability of hypnotic reaction must be recognized as primary, and in which formal acknowledgement is given to the different ways in which subjects process suggestions. Such a model seems most appropriately formulated in terms of the hypnotic subject being viewed as an active participant in the events of hypnosis. Interactions occurring among task or setting constraints, and person variables such as aptitude for trance and style of cognitive processing, are dynamic and complex in character; a reciprocal relationship most probably exists among person variables, situation and behaviour. If hypnosis is viewed as a problem-solving situation in which hypnotic subjects cognize actively to become attuned to variations in context and modify their interpretations about what is happening, we will need to assess behaviour and experience by proper measurement instruments. Subjects selectively employ cognitive strategies that will assist them to adapt and respond to the suggestions that are administered. These strategies need to be assessed. Emphasis in this approach should be away from the hypnotist, and from judgements about the competency of response to suggestion. Rather, focus needs to be more on the experience and interpretation of suggestion by the subject, and on the way in which suggestions are processed cognitively to arrive at outcomes that are expected.

A model based on individual differences in responsiveness should carefully evaluate the ways in which we assess hypnotic performance. We commenced this chapter by passing comment on the important role standardized scales of assessment have played in highlighting the profound differences in responsiveness to hypnotic suggestion that occur among subjects in the normal population. These same measures, however, are ill equipped to detect and quantify the essential diversity of hypnotic reaction, especially as it occurs among highly susceptible subjects. The standardized tests should nevertheless not be replaced. They should rather be supplemented by techniques of enquiry that are better attuned to assess hypnotic experience in its full complexity. Trance logic serves to make this point rather well. The hypnotic literature has for years reported trance logic in terms of the incongruity of the susceptible subjects' response. The essential paradox of the hypnotic subject who reports two of the same person (double hallucination) has never really been challenged, for instance. Yet data gathered from the Experiential Analysis Technique (Sheehan and McConkey 1982) suggest that such incongruity is more in the mind of the observer than of the experiencing subject, and that trance logic is less a defining feature of hypnosis than a form of response that is stylistically compatible with other aspects of the hypnotic subject's experiences.

Conclusion

Any model that advocates the primacy of individual variation in hypnotic reaction is difficult to state precisely. This chapter serves primarily to highlight the need to formulate a model that recognizes the essential richness and variety of hypnotic experience more sensitively than existing models. The mental abilities, perceptions and emotive responses of susceptible subjects are organized into a complex system of functioning and subtle cognitive processes occur in hypnotic subjects that clearly guide them towards what they personally view as an appropriate response. The full meaning of hypnosis is best understood by considering the hypnotic subject as an active, sentient being who uses the information that is available in a variety of ways. It is the future task of assessment and theory in the field of hypnosis to measure that variety and conceptualize the processes that are at work.

References

Bergerone, C., Cei, A. and Ruggieri, Z. (1981) Suggestibility and cognitive style. *International journal of Clinical and Experimental Hypnosis*, 29: 351–54.

Bowers, K. S. (1976) *Hypnosis for the Seriously Curious*. Monterey, Calif.: Brooks/Cole.

Crawford, H. J. and Allen, S. N. (1983) Enhanced visual memory during hypnosis as mediated by hypnotic responsiveness and cognitive strategies. *Journal of Experimental Psychology: General*, 112: 662–85.

Curran, J. C. and Gibson, H. B. (1974) Critique of the Stanford Hypnotic Susceptibility Scale: British usage and factorial structure. *Perceptual and Motor Skills*, 39: 695–704.

DePiano, F. A. and Salzberg, H. C. (1981) Hypnosis as an aid to recall of meaningful information presented under three types of arousal. *International Journal of Clinical and Experimental Hypnosis*, 29: 383–400.

Dhanens, T. P. and Lundy, R. M. (1975) Hypnotic and waking suggestions and recall. *International Journal of Clinical and Experimental Hypnosis*, 23: 68–79.

Diamond, B. L. (1980) Inherent problems in the use of pretrial hypnosis on a prospective witness. *California Law Review*, 68: 313–49.

Diamond, M. J. (1974) Modification of hypnotizability: a review. *Psychological Bulletin*, 81: 180–98.

Diamond, M. J. (1977). Hypnotiability is modifiable: an alternative approach, *International Journal of Clinical and Experimental Hypnosis*, 25, 147–66.

Ekehammer, B. (1974) Interactionism in modern personality from a historical perspective. *Psychological Bulletin*, 81: 1026–48.

Gill, M. M. and Brenman, M. (1961) *Hypnosis and Related States*. New York: International Universities Press.

Goldberger, N. I. and Wachtel, P. L. (1973) Hypnotizability and cognitive controls. *International Journal of Clinical and Experimental Hypnosis*, 21: 298–304.

Hilgard, E. R. (1965) *Hypnotic Susceptibility*. New York: Harcourt, Brace & World.

(1977) *Divided Consciousness: Multiple Controls in Human Thought and Action*. New York: Wiley.

(1978–9) The Stanford Hypnotic Susceptibility Scales as related to other measures of hypnotic responsiveness. *American Journal of Clinical Hypnosis*, 21: 68–83.

(1979) Consciousness and control: lessons from hypnosis. *Australian Journal of Clinical and Experimental Hypnosis*, 7: 103–16.

Hilgard, E. R., Weitzenhoffer, A. M., Landes, J. and Moore, R. K. (1961) The distribution of susceptibility to hypnosis in a student population: a study using the Stanford Hypnotic Susceptibility Scale. *Psychological Monographs*, 75: 1–22.

Klein, G. S., Gardner, R. W. and Schlesinger, H. J. (1962) Tolerance for unrealistic experiences: the study of the generality of a cognitive control. *British Journal of Psychology*, 53: 41–55.

Laurence, J. R. (1982) *Memory creation in hypnosis*. Unpublished doctoral dissertation, Concordia University, Montreal.

Laurence, J. R. and Perry, C. (1981) The 'hidden observer' phenomenon in hypnosis: some additional findings. *Journal of Abnormal Psychology*, 90: 334–44.

Levine, J. and Ludwig, A. M. (1965) Alterations in consciousness produced by combinations of LSD, hypnosis, and psychotherapy. *Psychopharmacologia*, 7: 123–37.

Morgan, A. H. (1972) Hypnotizability and 'cognitive styles': a search for relationships. *Journal of Personality*, 40: 503–9.

Nogrady, H., McConkey, K. M., Laurence, J. R. and Perry, C. (1983) Dissociation, duality, and demand characteristics in hypnosis. *Journal of Abnormal Psychology*, 92: 223–35.

Perry, C. (1979) Is hypnotizability modifiable? *International Journal of Clinical and Experimental Hypnosis*, 25: 125–46.

Putnam, W. H. (1979) Hypnosis and distortions in eyewitness memory. *International Journal of Clinical and Experimental Hypnosis*, 27: 437–48.

Reiser, M. (1974) Hypnosis as an aid in a homicide investigation. *American Journal of Clinical Hypnosis*, 17: 84–7.

Roberts, M. R. (1965) Attention and cognitive controls as related to individual differences in hypnotic susceptibility. *Dissertation Abstracts International*. 25: 4261.

Sanders, R. S. and Reyher, J. (1969) Sensory deprivation and the enhancement of hypnotic susceptibility. *Journal of Abnormal Psychology*, 74: 375–81.

Sarbin, T. R. and Coe, W. C. (1972) *Hypnosis: A Social Psychological Analysis of Influence Communication*. New York: Holt, Rinehart & Winston.

Schafer, D. W. and Rubio, R. (1978) Hypnosis to aid the recall of witnesses. *International Journal of Clinical and Experimental Hypnosis*, 26: 81–91.

Sheehan, P. W. (1971) Countering preconceptions about hypnosis: an objective index of involvement with the hypnotist. *Journal of Abnormal Psychology (Monograph)*, 78: 299–322.

      (1977) Incongruity in trance behaviour: a defining property of hypnosis. *Annals of the New York Academy of Sciences*, 296: 194–207.

      (1980) Factors influencing rapport in hypnosis. *Journal of Abnormal Psychology*, 89: 263–81.

Sheehan, P. W. and McConkey, K. M. (1982) *Hypnosis and Experience: The Exploration of Phenomena and Process*. Hillsdale, N. J.: Laurence Erlbaum.

Sheehan, P. W., McConkey, K. M. and Cross, D. (1978) Experiential analysis of hypnosis: some new observations on hypnotic phenomena. *Journal of Abnormal Psychology*, 87: 570–3.

Sheehan, P. W. and Tilden, J. (1983) Effects of suggestibility and hypnosis on accurate and distorted retrieval from memory. *Journal of Experimental Psychology: Learning, Memory and Cognition*, 9: 283–93.

      (1984) Real and simulated occurrences of memory distortion in hypnosis. *Journal of Abnormal Psychology*, 93: 47–57.

Shor, R. E. (1962) Three dimensions of hypnotic depth. *International Journal of Clinical and Experimental Hypnosis*, 10: 23–8.

(1979) A phenomenological method for the measurement of variables important to an understanding of the nature of hypnosis. In E. Fromm and R. E. Shor (eds.), *Hypnosis: Developments in Research and New Perspectives*, Hawthorne, N.Y.: Aldine.

Spanos, N. P. and Barber, T. X. (1974) Toward a convergence in hypnosis research. *American Psychologist*, 29: 500–11.

Spanos, N. P., Brown, J. M., Jones, B. and Horner, D. (1981) Cognitive activity and suggestions for analgesia in the reduction of reported pain. *Journal of Abnormal Psychology*, 90: 554–61.

Spanos, N. P., Radtke-Bodorik, H. L., Ferguson, J. D. and Jones, B. (1979) The effects of hypnotic susceptibility, suggestions for analgesia, and the utilization of cognitive strategies on the reduction of pain. *Journal of Abnormal Psychology*, 88: 282–92.

Wells, G. L. and Leippe, M. R. (1981) How do triers of fact infer the accuracy of eyewitness identifications? Using memory for peripheral detail can be misleading. *Journal of Applied Psychology*, 66: 682–7.

Whitehead, S. (1983) Factors influencing trance logic response. Unpublished honours dissertation. University of Queensland.

Wolberg, L. R. (1948) *Medical Hypnosis Vol. 1: The Principles of Hypnotherapy*. New York: Grune & Stratton.

Zelig, M. and Beidleman, W. B. (1981) The investigative use of hypnosis: a word of caution. *International Journal of Clinical and Experimental Hypnosis*, 29: 401–12.

WHAT IS HYPNOSIS?

Peter L. N. Naish

In this final chapter a brief attempt will be made to draw together the individual strands of discussion begun in the earlier chapters. The subject of hypnosis has been presented from various view points and with different emphases, and it must not be expected that this chapter will pick the 'winner'. If it were possible to decide upon the definitive theory of hypnosis, this book would not have had the present form; only the 'correct' account would have been given. However, certain common themes run through many of the contributions, and these will be highlighted, as each chapter is discussed.

Perhaps the most significant feature of the authors' contributions is their tendency to reflect movement from extreme positions towards a middle ground. For example, Waxman has previously seemed to place greater emphasis upon physiological explanations of hypnosis (Waxman 1981). In his chapter in this book he refers to the condition as being an altered state of awareness, which sounds very much like the psychologists' suggestion that there is a change in cognition. Wagstaff too appears to have adopted a less fiercly 'rational' position. In the past (Wagstaff 1981) his emphasis has been very much upon giving compliance-based accounts of hypnotic responding. Now Wagstaff not only accepts that subjects may, by cognitive means, actually experience some of the alleged effects, but he suggests that the adoption of cognitive strategies may be the option of first choice. Naish too has moved from accounts based solely upon criterion shifting (e.g. Naish 1983) to a description involving the interaction of perceptual and cognitive processes. There seems to be an indisputable meeting of minds in proposing that cognitive effects are an important part of 'being hypnotized'.

Chapter 2

As was pointed out earlier in the book, it is natural that an author with a medical background should tend to see hypnosis through a physiologist's eyes. David Waxman's account of the phenomenon was clearly grounded in physiology, and at some level such an account must be correct. Given that our experiences must always be mediated, or indeed represented by neural events, then it follows that hypnosis (however it is experienced) must have a neurological basis. However, as a number of the contributors have shown, there is little evidence available to support a stronger physiological account. In other words, the same general kinds of neural activity probably obtain in various other situations not labelled 'hypnosis'. There is a certain risk, when embracing the more sceptical views of hypnosis, of becoming too dismissive and 'throwing out the baby with the bath water'. Coming at the beginning of the book, Waxman's chapter is a useful reminder that there is a large body of practitioners who employ hypnosis as a useful tool in their work. It must be presumed that these trained therapists, who have many other techniques besides hypnosis, employ hypnosis because they find it to be effective. This conclusion does not, of course, explain why hypnotic techniques have therapeutic value, but to ignore the fact that they do is to put on the same blinkers as the commission that disposed of Mesmer.

David Waxman offers a number of explanations to account for hypnotic effects, and some of these set the scene for the accounts given in later chapters. For example, Waxman indicates that, even in the therapeutic setting, hypnosis cannot be relied upon as a miraculous key to the memories. As he points out, an uncovered 'memory' may not be accurate, although its expression may still be of therapeutic value. Again, when dealing with the question of hypnotic pain relief, Waxman states that the improvement may be due to an alleviation of the associated anxiety. Naturally, Waxman stresses that patients cannot be made to do things against their will, and that no therapeutic change can be effected, unless the patient really wants to change. The careful reader of this chapter must inevitably share Waxman's conclusion that hypnosis, although therapeutically useful, is in no sense a magical panacea.

Chapter 3

Brian Fellows further underlines the relative 'ordinariness' of hypnosis, and expressly points out that there are no physiological differences between a 'hypnotized' person and an appropriate control. For this and other reasons, Fellows comes down on the side of the non-state view, rather than a state description of hypnosis. However, Fellows spends some time in exploring other situations in which trance-like behaviour may be observed; he is particularly interested in the effects of poetry and painting. If a rapt reader of poetry is presumed to be an analogue of a hypnosis subject, then there seems to be something a little state-like about this view. Of course, it all depends upon one's terminology, for a poetry reader is not in a physiologically distinct state, as is for example an intoxicated person. However, to see common elements in the behaviours of different people is, in a weaker sense, to imply a common state. Clearly it is not a state *unique* to hypnosis, if poetry readers too can display it.

To show that there is a good deal in common between the behaviours traditionally found in hypnosis and those associated with other activities is useful. The fact that 'hypnotic' behaviour turns out to be comparatively widespread helps to set reasonable bounds for explanations of the behaviour. For example, the responses of a person privately reading poetry are not easily ascribed to compliance. Extrapolating to the hypnosis situation should therefore lead us to doubt that compliance is a major determinant of those behavioural responses. For a more reasonable explanation Fellows turns to the recent work of Barber, and themes emerge that recur throughout this book. That is, there appears to be a need to accept subjective accounts of hypnosis and to explain them by proposing that the hypnotically susceptible have particular cognitive skills and abilities.

Chapter 4

Graham Wagstaff also adopts a cognitive explanation of some hypnotic processes, but is first at pains to demonstrate the non-unique quality of the phenomena. There seems to be a degree of difficulty in bringing these two accounts together, since they appear to be directed at rather different aspects of the overall hypnosis 'package'. Thus the components of the hypnosis situation that are commonly found elsewhere are the overt behavioural responses, and the reader must by now be convinced (as Wagstaff would wish us to be) that 'hypnotic' behaviour is drawn from the normal repertoire. However, the putative cognitive effects are generally manifested in subjective accounts, and these do seem, at least from some subjects, to suggest an element of the unusual. In fact, as Fellows' chapter points out, although uncommon this kind of experience is not unique to the hypnosis situation.

If a theory of hypnosis is to be founded upon the unusual nature of the claimed *subjective* experiences, then it is of little relevance to the theory to note that the associated behaviours are *not* out of the ordinary. It is nevertheless important to establish that the behaviour is unexceptional, for two reasons. Firstly, it is to be hoped that such a frequent assertion, in books such as this, will gradually dispel the erroneous beliefs so commonly held concerning the 'power' of hypnosis. Secondly, to stress that the behaviour is normal is effectively to say that the only remaining area that could explain 'real' hypnotic effects is in the private world of the subject's information-processing strategies. The problem for this approach is that subjective accounts are very difficult to verify. To attempt to test the reality of a hypnotic experience of this sort is almost inevitably fruitless. For example, Wagstaff cites a study showing that an hallucinated colour does not lead to a coloured after-image, as a real colour would have done. However, this finding cannot enable us to distinguish between a subject who is lying and one who genuinely experienced an hallucination. After-images are generated at a very early level in the visual processing system, by the presence of a real image on the retina. A cognitively generated hallucination would be formed at a much later stage; and as the retina could not be involved, it follows that no after-image could be formed. To decide whether subjects do actually employ special information-processing strategies, to generate self-convincing experiences, requires tests of a more subtle nature.

Wagstaff is clearly of the opinion that subjects do not always succeed in using such strategies, and that they then resort to compliant behaviour to give the hypnotist what they believe he wants. One is reminded of the predicament of T. S. Eliot's Becket: 'The last temptation is the greatest treason:/to do the right deed for the wrong reason.' However, Wagstaff's point is another reminder of the ordinariness of hypnotic behaviour. Since there is no special ingredient, the behaviour can be produced to order, at any time and for any reason. This may be one of the causes of the low correlations commonly found between hypnotic susceptibility and other plausibly related characteristics. As susceptibility is normally assessed, a high scorer is one who *produces* the behaviour, the *reason* for its production remaining unknown. It is entirely likely that only some subjects produce the behaviour in response to cognitively induced experiences.

Chapter 5

Spanos also raises many of the difficult issues discussed above. He begins by reminding the reader of the state/non-state distinction, and suggests that a special-state theory would require mechanisms such as dissociation, or other special cognitive processes. Spanos presents ample evidence in support of the non-state view, but later (for example in the sections discussing susceptibility and pain control) proposes the existence of cognitive strategies. He presumably does not consider these to be 'special'; otherwise it must be imagined that he would have changed sides, to become a state theorist. This point underlines the closeness of the different approaches. Fellows described the convergence of hypnosis research, and it becomes apparent that many of the remaining differences in theoretical stances are a matter of semantics.

Chapter 5 included the interesting topic of hypnotic involuntariness. This is of particular concern to many potential subjects or patients, and was also addressed in Chapter 1. Spanos reaches the apparently paradoxical conclusion that subjects can succeed in convincing themselves that their own behaviour is involuntary, while at the same time carefully controlling the behaviour to achieve the desired effect. This again points to the adoption of an unusual cognitive style, which can permit the production of appropriate behaviour, while analysing it in a way that will make it seem externally controlled. It is known that people differ in everyday life in the extent to which they perceive themselves as having control over their destinies. Those who have a strong impression that their locus of control lies beyond them may become sufficiently distressed to require treatment. A sense of involuntariness in the hypnosis situation can be likened to an extreme example of perceived external locus of control. As such, there is a limit to the comfort that can be offered a nervous hypnosis candidate. The adivce must be to deal with a hypnotist who can be trusted, so that even if there is a sense of non-volition there will not be a corresponding fear of abuse.

In the context of hypnotic amnesia Spanos is again at pains to demonstrate that subjects do only what they believe is expected. However, demonstrations such as these should come as no surprise; it was stressed in Chapter 1 that hypnosis can be mediated only by what the subject makes of the situation and of the hypnotist's words. Subjects try to generate experiences that are concordant with their expectations. If a subject believes that amnesia should be total, then he or she tries to achieve that result; but if convinced that the amnesia should be breached, then that is attempted. None of these obervations addresses the question of how a subject goes about reaching the desired goals.

A central part of Spanos's chapter deals with his work on susceptibility training. For a subject's susceptibility to be enhanced, it is necessary to explain to him or her how the appropriate experiences are to be achieved. Since enhancement has been shown to be feasible, it is reasonable to conclude that to have hypnotic experiences is a skill, for which it is possible to be trained. Such a conclusion weakens claims that hypnotic responses are simple examples of compliance. An ardent supporter of the compliance position might suggest that the time spent in training makes a subject feel that he or she must reward the hypnotist by producing 'better' responses. However, as Spanos points out, it seems to require the right sort of training to produce the desired effects, not simply enough time to give the subject a sense of obligation.

Chapter 6

In the preceding chapters the claim was frequently made that cognitive processes are involved in the production of 'hypnotic' effects. However, the exact nature of these processes generally remained obscure. Naish went some way to redress this omission by spelling out, in fair detail, how hypnotic experiences might be generated. Moreover, the kind of oblique experiment he carried out, to test the theory, lends some support to the general concept of cognitive effects in hypnosis. This may be contrasted with the difficulty of making direct tests upon subjective experiences, a problem raised in the discussion of Chapter 3.

Although it is encouraging for cognitively based theories to see that precise mechanisms can be proposed to account for aspects of hypnosis, Naish's theory is not a full explanation of hypnosis. The signal detection account can certainly offer an explanation for many hypnotic phenomena, but Naish gives little indication as to how the putative criterion shifts are brought about. In other words, to adopt this concept is to change the area requiring explanation; a cause for the behaviour has been offered, but now a cause of the cause is required. Perhaps a strength of this position is that it moves the area requiring investigation into a domain very familiar to experimental psychologists. As with Wagstaff's or Spanos's use of social psychological descriptions, explanations founded upon well-tried concepts help to dispel the aura of mystery and magic surrounding hypnosis.

An essential component of the Naish position is that criterion shifts are presumed to act upon stimuli at a stage of processing before a conscious perception results. This interpretation of signal detection theory has been criticized by Gregg and Whiteley (1985). They claim that the theory has to do with the *conscious* decisions subjects make about stimuli, once they have become aware of them. Naish (1985) has accepted that signal detection theory addresses this issue, but denies that this is the sole application of the theory. At present it would seem that the Naish position is generally held to be acceptable, but clearly, were this interpretation of signal detection theory shown to be in error, then his account of hypnosis would be severely undermined.

Chapter 7

Sheehan's chapter reinforces many of the points raised in earlier sections of the book. Earlier ideas are drawn firmly into the cognitive net. For Sheehan, the future of hypnosis research should lie in the exploration of the cognitive processes involved. The plural 'processes' is used, since it is clearly demonstrated that subjects can find a number of means to reach the desired hypnotic end. This point is a reminder of the complexity of the perceptual mechanisms, referred to by Naish. A subtle change at any one of the many different levels might well lead to the same kind of end experience. To attempt an explanation of hypnosis in these terms is to acknowledge the validity of subjects' reported experiences, and Sheehan sees such reports as an important indicator of a subject's information-processing style. Whether discussing trance logic and age regression, or hidden observer effects and analgesia, Sheehan presents the phenomena as if they are genuine experiences for the subjects.

Sheehan is inclined to accept the general principle of stability in hypnotic susceptibility. At first this might appear to be in conflict with the evidence offered by Spanos, showing that susceptibility can be enhanced by training. However, these positions can be seen as two sides of the same cognitive coin. Research in cognitive psychology has demonstrated that different individuals can maintain different but relatively stable cognitive styles. Nevertheless, these styles can be modified with suitable training – a facility often employed in therapeutic settings. For example, an anorexic patient may employ a style that leads her to see her very thin body as being overweight; small quantities of food are perceived as excessive. In treatment the therapist will attempt to modify these misperceptions. Returning to hypnosis, if the phenomenon is a reflection of cognitive activities, then it is entirely to be expected that these activities will in general reflect a constant style. On the other hand, a suitably oriented training programme would be able to modify these styles.

It is tempting to see the analogy between medical and hypnotic cognitive shifting as offering an explanation for the therapeutic effectiveness of hypnosis. If medical conditions can sometimes be alleviated by promoting a change of cognitive style, then it seems reasonable that hypnosis should facilitate those changes, since it appears to rely upon cognitive shifts for its own effects.

In earlier discussion it has been accepted that behaviour which looks 'hypnotic' to the observer might be the result of a variety of factors. In some cases the behaviour may reflect simple compliance; in others the hypnosis may be more 'real', and involve cognitive effects. Sheehan's chapter implies that this distinction is too crude, since the cognitive processes themselves may be subdivided. His suggested third style of responding – 'constructive' – perhaps matches most closely the concept of 'genuine' hypnosis, in which the subject actually manages to generate the suggested experiences. Sheehan's description of the constructive style certainly bears a good deal of resemblence to Naish's account of hypnotic response. Sheehan's 'concentrative' and 'independent' styles appear to encapsulate some of the emphases of the other authors.

Summary

The above brief overview of this book's chapters inevitably reflects the prejudices of its author. In so short a space it is not possible to do the contributors full justice, and some may very reasonably feel that they have been misrepresented. These last few pages have been offered principally for the reader who was previously unfamiliar with the topics covered. It is hoped that they will have provided a framework within which to integrate the various views presented earlier. However, the reader is urged to re-examine the preceding chapters and to decide for him- or herself whether this closing outline is in any way an adequate representation of the wealth of information it attempts to embrace.

At the start of this chapter it was stated that no definitive theory of hypnosis could be offered. However, from the themes that have run through this book, it is possible to conclude with a list of characteristics which roughly define our current views.

(1) 'Hypnosis' describes a situation in which subjects are likely to produce behaviour that *they* believe to be appropriately 'hypnotic'.

(2) The behaviour is frequently unusual, but never unique.

(3) Hypnotic behaviour is produced for a variety of reasons.

(4) In some subjects, the outward behaviour (including verbal descriptions of subjective impressions) is a result of the unusual experiences achieved.

(5) Subjects generate their own unusual experiences, by employing appropriate information-processing strategies, which result in altered cognitions.

(6) A given hypnotic effect can be achieved by a variety of cognitive styles.

References

Gregg, V. H. and Whiteley, A. E. (1985) Hypnosis and signal detection theory: reservations concerning Naish's theory. *British Journal of Experimental and Clinical Hypnosis*, 3: 139–141.

Naish, P. L. N. (1983) Hypnosis: a signal detection approach. Paper given at January meeting of Experimental Psychology Society, London.

—— (1985) Is a signal detection account of hypnosis supportable? *British Journal of Experimental and Clinical Hypnosis*, 2: 147–50.

Wagstaff, G. F. (1981) *Hypnosis, Compliance and Belief*. Brighton: Harvester.

Waxman, D. (1981) *Hypnosis: A Guide for Patients and Practitioners*. London: Allen & Unwin.

FURTHER READING

Those readers wishing to keep abreast of developments in hypnosis research and applications could not do better than to consult the journals on the subject. Such journals are published in many countries. The *International Journal of Clinical and Experimental Hypnosis*, published in the USA, is widely available. In the UK the equivalent is the *British Journal of Experimental and Clinical Hypnosis*. These journals are most easily obtained through university libraries, although those who are eligible may join the associated societies and receive their journals direct. A number of books are available on the subject. Some of these, inevitably, are written in a sensational style and do nothing to advance the public's understanding of hypnosis. The reader is advised to examine the reference lists given at the end of each chapter of this book, in which details may be found of the books from which the contributors have quoted. To offer specific recommendations tends to be invidious, but it is perhaps acceptable to suggest one from each of three categories: a generally 'readable' book, a second that is strongly academic and a third that examines therapeutic applications:

K. S. Bowers, *Hypnosis for the Seriously Curious*. New York: Brooks/Cole, 1976.
P. W. Sheehan and C. Perry, *Methodologies of Hypnosis: A Critical Appraisal of Contemporary Paradigms of Hypnosis*. Hillsdale, N: Lawrence Erlbaum, 1976.
M. M. Miller, *Therapeutic Hypnosis*. New York: Human Sciences Press, 1979.

APPENDIX: SEEKING MEDICAL HELP THROUGH HYPNOSIS

Hypnosis is for many people primarily a source of therapy. It is likely that some readers of this book will wish to explore the possibility of employing hypnosis treatment for themselves, and it is appropriate that a little guidance should be offered.

First and foremost, it should be appreciated that hypnosis is a tool and not a therapy in itself. The blanket term 'hypnotherapy' is misleading and tends to be avoided by the medically qualified. For a person to set up exclusively as a 'hypnotherapist' is analogous to someone claiming to be a 'penicillin-therapist'; there are situations where penicillin would be one of a number of possible treatments, and other occasions when it would be completely inappropriate. Similarly, hypnosis can be expected to be effective only in certain circumstances, and even then it may be that a different approach would be more suitable. Considerations such as these, together with the general warnings that have been given previously concerning consulting 'quacks', make it clear that treatment is best sought from a well-qualified, accredited person. Since the therapist should be in a position to be able to decide whether hypnosis or another style of therapy is appropriate, it follows that he or she must be properly trained in medicine or psychology. Most countries have professional organizations, to which such therapists are likely to belong. In Great Britain there are two such bodies: the British Society of Medical and Dental Hypnosis, and the British Society of Experimental and Clinical Hypnosis. Members of these learned societies may be consulted in the confidence that they hold recognized qualifications in medicine, psychology and dentistry. There is also the advantage that the treatment offered is frequently available under the National Health Service.

AUTHOR INDEX

SUBJECT INDEX